# ARGYLL AND THE ISLANDS

## AN ILLUSTRATED ARCHITECTURAL GUIDE

Argyll and the Islands - what appears in our mind's eye when this area of Scotland is mentioned? It would be an unusual person who does not picture long narrow sea lochs, high brooding cliffs, islands jutting majestically out of the water, strands of white sand, romantic castles perched impossibly on rocky shards - but always water. It is an area dominated by the sea, dangerous, fascinating and challenging to mankind.

This wonderful book turns the reader's eye away for a time from the sea itself to the equally fascinating buildings erected throughout the centuries to provide shelter, strongholds, churches, work places and recreation for those people who could not resist the attraction of this remote and beautiful area. Surprises abound around this corner and along that track, on this islet and in that little harbour. This book takes the reader to them all, along the way not only providing illuminating detail regarding the construction and built form but also demonstrating the slow march of Scottish social history.

This is an area of the Glasgow Chapter of the Royal Incorporation of Architects in Scotland that is pretty well recognised from the sea but which deserves much more thorough investigation landward. Row ashore, take this book, march along the beach then turn inland - you won't be disappointed!

Joan Scott
RIAS Glasgow Chapter President

D1555852

Author: Frank Arneil Walker
Series editor: Charles McKean
Series consultant: David Walker
Cover design: Luise Valentiner
Index: Oula Jones

Cover illustrations (all © RCAHMS)
Front Tobermory
Back Detail of Iona Abbey cloister; Dunderave Castle; Kilchurn Castle; Poltalloch House by William Burn, 1849; Inveraray from the watch tower.

The Rutland Press
ISBN 1873-190-522
1st published 2003

Layout, picture scans and maps by
The Royal Commission on the Ancient and Historical Monuments of Scotland
Printed by Burns & Harris, Dundee

British Library Cataloguing in Publication Data.
A catalogue record for this book is available from the British Library.

*Castle Stalker.*

## INTRODUCTION

A journey in Argyll leads inevitably to the sea.
First come the long lochs – Loch Long itself, Loch
Fyne, even longer, and Loch Awe. From one to
the other the road climbs and falls. Up on the
hills, mist and moor. Down on the lochside, a
revelation of western light flooding up the valley,
glinting on white-harled walls or sharpening the
dark silhouette of rubble ruins. Finally,
squeezed through the Pass of Brander, the
traveller drops onto the soft shores of Loch Etive.
Below Connel Bridge run the Falls of Lora, a
frothy intimation of the Firth of Lorn. Over a
last hill lies Oban and the open sea. Out there
are the islands – Mull and Iona, Islay and Jura,
Coll and Tiree. On good days they seem to float
mirage-like on the horizon. Then again, no less
mysterious, they fuse in low lugubrious cloud,
drenched in melancholy. Further out, the lonely
lights of Skerryvore and Dhu Heartach flash
across the Atlantic swell.

*Left Corran Esplanade including The
Great Western Hotel, Oban c.1875;
Above MacMillan's Cross, Kilmory
Chapel.*

George Washington Wilson Collection,
University of Aberdeen

RCAHMS

   This view of the western sea brings
illumination. There is the realization that this is
not an end but a beginning. For this is the
threshold of Celtic Argyll. These are the waters
that baptised Scotland's Christianity. Columba
came here in the sixth century, leaving Ireland to
bring Christ to a pagan country. On these
islands and at landfalls on Kintyre and along the
shores of the narrow sea lochs cut deep into
Knapdale and Lorn he and his followers built the
timber chapels and rude rubble cells of a new
faith. There is considerable evidence for this
colonization, perhaps as much a matter of
territorial aggrandizement as religious concern,
but little that is architectural beyond the vestiges
of a beehive cell or the footings of some primitive
place of worship. What does survive is stone
carving; simple cross-incised slabs, inscriptions in
the Irish ogham alphabet, and above all the great
high crosses of Iona, Kildalton and Keills. These
are more than enough to show both the piety of
the Celtic church and the sophistication of

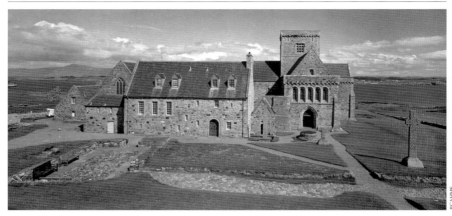

*Iona Abbey.*

Dalriadan culture in Argyll. Later, as the fortunes of Dalriada swung to mainland Scotland rather than Ireland, the Roman church began to extend its diocesan and monastic control. By the second half of the twelfth century the Cistercians were building an abbey at Saddell. On Iona, only a few decades later, an Augustinian nunnery was under construction while the Benedictines were building a new abbey to replace the old Columban foundation.

None of this was achieved without danger or delay for whatever temporal polity prevailed along Scotland's western seaboard towards the end of the first millennium AD it did not do so without challenge. From the middle of the ninth century Norse raiders had ravaged the coast. Here once more the evidence of the landscape is crucial. On countless rock-gnarled promontories traces of ancient fortification testify to a need for defensive security. In the centuries-long struggle for control of the Atlantic marches several of these duns became strategic strongholds alternately invested by Norseman and Gael. Dunaverty, Castle Sween, Duntrune, Dunollie, Dunstaffnage, Duart, Achadun and Dunivaig –

*Castle Sween.*

all are, or were, fortified masonry curtains wrapped around some defensible rocky outcrop. In time, with the final defeat of the Viking invaders in the thirteenth century, all were nominally Scottish. Yet suzerainty in the Gaedhealtachd remained in doubt. In Argyll and the Islands clan loyalties counted for much – and still do. In Lorn and Mull effective governance lay with the Clan Dougall while from their *well biggit* power-base at Finlaggan on Islay (now much reduced) the MacDonald Lords of the Isles for long held sway over much of the western seaboard. Not until the end of the fifteenth century was the monarchy finally in command.

Royal power introduced a new force in the region. The Clan Campbell, ancient in origin but hitherto subservient to MacDougalls, MacDonalds and MacLeans, now rose to pre-eminence. Installed as keepers of several important royal fortresses, the family ruled Argyll as the king's men. As their territories expanded through Mid Argyll into Lorn, Kintyre, Islay, Mull and Morvern, so did their ambitions. Favoured at Court and thirled to the Protestant cause, they shrewdly consolidated their power at both local and national level. Locally, this prestige was visible in the increasing architectural sophistication of the houses raised by the many individual branches of the family spread across the county; a range of domestic design that stretched from the gabled towers of Carrick, Kilchurn, Kilberry and Achallader to the pedimented façades of later classical mansions like Airds, Strachur, Asknish and Barbreck. But it was evident in grander projects too. In 1607 the plantation settlement of Campbeltown was founded. By the 1750s, the Campbell Dukes of Argyll were building not just a new clan castle at Inveraray but a new town with town-house, inn and a bi-axial plan at the crossing of which a unique *double-church* would be built. Agricultural improvements were underway in Glen Aray and Glen Shira. Steps were taken to

*Silvercraigs's House, Inveraray.*

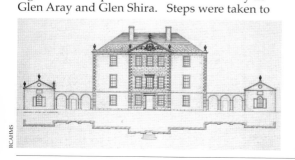

*RCAHMS drawing of Barbreck House.*

RCAHMS

Courtesy of St Andrews University Library (Valentine Collection)

From top *Aerial view of Tobermory,
Mull; Basin of the Crinan Canal, c. 1900.*

introduce the textile industry. Through the
British Fisheries Society the 5th Duke of Argyll
fostered the development of Tobermory on Mull,
while on Islay a succession of Campbell lairds
was responsible for the island's distinctive
planned villages. No other family has left its
mark so clearly on the man-made landscape of
Argyll and the Islands.

Such built developments, whether prompted
by Campbell initiative and innovation or, like the
early ironworks at Bonawe and Furnace, the
result of some other enterprise, relied on
maritime transport. Even at Inveraray, almost all
the materials needed for building were brought
by boat up Loch Fyne. The sea remained
Argyll's principal highway. Throughout the
eighteenth century and into the nineteenth, roads
constructed first by the military and later by

RCAHMS

North Pier, Oban.

Nick Haynes

Rothmar, Campbeltown.

statute labour did greatly improve communications across the county, many establishing the routes that are still followed. But the importance of the sea was little diminished. Indeed, at the beginning of the nineteenth century, the construction of the Crinan Canal coupled with the advent of steam navigation, the one completed at precisely the moment of the other's birth, served only to underscore what vital arteries the lochs and firths were. Then came the railways augmenting the links from Central Scotland to Oban and the steamer services to the Western Isles. By 1900 the combined convenience of travel by road, rail or steamer had transformed the county. At first no more than the distant destination of a few intrepid travellers lured by the romantic thrill of the sublime, by the end of Victoria's reign Argyll and the Islands were in thrall to tourism. Remote on the moors and in the wilder glens, the country-houses and shooting-lodges of *parvenu* lairds filled up with weekend house-guests. In the few towns, hotels and guest houses opened their doors to trippers pouring off steamer or train. Oban and Campbeltown, in fast and regular communication with Glasgow by rail and sea, took on a genuinely urban character with some of their finest buildings designed by the city's leading architects. J J Burnet, Henry Clifford, William Leiper, T L Watson and Charles Wilson all made significant contributions to the streetscape of Argyll's two main towns. Included in this legacy, a precious handful of magnificent tenement ranges in polychromatic stonework scarcely surpassed elsewhere in Scotland.

The Edwardian years marked the high point in Argyll's prosperity. Since then the twentieth

*Cairns and standing stone in Kintraw.*

century has seen a gradual decline accelerated in mid-century by the removal of steamer services from the Clyde and the reduction of rail services on the West Highland line. Tourism is still important to the local economy though the tourists no longer come *en masse*. Now they are hill-walkers, yachtsmen, fishermen, bird watchers, castle spotters. The Road to the Isles may be quiet but this is its attraction. The journey winds back in time past the Victorian and Georgian mansion-houses of great estates, past white-walled villages, deserted rubble townships, battlemented castles, gaunt abbeys and tiny ruined sanctuaries, back finally to the burial cairns and standing stones of pre-history, back to strange cup-and-ring-marked rocks, remote and runic. A journey through time – and through space too. Man-made spaces: the geometry-shaped streetscapes of Inveraray, Lochgilphead and Bowmore; sea-prospect promenades at Oban and Campbeltown; cottage rows at Arinagour, Ellanabeich and Portnahaven, unpretentious and beautiful. And the wide-open spaces of the natural landscape: the slow, vaguely anxious ascent to the Rest and Be Thankful, distant resonances in Kilmartin Glen, long polder-flat perspectives across Moine Mhor, hidden anchorages along the ragged rock-girt shores of Loch Sween, and the soul-searching walk over lonely strands on Coll and Tiree, ochre touching turquoise under endless skies. These are journeys worth making.

**Organisation of the Guide**

Most travellers reach Argyll from Central Scotland by way of three possible routes. They may follow the south shore of the Clyde (see *South Clyde Estuary* in this series) to Greenock and Gourock where car ferries cross the Firth to Cowal. They may take the north shore (see *North Clyde Estuary* in this series) to Dumbarton and the Vale of Leven, continuing by Loch Lomond and Loch Long before crossing the Rest and Be Thankful into Mid Argyll. A third approach holds to the Loch Lomond shore all the way north to Glen Falloch and Crianlarich where, joined by the road from Perthshire and Stirlingshire (see *Stirling and the Trossachs* in this series), the road west heads on to Dalmally and Lorn.

This guide has five main sections - **Cowal, Mid Argyll, Kintyre, Lorn,** and **the Islands.**

**Cowal** is approached from the north. First, from the Rest and Be Thankful, the dead-end route to Lochgoilhead and Carrick Castle is explored. From Strachur there are three roads south: down the Loch Fyne shore to Ardlamont; by Glendaruel to Tighnabruaich and Kames; by Loch Eck to Benmore. For coastal Cowal, see *North Clyde Estuary* in this series.

The description of **Mid Argyll** begins with Loch Fyne and Inveraray, then Loch Gilp and South Knapdale. Following the Crinan Canal, the guide continues to North Knapdale, Kilmartin Glen and Loch Craignish.

**Kintyre** begins at Tarbert on Loch Fyne. From here the west and east coast roads south are followed. Then comes Campbeltown and, at the foot of the peninsula, Machrihanish and Southend.

There are two routes into **Lorn**. The first from Dalmally runs by Loch Awe and on over the Pass of Brander to Loch Etive. From Connel a road goes north to Benderloch and Appin. The second route from Kilmartin Glen reaches the coast at Loch Melfort and continues north by way of the small islands of Seil and Luing. Both routes converge on Oban.

Oban is the departure point for **the Islands**. Lying close to the mainland, Kerrera and Lismore are described first. Next come Mull, Iona and the Treshnish Isles. Then Islay, Jura, the Garvellachs and Colonsay. Finally the guide reaches the outlying islands of Coll and Tiree.

**Text arrangement**
Entries for principal buildings follow the
sequence of name (or number), address, date and
architect (if known). Lesser buildings are
contained within paragraphs. Both demolished
buildings and unrealised projects are included if
appropriate. In general, the dates given are those
of the design (if known) or of the beginning of
construction. Entries in the small column
highlight interesting biographical, historical and
social aspects of the story of Argyll and the
Islands.

**Map references**
Maps are included in the text for the towns, with
a sequence of larger maps covering the whole
area appearing on pp. 211-215. A key to these
maps appears on the inside front cover. Numbers
on the maps do not refer to pages but to the small
numbers adjacent to the text itself. Numbers in
the index refer to pages – those in italics refer to
pictures in the colour section.

**Access to properties**
The majority of buildings in this guide are visible
from public roads or footpaths. However, only a
few of them are normally open for public visiting,
and readers are requested to respect the
occupiers' privacy.

**Sponsors**
The support of the following is gratefully
acknowledged: Argyll and the Islands, Loch
Lomond, Stirling & Trossachs (AILLST) Tourist
Board; North British Trust Hotels; The Oban
Times; Blair Atholl Estates; PF Charitable Trust;
Raven's Charitable Trust; Michael Blakenham;
Patrick Lorimer; Angus Macdonald; and Mr &
Mrs D Stewart.

## LOCHGOILHEAD

1 **Lochgoilhead and Kilmorich Parish Church**,
18th century (see p.25)

A harled, skew-gabled kirk, its T-plan
arrangement evidently 18th century in
provenance.   Much of the walling of the east and
west aisles, however, survives from the
longitudinal plan of the 14th century Church of
the Three Holy Brethren.   The north aisle belongs
to the radical remodelling carried out in the 18th
century when the two tall round-arched windows
flanking the south pulpit were introduced.
Other window openings, square-headed, have
been regularised.   In 1832, the session house with
its pyramid-topped birdcage bellcote on the
gable, was built against the south wall and in
1894 Campbell Douglas added the north porch.
The interior was refurbished by Ian G Lindsay in
1957.   Of two earlier galleries only the west
remains, the Drimsynie Loft, early 19th century.
Pulpit, 1791, from Kiltearn, Ross and Cromarty,
installed in 1955.   In the east aisle a drop in floor
level indicates the medieval chancel.   There is a
tomb recess framed by a semicircular arch in the
north wall and against the east gable the
**Campbell of Ardkinglass Monument**, late 16th
century, a symmetrical compilation of naively
classical elements with a triangular upper zone
incorporating tiers of squat finials linked by
scrolling.   At the centre of the lower zone is a
doorway, now blocked, which originally led to
the Ardkinglass burial aisle, demolished in 1850.

From top *Campbell of Ardkinglass
Monument; Lochgoilhead and Kilmorich
Parish Church; Drimsynie House.*

**Lochgoilhead Free Church**, 1883, Campbell
Douglas & Sellars
Basic Gothic, though the west porch has a spirelet
bellcote.   In 1952 the church became a hall but it
is no longer in use.

2 **Drimsynie House**, mid 19th century,
James Smith(?)
Early photographs show a rather cubic
crenellated mansion rising above the trees on the
west side of the loch.   Besides a square entrance
tower with a corbelled castellated parapet,
slender square turrets stab the battlemented
skyline at the corners.   Hood mouldings and
cross-loops add to the conceit.   Today all sense of
lonely romance has vanished, in a sea of
caravans, chalets and the flat roofs of late 20th
century leisure buildings.   Though radically
converted, the symmetrical façade range of a
**court of offices** antedating the Victorian

mansion can still be discerned nearby.

**Village Hall**, 1898, James Salmon & Son
Despite roughcast and slates, stained timberwork
in the verandah and gables betray the spell of
English Arts and Crafts.

**Lochgoilhead Hotel**, an 18th century inn, altered
and extended to the east, is at the centre of the
village, close to the water's edge. **The Cottage**,
mid 19th century, harled, with a porch crested
with decorative ironwork, also enjoys the view
down the loch. A succession of villas spills
down the east shore. The earlier houses, c.1840,
have attic dormers and open eaves. **Alma**,
c.1860, has a fine ironwork verandah with
filigreed spandrels. With arched windows,
bargeboards and a tall Italianate tower,
**Burnknowe**, c.1875, recalls the Clydeside houses
of Alexander Thomson. **Invermay** and
**Woodlands** are plain piend-roofed houses, c.1880,
the latter prettified by added shutters and
balconies to the loch. On the opposite shore, two
kilometres south of the village, **The Lodge** seems
to have been begun in 1863-64, probably by
Boucher & Cousland, but a decade later was
enlarged by William Leiper with balconies,
verandahs and overhanging eaves in a light-
fingered Swiss Cottage transformation.

*From top Lochgoilhead Hotel; The Lodge.*

### CARRICK CASTLE
3 **Carrick Castle**, late 14th century
Built by the Campbells of Lochawe who later
became Earls of Argyll. Set on a massive rock
base on the west shore of Loch Goil, the castle
walls of pinned rubble rise almost 15 metres on
all sides. The plan is oblong, almost a double
square, though cut obliquely across the north-
west corner. There were three high storeys
reached by mural stairs and lit by a variety of
randomly placed windows, some lintelled, some
with moulded pointed arches. Impressive
externally, the interior was destroyed when the
castle was fired during the Earl of Argyll's
rebellion of 1685. Ruinous outer works on the
east comprise a rectangular north range, early 17th
century, the raggled roof-line of which can be
seen on the east wall of the castle, and a
courtyard wall, 16th century, which narrows the
courtyard approach towards the entrance gate at
the south. Neglected for more than two
centuries the castle was partially repaired in the
early 1900s. In 1988 Ian Begg created living

Above *Carrick Castle drawn in the mid 19th century;* Left *Carrick Castle before reoccupation.*

accommodation at first- and second-floor levels under a steeply pitched attic; a lower caphouse roof advances over the stair rising at the north-east corner.

There is not much more to the village. The old timber **pier**, 1877, which closed in 1945, has been superseded by a Ministry of Defence quay constructed in the 1950s. Bereft of steamer links to the Clyde and shorn of its bartizan roofs, **Hillside**, 1877, the one lonely Baronial tenement, is doubly incongruous. One or two Victorian villas along the shore road catch the eye: **Rhumhor** has fun with canted bays; **Craigard** is more seriously Scots.

## STRACHUR

The village stretches from the almost Gothic **school** of 1912, by Archibald Fergusson (two-storey classroom wing by Argyll County Council, 1956) down to the Loch Fyne shore. The oldest part lies to the north of the A815. The Old Inn, now known as **Strachur Hall**, dates from the 1790s. It has a roughcast bow-front to the north-west on which a gabled second floor has been corbelled. In 1804 the north-east gable was reduced when the village street was widened. Nearby is the inn's **coach house**, its rubble walls cut with ventilation slots.

*Strachur Hall.*

4 **Strachur Parish Church**, 1789; reconstructed 1902-03, Archibald Fergusson
An oblong kirk in an ancient burial enclosure elevated above the street. A short belfry tower advances at the centre of the south front. This frontispiece, which is pedimented above what

was originally the entrance but is now the vestry, carries an ogee-topped bellcote. The west and east gables were constructed at the start of the 20th century when the church was recast and a new porched entrance created on the east. Internally, this change in the liturgical axis has left only the east gallery from the 18th century arrangement. In the graveyard, some **tapered slabs**, 14th-15th century, and many **headstones** with armorial and craft carving, 18th-19th century.

5 **Strachur House**, *c.*1785 (see p.25)
General John Campbell's five-bay wide classical mansion-house is pedimented on the south-west. At the centre, tripartite windows and pilastered entrance, the latter hidden by a rounded porch, added early 20th century. Lower flanking wings, originally flat-roofed and castellated, were altered and given dormered mansards at the same time. The garden front is boldly bowed through three storeys and retains its crenellated parapet. Many of the interior features are original; cornices, door casings, chimneypieces. The freestanding columned screens at the rear of the bow-fronted dining-room and study on ground and first floors are particularly graceful. The **formal garden** on the north-east is early 20th century but the **walled garden** beyond is original. There are several estate buildings from the last years of the 18th century. Among them, the **West Gateway**, a round-arched rubble portal on the A815, the exceptionally well-appointed, two-storey **court of offices**. These are approached across a delightful **bridge** (see p.25) of the most sophisticated classical elegance, its segmental arch set between urn-carrying pedimented abutments penetrated by riverside passageways. Similarities with bridges by John Adam and Robert Mylne at Inveraray cannot be accidental, though the designer is unknown. **Betty Jenkins's Bridge**, which crosses the Eas Dubh, is also segmental in span but decidedly rough and rural in treatment.

From top *Strachur Parish Church; Strachur House; Strachur House, garden front; Strachur House bridge.*

## LOCHFYNESIDE EAST

From Strachur the A815 continues north-east along the Loch Fyne shore to St Catherines, once a ferry point for the short crossing to Inveraray but now no more than a straggling hamlet. **St Catherines Hotel** is the coaching inn of 1756 enlarged with a dormered attic and a wide, but far from enhancing, glazed porch. The road then veers inland to meet the A83 coming down Glen

Kinglas from the Rest and Be Thankful. South-west from Strachur the A886 also follows the shore almost as far as Newton, a side-lined row of early 19th century lochside cottages and a few detached fishermen's stores. A swing south brings the main road into Glendaruel (see below). But, after passing through Strathlachlan, a secondary route, the B8000, maintains the coastal route down the east shore of Loch Fyne.

## GARBHALLT

**Strathlachlan Parish Church**, *c*.1792
A simple hall church rudely Gothic in aspiration. Harled with roughly cut stones projecting in a naively rustic manner at the quoins and around lancets and quatrefoil in the south-west gable. The roof is late 19th century, a renovation that may explain the bargeboarded gable to the north-east.

**Old Parish Church**, Kilmorie, 15th century
Only the roofless rubble shell of the **MacLachlan Burial Aisle**, late 16th century, survives. Its west gable appears to be the chancel gable of the earlier church. In the surrounding burial enclosure are some **grave slabs**, 14th-16th century, and a re-erected 15th century **cross-shaft** with a damaged foliated head.

6 **Old Castle Lachlan,** from early 15th century
Though the castle is not large, its massy ruinous profile silhouetted against the sky as it erupts from a promontory at the mouth of Lachlan Bay is wonderfully evocative. The plan is simple; an oblong curtain reminiscent of Castle Sween, though much later and smaller. Much of this curtain remains with walls standing to a height betrayed as four storeys by the window openings of two inner ranges, reconstructed *c*.1500. These ranges, separated by a narrow central yard, are floorless but preserve vaulted chambers at ground-floor level. The castle was inhabited until the end of the 18th century when New Castle Lachlan was built. (see p.25)

**New Castle Lachlan,** *c*.1790; remodelled 1903
Unrecognizable as the modest classical mansion-house which Robert MacLachlan built with a flying stair and a crenellated parapet to recall its castellar predecessor, the present house is the result of extensive enlargement and alteration in a vigorous Baronial idiom carried out at the start of the 20th century. The result, impressive if by

**The construction of a military road from Dumbarton to Inveraray** began in 1743 under the direction of Major William Caulfield. The route went by Loch Lomondside to Tarbet, thence to Arrochar on Loch Long and then through Glen Croe to Cairndow and Loch Fyne. By 1748 the road had been laid as far as the Rest and Be Thankful summit in Glen Croe, a wild and desolate climb up the glen in a series of serpentine turns. Robert Southey found the track *descending from the immediate summit . . . with such volutions that a line drawn from the top would intersect several times in a short distance. In mountainous countries,* he wrote, *a fine road is a grand and beautiful work, and never so striking as when it winds thus steeply and skilfully.* Now bypassed at higher level by the modern carriageway, the old military road can still be seen, a thin thread woven back and forward on the valley contours below.

From top *Strathlachlan Parish Church; Old Castle Lachlan; New Castle Lachlan.*

From top *The Oystercatcher; Ballimore House; Barnlongart.*

The gardens at Ballimore were largely the responsibility of **Thomas Mawson** (1866-1933). He developed a highly successful garden design practice with commissions in Britain, continental Europe and the USA. In 1900 he published *Art and Craft of Garden Making*. At Ballimore he combined both formal and informal approaches to landscape: terraces, obelisks, geometrical bedding and clipped yews were used to define areas close to the house while these were subtly merged with freer planting and winding woodland walkways beyond. The creation of pools, waterfalls and rock gardens and the introduction of choice species of rhododendrons, etc., all contributed to what Mawson himself referred to as *a somewhat extensive piece of work*. Almost all of this magnificent achievement is now neglected and overgrown.

that time barely fashionable, is again castellar in allusion with a high battlemented tower at the centre of the south-west front, the culmination of an asymmetrically contrived composition. The **court of offices** built *c.*1800 survives in dilapidated condition at the rear. Beyond is an overgrown **walled garden**.

### OTTER FERRY
Despite the name, there is no ferry. The old rubble **quay** and **slipway**, a late 18th century replacement for an earlier jetty built for the Commissioners of Supply in 1773, is still in occasional use but the ferry across Loch Fyne to West Otter and Loch Gilp was long ago discontinued. Nor, of course, do steamers call; in 1948 the steamboat pier, 1.6 km. north, was closed. Of the few houses clustering near the old pier, The Oystercatcher with its pedimented three-bay front, appropriately painted in black and white, is, in fact, the oldest, the late-18th century **ferry-house**. An estate track leads west from the quay towards the sand spit (Gaelic *oitir*) which gives the place its name. Continuing south by the shore, it reaches Ballimore House.

7 **Ballimore House**, *c.*1832, David Hamilton; recast by William Leiper, 1898-99
The early 19th century character of the original house is still apparent in the underlying symmetry of the composition and in Hamilton's fine porch. The later work is no less evident and yet Leiper's hefty Baronial corbels, rounds and castellated parapet emerge seamlessly from the older masonry. The still Scottish extensions to the north-east, 1914, probably by Leiper's partner and successor William Hunter McNab, are roughcast and altogether lighter in touch but all too clearly additions. Behind the house is Hamilton's **court of offices** carrying a tall birdcage belfry corbelled over the carriage pend. Uphill to the south-west, **Barnlongart**, *c.*1899, a charming Arts and Crafts house by Leiper, lies sadly abandoned. Forgotten and neglected, too, the astonishing terraced and woodland **gardens** laid out by Thomas Mawson, 1900-01; only a few overgrown beds and a small roofless summer-house give clues to what must have been perhaps the finest garden in Argyll.

### KILFINAN
A pleasant village about 5 km. south over the hills from Otter Ferry. Church, hotel, manse and

cottages group attractively round a bend in the B8000.

8 **Kilfinan Parish Church,** from late 12<sup>th</sup> or early 13<sup>th</sup> century

Similarities of elongated plan and orientation with ruined churches at Kilkivan and Killean in Kintyre and Kildalton in Islay substantiate an early medieval date. The north aisle or **Lamont Aisle** was added in 1633. The church itself, however, required repairs before the end of the 17<sup>th</sup> century and was largely rebuilt in the second half of the following century when the upper floor of the Lamont Aisle became a laird's loft (now blocked) accessible by a forestair. Birdcage gable belfry, 1837. Renovation by John Honeyman, 1881-82, introduced a number of lancets, an Early English east entrance door and a new open-trussed roof.

In the burial vault of the Lamont Aisle are several funerary monuments including **tapered slabs,** 14<sup>th</sup>-15<sup>th</sup> century and fragments of a **freestanding cross** of similar date. West of the church is the **MacFarlane Burial Enclosure,** c.1830, which has a pedimented sarcophagus in the west wall. To the south, through neo-Greek gate-piers, the **Rankin Burial Enclosure,** c.1900, entered through a round arch framed by a pilastered aedicule of pink marble.

**Kilfinan Hotel** appears to be the aggregation of four gable-to-gable roadside dwellings all with bargeboarded eaves dormers; most seem Victorian, though the south house is dated 1760. The tall two-storey-and-garret **manse** of 1808 sits across the road from the church. Doorpiece and dormers are mid 19<sup>th</sup> century. **Fearnoch Mill,** 1 km. north of the village, is a mid-19<sup>th</sup> century threshing mill now converted to a dwelling but retaining its iron overshot wheel.

9 **Ardmarnock House,** c.1826

Some six kilometres south of Kilfinan on a narrow road branching west from the B8000; small, cubic and classical, a three-bay, piend-roofed mansion raised on a basement and dignified by a simple porch of fluted Ionic columns reached across a flying stairway. A central blocking piece serves instead of a pediment. Baronial north-east wing added c.1880.

*From top* Kilfinan Parish Church; *armorial slab in the Lamont Aisle of* Kilfinan Parish Church; *Rankin Burial Enclosure;* Ardmarnock House.

The following is noted in the image margins: RCAHMS (repeated beside images).

From top *Ascog Castle; Kilbride Church;*
Right *Ardlamont House.*

## MILLHOUSE

A village cluster at the cross-roads of South
Cowal. A few brick cottages, rubble ruins and
overgrown foundations are all that remain from
the gunpowder works which operated here
between 1839 and 1921. To the north is Kilfinan.
To the east, Kames, Tighnabruaich and the Kyles
of Bute (see below). To the west, the shattered
shell of **Ascog Castle**, mid 15th century, like
Toward Castle (see *North Clyde Estuary* in this
series) a Lamont seat destroyed during the Earl of
Argyll's rebellion in the late 17th century. Further
west, at the ferry point for Tarbert, a deserted
village. This is not some lost rural idyll but the
putative industrial settlement of **Portavadie**
located close to the deep waters of Loch Fyne to
accommodate the hundreds of men that should
have built (but never did) concrete oil platforms
for the oil industry. Monopitch ranks of
dormitory blocks, recreation rooms, restaurant
and other amenity buildings, by Thomas Smith,
Gibb & Pate, have stood unoccupied for more
than two decades, hollow and haunted, echoing
with reproach.

### Kilbride Church, 1839

A gabled Gothic box with an entrance gable
carrying a corbelled castellated bellcote. No
longer in use.

### Ardlamont House, 1819-20, Thomas Napier

The core, a T-plan five-bay mansion with a
piended roof, is early 19th century but parts of the
gabled west and east wings survive from an older
house probably built a century earlier. A boxy
porch, pilastered but flat-roofed, perches at the
centre of an otherwise disappointingly flat south
façade, a flying stair advancing across the sunk
basement area below. The north front, originally
the rear, acquired precedence in 1970 when a hip-
roofed columned portico was wrapped around
the projecting stem of the T. By the roadside is
the **court of offices**, early 19th century, the main
south range symmetrical with end pavilions and

a gabled centre with arched pend and doocot entries. In the **walled garden**, early 19th century, there is an obelisk **sundial**, early 18th century. (see p.26)

## GLENDARUEL

12 **Dunans House**, *c*.1864-65, Andrew Kerr
Well set Baronial mansion of three tall storeys with a large cylindrical tower at the south-east corner and pedimented eaves dormers west and south. The house is approached over a spectacularly high rubble **bridge**, 1815, which crosses the gorge of the River Ruel, more than 13 m. below, in three pointed-arch spans. Downstream, on a wooded bluff above the river, is the **Fletcher Mausoleum**, a small, late 18th century Gothic burial chapel with open tracery and a gated entry in the east gable.

The main route down the eastern side of the valley is straight and fast. On the opposite side of the river, however, a slower narrower road has more to offer. Past Achanelid farm, surrounded by trees on a steep knoll to the left of the road, is a small **burial enclosure** with several mural tablets, 19th century, built by the Campbells of Glendaruel. Further on is Glendaruel Park. A crenellated rubble wall with a pointed-arch **gateway**, early 19th century(?), gives some idea of former grandeur. But both the mansion-house of 1762 and its Baronial successor by William Leiper, 1900-03, have gone, the latter destroyed by fire in 1970. The early **estate offices** and **stables**, remodelled by Leiper in a roughcast vernacular idiom, survive to serve a caravan park. So, too, do Leiper's **Home Farm**, **Watermill Cottage** and **Laundry Cottage**, all endowed with a soft rural charm. Concealed off a rough track uphill is **St Sophia's Chapel**, 1912, buttressed Gothic in miniature, designed by Leiper's partner, W H McNab, for the Catholic wife of the estate laird, William Harrison Cripps. An inelegant extension mars its conversion to residential use.

## CLACHAN OF GLENDARUEL

A hamlet on the east side of the valley where the older, narrower road rejoins the A886. There are a few rudimentary rubble **cottages**, a **smiddy**, a symmetrical **steading** adapted as housing, and an inn, **Glendaruel Hotel**, all of which date from the early years of the 19th century, though they are much altered.

From top *Dunans House; Dunans Bridge; Glendaruel gateway; St Sophia's Chapel.*

*Kilmodan Parish Church.*

### 13 **Kilmodan Parish Church**, 1783

A harled T-plan kirk with sandstone quoins and margins. The main south façade is characteristically Presbyterian: a central pedimented projection set between tall round-arched windows with smaller superimposed windows lighting the west and east galleries. The doorway at the centre of the south front has been blocked and access is now gained through doors in the gables. The interior was handsomely renovated in 1983. It retains galleries in the three arms of the T, each of which originally served as a laird's loft for separate branches of the Campbell family resident in the parish. In the graveyard is a small rubble building, mid 18th century(?), which may have been the Burial Enclosure of the Campbells of Auchenbreck but, given a slated pyramid roof in 1970, is now a **lapidarium**. It houses several **tapered slabs**, 14th-15th century, carved with swords, plant interlacing and effigies.

*Bealachandrain Bridge.*

South of Clachan, the two segmental arch spans of **Bealachandrain Bridge**, 1808, by Thomas Telford, take the hill road west to Otter Ferry across the River Ruel. Attractively white on the hillside, **Bealachandrain Farm**, a typical, early 19th century, three-bay farmhouse with a U-plan **steading** built round a cobbled yard.

Past Bealachandrain Bridge the valley narrows suddenly. Here the road divides. The A886 continues down the east side of Loch Riddon (also known as Loch Ruel) to the Kyles of Bute and the ferry for Bute at Colintraive (for Bute itself, see *North Clyde Estuary* in this series). The A8003, on the other hand, crosses the river taking the west shore to the Kyles and on to Tighnabruaich, Kames and South Cowal.

*Kilmodan and Colintraive Church.*

### COLINTRAIVE

Ferry point for the short crossing to Rhubodach on Bute. The village straggles along the A886 and its continuation south-east to the mouth of Loch Striven. Most of the older cottages have gone (an 1808 datestone from the old smiddy is now in the wall of the local Community Centre) but there are some attractive villas. **Faolinn**, 1908, has an English look: red-tiled roofs and an arcaded verandah. The harled **Old Manse**, *c.*1900(?), is much more Scots with its crowstepped entrance gable and Lorimer-like eaves dormers. Grandest of all is **Caol Ruadh**,

late 19th century(?), an appropriately named red brick and sandstone assemblage of bays and oriels terribly mauled by flat-roofed brick extensions which seem an ill-deserved penalty for conversion to a residential centre in the 1960s.

**Kilmodan and Colintraive Church**, 1840
A lancet Gothic kirk with aspiration to greater things; at the apex of its white seaside gable is a tall birdcage bellcote carrying a taller obelisk.

On the west side of the River Ruel the A8003 passes **Ormidale House**, a cluster of Victorian gables which engross and obscure almost all trace of the 18th century mansion they supersede. At the rear right, the walls of the original **court of offices** still stand. Farther on, down a side road that runs with the water's edge, is **Ormidale Lodge**, late 19th century, a four-storey L-plan house with a cone-topped turnpike stair in the re-entrant. It stands close to the old steamboat **pier**, 1856, built at the northern limit of deep water in Loch Riddon. From the Tighnabruaich road which winds and climbs south there are spectacular views across the narrows to Bute and the Firth of Clyde beyond.

## TIGHNABRUAICH

The first of three contiguous villages whose separate existence is only revealed by three piers, two of which are now rarely in use and one barely visible. Tighnabruaich's **pier**, 1843, rebuilt 1884-85, is still occasionally in service. The roughcast **pierhead building** began as a shop and house, c.1857, was extended as a tearoom with a half octagon roof to the north and a wide piended dormer south, c.1905, and is once again a dwelling.

**Tighnabruaich Parish Church**, 1863, Boucher & Cousland
Gabled rubble with round-arched windows and doorway. A tall gabled bellcote rises from the apex of the gabled front. (see p.26)

14 **Tighnabruaich House**, 1895, William Leiper
A large Arts and Crafts villa busy with gables and bays, tall chimneys and leaded lights in mullion-and-transom windows. Evidently part of the stylistic legacy of Norman Shaw but with minimal half-timbering and no tile-hanging. English in allusion, the design is unmistakably Scots in execution, for the house is built in rough

RCAHMS

RCAHMS

From top *Ormidale Lodge;*
*Tighnabruaich Parish Church.*

The architect **William Leiper** (1839-1916) is perhaps best known for his work in and around Helensburgh where he lived all his life (see *North Clyde Estuary* in this series). There he designed a number of villas in a manner at times Baronial, but more often in a softer Anglicised idiom much influenced by the Arts and Crafts style of Norman Shaw. These approaches were evident too in commissions won further west in Argyll. In the enlargement of Ballimore House, carried out 1898-99, and particularly in the vast pile of Glendaruel House, built 1900-03 but subsequently demolished after a fire in 1970, round towers, conically capped roofs and crowstepped gables are all deployed. On the other hand, at Tighnabruaich House, 1895, as at Ganavan House, Oban, 1888, tiles, half-timbering, red brick and sandstone evoke more English precedents. Something of both seems suitably infused in the inclusively named Argyll Mansions, 1905-07, the magnificent four-storeyed corner tenement which Leiper and his partner William Hunter McNab designed on the harbour front at Oban.

**A wonderful view south to the Kyles of Bute** can be had from the heights of the Tighnabruaich road above Loch Riddon. If this prospect, like much of the romantic scenery of the Highlands and Islands, is often at its best in the half-light of dusk, these are also the most dangerous moments for the unsuspecting traveller. It is then that the **midge**, hunting in clouds of countless thousands, strikes. This all but invisible scourge of the Celtic twilight comes in over 30 varieties, though one only, the Highland midge, or *culicoides impunctatus*, (and then only the female of the species) is responsible for blood-sucking attacks on humans. It is found all across Scotland but nowhere is it more at home than in Argyll.

*The Congo's no' to be compared wi' the West o' Scotland when ye come to insects,* avers Neil Munro's Para Handy. *There's places here that's chust deplorable whenever the weather's the least bit warm. Look at Tighnabruaich! – they're that bad there, they'll bite their way through corrugated iron roofs to get at ye!*

whinstone, red sandstone dressings and hard red brick. Interior panelled in Kauri pine. Hillside garden.

The village centre seems to coincide with the only stretch of double-sided street on the Kyles shore; a few shops with flats above date from *c*.1860. Beyond the Parish Church the village's villas are scattered along the coastal slopes. **The Grove**, 1876, is attractively fringed with good ironwork ornament. **The Square** probably has an 1840s core; if so, later enlargements in the 1920s give it little respect. Gothic details add interest to **Creagandaraich**, *c*.1855, and **Dunmar**, *c*.1855. At **Wellpark House**, 1864, there are fretted bargeboards and at **Eden Kerry**, 1857, more decorative ironwork. A hillside site and widely overhanging shallow-pitched roofs give **The Chalet Hotel**, 1857, its eponymous Alpine character; it was originally, fashionably and not surprisingly, known as Swiss Cottage. Farther north is **Argyll Villa**, 1868, an unremarkable, two-storey-and-attic, gabled house made extraordinary by the addition of castellated toy turrets at each corner. **Sherbrooke**, 1878, is in grander classical manner, symmetrical with a central porch flanked by tripartite windows with bipartites above.

### AUCHENLOCHAN
The link between Tighnabruaich and Kames. An iron **pier**, *c*.1878-79, remained in use until 1948 but is now almost entirely destroyed. The **High Church**, late 19th century, has fared only slightly better, its Decorated Gothic an incongruous addendum to the local school.

**Tighnabruaich Primary School**, 1874-75, James Boucher(?)
A gabled E-plan block to which Argyll & Bute Council have added a hip-roofed **hall** with glazing along the eaves, 1997-98.

The three-storeyed **Royal Hotel**, *c*.1865, extended south *c*.1900, rises high to enjoy the views. Previously fronted by a verandah canopied in fine ironwork. Nearby is a draper's **shop**, 1886, with the gabled bays and dormers of the house above tiered over its full-frontal fascia. Along the front are several villas built in the 1870s and 1880s. **Nodfa** has an arcuated entrance balcony between bays. **Allt Mor** and **Ardvaar** both have decorative bargeboarding.

*Royal Hotel, Auchenlochan, c.1900.*

*Kames Pier.*

## KAMES

An unprepossessing place from which a road goes west to Millhouse and Portavadie. There is a ruined **pier**, 1856 and 1880, and another jetty, the **Black Quay**, 1839, built for the powder works at Millhouse. Above the now far from picturesque pier is **Kames Hotel**, mid 19th century, unremarkable save for its ironwork entrance canopy of tapered and fluted Ionic columns. At **Rockholme**, 1900, the ironwork porch arches on Corinthian columns. Bay windowed and dormered like many along the Kyles shore, **Netherton**, 1900, is distinguished by a half-timbered first floor.

**Kyles Parish Church**, 1898-99
Framed in red sandstone dressings at the projecting centre of the east gable is a cusped four-light window under a segmental arch. Below it, under a similar arch, a splayed entrance doorway.

## BY LOCH ECK TO THE HOLY LOCH

From Strachur the A815 runs south along the valley of the River Cur to follow the east shore of Loch Eck to the Holy Loch and Cowal coast (for Cowal's Clyde coast, see *North Clyde Estuary* in this series).

Near the hamlet of **Glenbranter** is **Glenshellish House**, late 1820s, a piended farmhouse with a pediment front and lower symmetrical wings curving around a yard at the rear. Five kilometres further south, a neat three-bay house can be seen, starkly white against the dark hillside across Loch Eck on the west shore. This is **Bernice**, an 18th century dwelling, isolated, simple, but somehow archetypally architectural.

15 **Benmore House and Gardens**, from 1851, John Baird and Charles Wilson (see p.26)

*Glenshellish House.*

Right *Benmore House in 1925;* Below *Benmore House sundial.*

Set at the heart of a richly planted estate that is now the Younger Botanic Garden outstation of the Royal Botanic Garden in Edinburgh. By 1851, James Lamont, who had newly acquired the estate, had replaced a much decayed older mansion with a new house, by *Mr Baird, of Glasgow*, probably the rather strange crowstepped core evident at the centre of the present south front. Just over a decade later a new American laird engaged Charles Wilson to design the unequivocally Baronial four-storey tower added at the north-west angle, 1862. David Thomson added the Baronial service wings around a courtyard to the north. Later still, possibly in the 1890s, the present east wing was constructed. Adaptation as a Leisure Centre in the 1960s explains the unfortunate appearance of a harled escape stair at the rear of Wilson's tower-house.

A **formal garden** has been created in what was once the estate's walled garden. Although the great Victorian greenhouses have gone, there are many rare species of trees and plants. The shingled bell-shaped roof of **Puck's Hut**, 1928, by Sir Robert S Lorimer, commands the central axis of the garden layout; it was moved here from Puck's Glen in 1968. Armillary **sundial**, 1978. Baronial coach-house and stables of **Benmore Steading**, 1874-75, by David Thomson(?), carefully and convincingly restored by the Property Services Agency and James Taylor Partnership, 1990-91. Elsewhere in the estate: golden ironwork **gates** bearing the initials JD for James Duncan who had them fabricated for the 1871 Paris Exhibition, a rubble **fernery**, 1874, and the **Wright Memorial Shelter**, 1990, by Robin Lorimer, modest but elegantly classical. The **South Lodge**, with its corbelled eaves and gables similar to those on the original house of 1851, is probably by Baird. *Open to the public.*

At Dalinlongart, a road branches west through the hamlet of **Clachaig**, a scatter of white-painted rubble cottages built to house the workers

Top *Strachur House Bridge;* Middle
*First floor study of Strachur House;*
Bottom *Lochgoilhead and Kilmorich
Parish Church;* Above *Castle Lachlan.*

Top *Ardlamont House;* Above *Stained glass window in Tighnabruaich Parish Church;* Middle *Tighnabruaich Parish Church and manse;* Bottom *Golden gates at Benmore House.*

Top and Above *Dunderave Castle;*
Middle *Dubh Loch Bridge;* Bottom
*Garron Bridge.*

Top *Inveraray seen from the Watch Tower;*
Bottom *Inveraray seen from Duke's Tower.*

employed by the gunpowder works established here in the 1830s, passes through Glen Lean to reach the head of Loch Striven and then continues to Loch Riddon and the Kyles of Bute.

From the Rest and be Thankful the road into Mid Argyll falls west through Glen Kinglas to Loch Fyne.

Left *The Rest and be Thankful road.* Below *Inscribed stone at Rest and be Thankful.*

## CAIRNDOW
16 **Kilmorich Church**, 1816

A white-harled octagonal church entered through a square west tower with a traceried parapet and corner finials. Wall planes and pointed-arch windows are edged in sandstone. A gabled session-house was added at the east end in the late 19th century. The church's slated pyramidal roof is reflected in the boarded ceiling slopes of the interior. A single small gallery, the Ardkinglas loft, opens from the tower through a semicircular archway.

Above *Kilmorich Church.*

The village is a run of modest lochside dwellings. At the north end, some strongly vernacular **cottages** by Ian G Lindsay, *c.*1950; at the south, close to the church, a pleasantly unassuming group of dormered **houses**, early 1990s, by John Boys. **Cairndow Inn**, an 18th century staging-post, two storeys high and three bays wide, has sacrificed its original dignity to later expansion. A little uphill to the south is **Strone House**, *c.*1930, a rubble-walled residence with a high hipped roof carried on eaves brackets at the corners.

17 **Ardkinglas House**, 1906-08, Robert S Lorimer
A house with a history of many antecedent

mansions – mostly unbuilt. A Campbell residence of uncertain medieval and later date survived in ruins almost to the end of the 18th century. Proposals for its replacement from Colin Campbell in the 1720s, Robert Adam, 1773, and several from James Playfair, 1790, all foundered. A pedimented seven-bay mansion, dull but respectable, was finally built *c.*1795, only to be burnt down in 1831. Immediately, a new house was envisaged and proposals first in Tudor-Jacobean style and then in Baronial were obtained. But nothing was done beyond the adaptation of the 18th century stables as *Old Ardkinglas House* and it was only in the early years of the 20th century that the then new owner of the estate, Sir Andrew Noble, commissioned Lorimer.

The result is recognizably Lorimer Scotch: a complex aggregation of crowstep-gabled roofs set at different heights, peppered with chimney-stacks and the architect's typically idiosyncratic pedimented eaves dormers. Two bell-roofs accent the flanks while a tall caphouse tower with a cone-capped double-height bartizan rises above the valleys and gables of the roofscape below. The walls, which were meant to be harled, are in fact of local granite rubble with sandstone dressings. Splendid interiors, more classical than medieval in spirit, with Mannerist and Baroque touches in the decorative detail. Plasterwork by Thomas Beattie and Sam Wilson. In the grounds of the estate are a D-plan **walled garden**, early 19th century, and a magnificent **arboretum** in the valley of the Kinglas Water.

From Cairndow the A83 runs north-east to cross the River Fyne before swinging around the head

*Bridge of Fyne.*

of the loch to continue towards Inveraray down the opposite shore.

18 **Bridge of Fyne**, 1754, John Brown
A four-arched bridge with cutwater piers and projecting refuges carrying the old road over the river. The schist coping stones of the low parapet walls are incised with a fascinating variety of dates, initials and images.

*Left Dunderave Castle; Below Entrance door of Dunderave Castle.*

### LOCHFYNESIDE WEST

19 **Dunderave Castle**, 1598; restored 1911-12 by Robert S Lorimer (see p.27)

An L-plan house, seat of the MacNaughton clan. A square entrance tower containing a circular turnpike stair sits in the re-entrant, protected from the prevailing winds. This sheltered outdoor space is greatly enhanced by the lower wings which Lorimer added against the north-east and south-east gables and by his subtle dishing of the cobbled courtyard through which the house is approached. Above the entrance door is a mural panel carved with a cautionary text and above it a second smaller panel bearing the date 1598. On each side of the door, fragmentary carved heads have been incorporated (salvaged perhaps from some earlier building). Lorimer's restoration of the tower was extensive and included crowstepped gables, chimneys, most of the pedimented dormers and a number of gunloops. His work on the lower wings, while maintaining textural and decorative links to the original, is more inventive. A bellcast cone over a turnpike stair, a columned loggia reached by a forestair, a vaulted pend connecting the driveway to the inner yard of the castle; these and more, not least some robustly moulded details, enliven what is a comprehensively Scottish conceit. All of this merges imperceptibly against the old and sits so securely in the landscape that it seems as if Lorimer's driveway wall, tiered **garden**, pyramid-roofed **summer-house**, curving **sea-wall** and **slipway** had always been there.

20 **Garron Bridge**, 1747-49, Roger Morris. (see p.27) A single segmental-arch span of almost 20m. with part-balustraded parapets, by the designer of Inveraray Castle. Nearby an arcaded **screen wall** connects with **Garron Lodge**, 1783-84, by Robert Mylne, a harled gabled block sandwiched between lower wings but evidently only one of the two end pavilions of the symmetrical scheme the designer intended to build.

*Garron Bridge.*

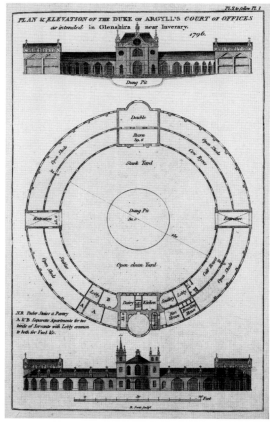

*Maam Steading engraved by John Smith, 1798.*

There are more bridges in Glen Shira: the hooded segmental-arch of **Dubh Loch Bridge**, 1785-87, by Robert Mylne (see p.27), and **Kilblaan Bridge**,

1760-68, by John Brown, a double span with cutwater piers. Mylne's **Maam Steading**, 1787-90, is again only half built for the original design envisaged a vast *round square* with arcading, towers and Gothic detail. Yet what has been realized, a semicircle of sheds with a two-storey barn at the centre is testimony enough to the ambitious estate improvements carried out by the reforming 5th Duke of Argyll.

South along the Loch Fyne shore the road passes **Kilmalieu Burial Ground**, site of the medieval church of Inveraray. The graveyard is rich in **headstones, table-tombs** and **mural monuments** with well over 300 dating from before the middle of the 19th century. Then comes Robert Mylne's **Aray Bridge**, 1773-76, two segmental arches separated by a triangular cutwater pier above which the masonry of the bridge is pierced by a dramatic porthole void. The architecture of this elegant crossing passes unnoticed for ahead, holding the eye, is Inveraray.

## INVERARAY

Seen from the north, the white town lies low between sea and sky stretched out along Front Street in a succession of symmetrical facades from The Great Inn to the pier. There is, at first, a Potemkin-like ambiguity about this sudden urban prospect, as if these harled walls were no more than walls, flat planar screens contrived to delude the distant viewer. But the road comes nearer. The view sharpens, moving out of elevation into perspective. To be sure, the effect is calculated. Moreover, for part of its length, the white street wall is indeed a wall, two-dimensional, an arcaded screen acting as a portal to the long open driveway known as The Avenue. But, otherwise, the facades have substance; these are solid Scottish houses, classical in provenance if austere: two or three storeys high; three, five, or, in the case of The Great Inn, nine bays wide.

Travelling south down the west shore of Loch Fyne, Dorothy and William Wordsworth came upon Inveraray with much the same surprise and pleasure that the traveller still experiences today. In her *Recollections of a Tour made in Scotland AD 1803* Dorothy records *When we had travelled about seven miles from Cairndow, winding round the bottom of a hill, we came in view of a great basin or elbow of the lake. Completely out of sight of the long track of water we had coasted, we seemed now to be on the edge of a very large, almost circular, lake, the town of Inverary* (sic) *before us, a line of white buildings on a low promontory right opposite, and close to the water's edge; the whole landscape a showy scene, and bursting upon us at once . . . With the expanse of water and pleasant mountains, the scattered boats and sloops, and those gathered together, it had a truly festive appearance. . .*

*Inveraray from the north.*

This is, in fact, the peripheral face of the new town created by the 3rd Duke of Argyll in the extensive estate reforms he set in train in the 1740s.

Before the great changes of the 18th century, Inveraray had been an unremarkable castletoun developed in a roughly triangular plan close to the tower-house which Sir Colin Campbell of Glenorchy had built in the1450s near the mouth of the River Aray. Its position on Loch Fyne and its proximity to a number of routes through the glens to the north and east gave it some trading advantages, a potential confirmed by its designation as a burgh of barony in 1472 and a royal burgh in 1648. It became the only market town in Argyll outside Kintyre. By the 18th century much of the administrative and legal business of the county was being conducted here, while the herring fishing had given a boost to the local economy. Though small, the place could boast a tolbooth, two schools, a double church (part Highland or Gaelic-speaking, part Lowland and English), as well as several stone-built, slated town houses. It had *quality and charm*. The old castle, however, was in ruins and although a new dwelling, the so-called *pavilion*, had been added in 1720-22 to provide some habitable accommodation, this failed to find favour with the 3rd Duke on his accession to the estate in 1743. A new castle was now envisaged and with it a new town.

*Above* Inveraray Castle engraved by H. Adlard, 19th century; *Right* Inveraray Castle seen from Aray Bridge.

21 **Inveraray Castle**, begun 1745, Roger Morris
The first sighting is brief, an oblique glimpse through the trees from the sudden elevation of Aray Bridge. The impression is fleeting but romantic; candle-snuffer roofs, turrets, battlements, spiky dormers. Approaching up the drive past the low, piend-roofed **Main Lodge**, 1795-96, the closer view confirms this quasi-medieval character, for the windows of the Castle are almost all set in hooded pointed-arch

openings, the skyline agitated with crenellations, sharp dormer gables, chimney stacks and steep slated cones. But the organisation of Morris's design, which was preferred to earlier, by no means dissimilar, proposals from Sir John Vanbrugh, *c.*1720, and Dugal Campbell, *c.*1744, is decidedly symmetrical, classical even, with none of the contrived picturesqueness later associated with Gothic caprice. The plan is rather larger than square (seven bays wide on the south-west and north-east, five on the south-east and north-west) with round towers at each corner. The building sits in a broad shallow fosse, the retaining wall of which responds to the curves of the round towers. Between the towers the walls rise two full storeys over the basement and were originally corbelled to a battlemented parapet above the first floor. The towers rise an extra storey, while at the centre of the plan a galleried hall emerges as a tall castellar clearstorey lit by large pointed-arch windows. (see p.93)

Work on the realization of Morris's design was at first in the hands of William Adam but, after his death in 1748, John Adam supervised further progress. By the time of the 3rd Duke's death in 1761 the major building work was complete. From 1770-72 William Mylne was involved, changing the Castle entrance from the south-west front to the north-east. A century later, following a fire in 1877, Anthony Salvin built the dormered attic storey, reconstructed the roofs, and gave the Castle its fairy-tale silhouette by adding chimneys and tall slated cones over the corner towers. In 1975, after fire had again ravaged the roof and attics, restoration was carried out by Ian G Lindsay & Partners.

The Castle is entered at the centre of the north-east front over a Gothic **bridge**, 1755-56, which vaults the fosse in two pointed-arch spans. There is a similar bridge on the south-west façade, though it has retained its trefoil parapet. The glazed ironwork porch over the north-east entry is by Sir Matthew Digby Wyatt, 1871. During the 1770s and 1780s Robert Mylne was responsible for the lavish interiors of the main public rooms. Plasterwork executed by John Clayton, 1780-82; late Gothic motifs in the north-east Entrance Hall, refined classical detail in the Dining Room and Drawing Room. The ceilings of the Saloon are probably by Thomas Clayton after late 1750s designs by John Adam. On the Drawing Room walls are seven large Beauvais tapestries hung in gilded frames, pastoral scenes

RCAHMS

NE *bridge from east, Inveraray Castle.*

On Monday 25th October 1773, **Samuel Johnson** and **James Boswell** were the guests of the Duke of Argyll at Inveraray Castle. *We were shewn through the house;* wrote Boswell in his *Tour to the Hebrides,* adding that *I never shall forget the impression made upon my fancy by some of the ladies' maids tripping about in neat morning dresses . . . their lively manner, and gay inviting appearance, pleased me so much, that I thought, for a moment, I could have been a knight-errant for them.* Dr Johnson's mind was evidently less frivolously preoccupied for he was *much struck by the grandeur and elegance of this princely seat.* He thought, however, the castle too low, and wished it had been a story higher. It was an observation that proved curiously prescient, though it would be just over a century before the English architect Anthony Salvin added a dormered attic storey to the castle roof. Whether Boswell's characteristic musings attained a more immediate consummation is not recorded.

by Jean Baptiste Huet, commissioned 1785. The display of weaponry fanned across the walls of the Armoury Hall was originally devised by Mylne, though it was reordered and increased in 1952-53.

*Open to the public.  Guide book available.*

*Aerial view of Inveraray Castle and formal gardens.*

RCAHMS

The Castle is orientated to the south-west, the original entrance on that side (now private) aligned with the axis of the **Lime Avenue** first planted in the 17th century.  Close to the house are the symmetrically planned lawns and beds of a **formal garden** laid out in the third quarter of the 19th century.

**Inveraray Castle Estate**

The built legacy of the extensive agricultural improvements carried out at Inveraray during the second half of the 18th century is concentrated along the fertile valley of the River Aray from the Castle north as far as **Carloonan Bridge**, 1755-57.

22 The **court of offices** at Cherry Park, a courtyard enclosed by four ranges raised to pyramid-roofed pavilions at each corner, was designed by John Adam, 1759, but only completed by William Mylne in 1772.  Brick-domed **ice-house** nearby,

1785-86.  The **Campbell Monument**, 1754, a
pedestal pillar carrying an urn, commemorates
Covenanting martyrs of the late 17th century; it
stood on Church Square, Inveraray, until 1983.  A
little to the north, **Frew's Bridge** (also known as
the Garden Bridge) crosses the Aray in a single
elliptical arch.  It too was designed by John
Adam, 1758, but built by the eponymous
Edinburgh mason, David Frew, 1759-61.
Elegantly classical, it sets up a long vista north,
at the end of which is **Carloonan Doocot** (see p.94),
by Roger Morris, 1747, a white harled cylinder
with a slated cone roof rising into a domed
pigeon entry at the apex.   Halfway to Carloonan
is **Maltland Square**, a large working courtyard
around which were disposed a **coach house** by
John Adam; a **south range** of stables, byres and
cottages and, on the north, an immense **barn**,
both probably by William Mylne, 1760-61; **The
'Great Shade'** on the west, 1774-75, and, closing
the Square on the east, the **riding school**, 1780,
both of these, like the Barn, large, high, hip-
roofed buildings with tall round-arched bays on
each lateral elevation.   Much of this ambitious
layout is now in ruin.   Only the abused Coach
House, the stores and workshops of The Great
Shade and the rehabilitated riding school,
destroyed by fire in 1817 but reconstructed as
**The Jubilee Hall** in 1897, are still roofed.   A few
cottages remain from the south range while the
tall arches of the barn stand ruinous and roofless
like some disregarded relic of Roman
engineering.   On the south side of the Square is

Left *Court of offices at Cherry Park;*
From top *Frew's Bridge; Maltland
Square; Beehive Cottage;* Below left
*Watch tower overlooking Inveraray.*

the **walled garden** laid out by James Potter, 1752-55. East of Maitland on the lower slopes of Dun na Cuaiche is **Beehive Cottage**, 1801, by Alexander Nasmyth, a small circular dwelling with a conical roof pierced at the apex by a chimney tube. At the summit, a **watch tower** folly by Roger Morris, 1747-48, circled by an earth bank which may have some connection with John Adam's intention to build a hilltop ruin. On the right bank of the Aray at Carloonan there is a charming **fishing pavilion**, 1802-03; hexagonal in plan with a pyramidal roof, it is cast in the same mould as Beehive Cottage, its geometries simple and powerful enough to suggest the hand of Alexander Nasmyth. Across the river are the ruins of **Carloonan Mill**, probably late 18th century.

**Inveraray Town** (see p.28)

Set back from the loch shore, **Front Street** is all that its name suggests - an urban façade, the straight-line edge of a straight-lined plan that evolved in the 1740s and 50s. Its white-harled houses pack together in symmetrical groups. To the right, linked obliquely across the Dalmally road by a round-arched **screen** to buildings that first served as **smithy**, 1772, and **bakehouse**, 23 1752, is **The Great Inn**, designed in 1750 by John Adam. A three-storey, nine-bay front, its otherwise simple vernacular façade is relieved by two Venetian window arrangements in round-arched recesses set symmetrically at ground floor. The glazed vestibule entry is a later addition,

From top *The Great Inn, now the Argyll Arms Hotel; The former Town House.*

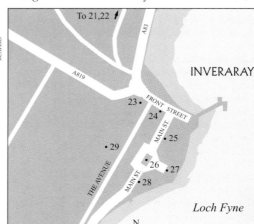

INVERARAY

*Loch Fyne*

N

300m

To 30

*c.*1900. Then another **screen**: five round arches with portholes in the spandrels, by Robert Mylne, 1787-88. The central arch marks the entry to **The Avenue**, a long tree-lined walk running south-west from its right-angled junction with Front Street. Next, three gabled houses by John Adam, 1755-57. At the centre, the former **Town House**, designed 1750 but not completed until 1757; three storeys high and five bays wide with a pedimented three-bay centre arched and rusticated at street level. Once the town's Court-house and Jail, it now serves as the local Tourist Information Office. Right and left are **Ivy House** and **Chamberlain's House**, identical three-bay dwellings with piended dormers at second floor level and added porches. Then, an opening in the street wall: Main Street, the central axis of the new town plan.

Across this gap, Front Street continues with another three-house group, lower in scale but no less symmetrical in disposition. **Gillies's House**, 1759-60, probably also by John Adam, rises at the centre; two tall storeys high and five bays wide, harled,with schist margins and rusticated quoins. Flanking this are two three-bay **manses**, by Robert Mylne, 1776. Ending Front Street, the second of these, now the Pier Shop, has an attractive arched entrance with segmental fanlight.

*Gillies's House.*

*Inveraray Cross drawn by A Gibb, 1859.*

**Pier**, begun 1759-62, John Adam
By 1771 the first jetty was already ruinous. James Gillespie Graham effected repairs in 1805 and the quay was again enlarged in 1809. Extended to serve the herring fishing industry in 1836. T-plan steamer pier built 1877.

**Cross**, late 14th or early 15th century, Iona School
Once the market cross of the old burgh and before that probably held in the now vanished medieval church at Kilmalieu. Shaft and armpitted cross-head are delicately carved with plant and animal forms though all figural imagery has been removed. Sited near the loch shore, it marks the axis of Main Street

**Main Street** runs south-west from Front Street. It is the busy, densely built-up spine of the town. On the landward side the houses back on to the long wall of **The Avenue**, 1757. To the loch, behind the straight street wall, an irregular arrangement of lanes and dwellings crushes around Crown Point confined by a partially

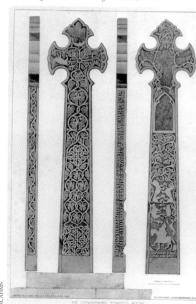

fortified sea-wall first envisaged in a town plan conceived by William Adam, *c.*1747. Halfway down the street, positioned in such a way as to create a dominant cross-axial focus in the townscape, is Inveraray's *double church*. It, too, is a legacy of William Adam's plan, though he imagined it in circular form. The idea survived in John Adam's plans of 1750 to be realized in Robert Mylne's double-fronted temple church half a century later (see below).

**Main Street North** varies in eaves height from two to three storeys; flatted houses, now with intermittent shops. Built between 1750 and 1780, it is consistent in materials and form: white-harled walls with black margins and dressings, thoroughly Scottish in its hard, heel-of-the-pavement planes and slated roof slopes. **MacPherson's House**, recognizable by its rusticated doorpiece and first floor keystone, is the earliest dwelling on the west side, completed in 1756 to a design probably by John Adam. On 25 the east is the grandly unassuming **Silvercraigs's House**, 1773-80, a substantial residence, seven bays wide with a central pend and chimneyed gablet, built for the town's provost. Further along is the **George Hotel**, formed from two three-storey, three-bay houses, 1776-79, by Robert Mylne. The northern house has ground-floor tripartite windows with unusually low side-lights.

*George Hotel.*

26 **Glenaray and Inveraray Parish Church**,
1792-1802, Robert Mylne
What might be mistaken for a temple to the Roman god Janus, since identically pedimented and pilastered classical facades, part ashlar, part

*Glenaray and Inveraray Parish Church.*

panelled harling, look north and south up and down Main Street, is in fact the town's *double church*, one half planned to house the Highland, or Gaelic, congregation, the other the English-speaking Lowlanders. Today, all worshippers meet in the north church, a four-bay space with king-post trusses, its reflection functioning as a hall since 1957. At the centre of the plan the two original pulpits backed on to a steeple tower which rose to a domed belfry and obelisk spire until 1941 when everything above the roof ridge was demolished. This loss removed the skyline linchpin in Inveraray's townscape. As built, the west and east walls of the church are plain, though still symmetrical enough with two tall round-arched windows and open corners where the entablature of each of the two principal facades returns recessed behind a single free-standing column with fluted capital. The cross-axis of Church Square survives.

*Pulpit, Glenaray and Inveraray Parish Church.*

Around **Church Square,** however, there is little response to the signals implicit in Mylne's geometries. On the west is the former **Grammar School,** single-storeyed with three gables, 1905-07, by E J Sim, and the **Royal Bank,** 1865, three-storeyed with a single chimneyed gable. On the east, a **fountain** by J & G Mossman, 1893, does pick up the transverse axis but harled buildings north and south eschew any reflected balance. The **Bank of Scotland**, mid 19th century, is little more than a cottage, though the **Bank Manager's House,** late 18th century, is altogether more ambitious with railed steps rising to a corniced door set between bipartite windows.

27 **Court House**, 1813-20, James Gillespie Graham At the east end of Church Square, a splendid classical façade finally reasserts the town's cross-

**Neil Munro** (1863-1930) was born in Crombie's Land, Inveraray. Aged 13, he found work with a local lawyer. Moving to Glasgow as a clerk, he began a tentative career as a journalist. By the late 1880s he was writing full-time for the *Evening News*, the newspaper he was later to edit. His first book, a collection of short stories, was published in 1896 and in half a dozen years spanning the turn of the century his first five novels appeared. In these he drew much on his early life in Inveraray. *The things we love intensely are the things worth writing about. I could never keep Inveraray out of any story of mine and I never will.* While the novels written in the first two decades of the 20th century were only modestly successful, their Celtic Twilight style a little out of kilter with the times, his humorous writings, especially the Para Handy stories dealing with the crew of the Clyde coast puffer, *The Vital Spark* (title of the first collection which appeared in 1906), captured the public imagination.

*Court House.*

axis. On a rusticated ground floor, an ashlar *piano nobile* with tall Tuscan pilasters carries entablature and balustraded parapet. At the centre, flanked by coupled pilasters, is a grand Venetian window that might have been designed by Robert Adam. It lights the staircase, from the upper landing of which column-screened lobbies lead left and right to the Court Room. This, the principal apartment, projects at the rear of the building in a semicircular drum, reflected in turn by the swelling of symmetrical bastion walls built to raise the foundations above the waters of the loch. In the courtyard between are two added **prison buildings**: south-west by Gillespie Graham, 1820; north-east by Thomas Brown, 1843-45. *Open to the public.*

To the north of Church Square, a little crushed between the backlands of Main Street North and the shore are **Factory Land**, built in 1774 with a large spinning workroom on its upper floor, and **Ferry Land**, 1777, a three-storey tenement with rear forestair. Both white-harled buildings restored by Ian G Lindsay, 1960. North of these, set obliquely by John Adam's plan of 1750, **Fernpoint Hotel**, 1752-53, has a turnpike stair tower with a pedimented timber doorpiece. Beyond, close to the end of Front Street, is **The Poacher**, *c.*1880. Harled, but with decorative ashlar details and a fine curvilinear gable, it was erected as a Public Reading Room and Coffee House. South of the Court House are **Crown Point House**, 1869-71, built as the Police Station, and two ranges of vernacular dwellings: **Crombie's Land**, 1822-25, restored by Ian G Lindsay, 1959, and **Fisher Row**, built by Lindsay in 1962 to replace an earlier building.

**Main Street South** is short but austere and powerful. Harled, slated, and consistently three storeyed, it raises vernacular craft to urban distinction. On the east is **Relief Land**, 1775-76, a white wall of five three-bay flatted dwellings. On the west, **Arkland**, 1774-75, an identical street façade save for its black-painted margins and the intrusion of a few small shops. Both are by Robert Mylne. Behind Arkland is **Arkland II**, late 18th century, simpler still, and a few piended **outhouses** on **Back Lane**. From the south end of Arkland, the street becomes one-sided, open to the loch. The harled street wall, now two storeys high, continues: **Black's Land**, *c.*1777, and **Mackenzie's Land**, 1775. Then, at right angles,

28

*From top Factory Land; Relief Land; Cross Houses; All Saints Church.*

**Cross Houses**, 1776-77, restored *c*.1958, three cottages with a strongly coved eaves and hipped dormers.

29 **All Saints Church**, 1885-86, Wardrop & Anderson
Nave and chancel First Pointed Gothic. The church's wayside modesty is confounded by the outrageously tall **Duke's Tower**, designed by Hoare & Wheeler and erected 1923-31 in memory of the Campbells who fell in the Great War. At more than 38m. high, it dominates church, town and countryside with its lofty presumption. The interior of the church, arranged for Episcopal worship, contains a pre-Reformation stone bowl **font**. *Open to the public.*

A short distance south of the planned town is **Newton**. Suburban Inveraray? In fact, a village constructed from 1749 to house the displaced while the new town took shape. Perhaps a few houses survive from the late 1700s but almost all are 19th century. There is a plain three-bay Georgian **house**, early 19th century, a former **manse**, *c*.1810, harled, with tall windows, and **The Old Rectory**, *c*.1810, not dissimilar but grander in ashlar, with a doorpiece framed by Ionic pilasters. Gabled **Free Church School**, 1848, with a symmetrical extension, 1880. The **Free Church**, 1895, now the Masonic Hall, is conventionally Gothic. St Malieu Hall, on the other hand, once the **United Secession Church**, 1836, has a harled curvilinear gable carrying ball skewputts. Finally, faint flavours of Gothic
30 return in **Loch Fyne Hotel**, *c*.1865, by George Devey.

The A83 follows the shore of Loch Fyne passing **North Cromalt Lodge**, 1801, a harled, hip-roofed house with lower piended appendages, perhaps by Alexander Nasmyth, and **South Cromalt Lodge**, late 18th century, a tiny doll's house dwelling less than 6m. square under a pyramidal roof. At the Wildfowl Park the road swings inland. **Claonairigh**, late 18th century, sits severe and symmetrical like a child's drawing. Beside it, little or nothing now of the workshops set up here, 1776-78, as part of the Duke of Argyll's efforts to establish a local textile industry.

### AUCHINDRAIN
31 A township of scattered cottages, byre-dwellings, barns, stables, etc. which has survived to become

Nothing disrupts the balanced eighteenth century reserve of Inveraray more than the **Tower of All Saints Church**. The Church itself, built in 1885-86 for Amelia, the Episcopalian second wife of the Presbyterian 8th Duke of Argyll, preserves a duly modest scale. But the Duke's Tower, left incomplete in 1931, is monstrously tall on the skyline. Raised as a war memorial, it contains a splendid ring of ten bells. Originally hung in the Bell House beside the Church, they were cast in Loughborough in 1920. They are inscribed in Latin with the names of Gaelic saints: Maluag, Columba, Mundus, Brendan, Maelrubha, Blaan, Murdouche, Brigida, Molaise and Mary, Star of the Sea.

From top *Loch Fyne Hotel; Old mill at Claonairigh; Claonairigh.*

AUCHINDRAIN

From top *Auchindrain township;*
*RCAHMS plan of Auchindrain.*

a valuable Museum of Country Life. The layout
seems arbitrary and without order, yet wind,
water and subsoil conditions evidently played a
part in the way the community utilised the site
for building and cultivation. The low, mainly
gabled buildings vary in length but have a
consistent width, *c.*6m. All are rubble structures
dating from the years between 1770 and 1840 and
several retain cruck roofs. Some have been re-
thatched but corrugated iron is common. The
typically linear plan arrangement of room,
kitchen and byre recurs frequently. (see p.94)
*Open to the public.*

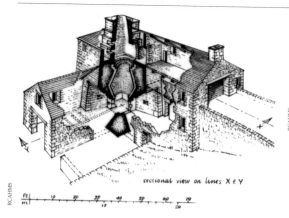

Above *Craleckan Ironworks furnace-stack;* Left *RCAHMS sectional drawing of Craleckan Ironworks furnace.*

*sectional view on lines X & Y*

## 32 FURNACE

Lochside village clustered by the Leacann Water. The name, which superseded the old name of Inverleckan, betrays its industrial history. In 1754 **Craleckan Ironworks** was founded using charcoal from the Argyll woods and imported iron ore brought up Loch Fyne. The battered granite rubble walls of the **furnace-stack** still stand, almost 8m. high, a monumental memory of 18th century enterprise. Alongside is the re-roofed **Casting-House** and to the east the roofless three-storeyed **Blowing-House**. Operations ceased in 1812. But thirty years later a second industrial venture began when the Lochfyne Powder Works was established. For forty years the manufacture of gunpowder was carried on until in 1883 a catastrophic explosion brought production to a halt. At the north end of the village are **Powdermills Cottages** (see p.94), a mid 19th century row of workers' dwellings. Of the factory buildings only a few ruinous shells survive.

## 33 Kenmore Village, 1771-72, William Douglas

Two parallel rows of cottages with a village green between, founded as a fishing community by the 5th Duke of Argyll on the loch shore some 4km. north of Furnace. Another of the Duke's proposals for a planned village to house the ironworkers in Furnace itself came to nothing.

**Cumlodden Parish Church**, 1841, James Nairn
A small gabled kirk, only tentatively Gothic. Above the east gable, through which twin doors now converted to windows originally gave access to the church, a sharp birdcage bellcote. The church houses a carved Early Christian **cross**

Below *Plan of Kenmore village in 1775;* Bottom *Cumlodden Parish Church.*

A PLAN of a Village

*From top Killevin Burial Ground mausoleum; Lochfyneside Free Church; Lochfyneside Church; Right Minard Post Office Building.*

**shaft**, 8th or 9th century, brought here from Killevin Burial Ground at Crarae. (see p.95)

## MINARD
**Killevin Burial Ground**, Crarae
No trace of the ancient chapel can now be found in the medieval graveyard on higher ground above the burn. **Campbell Enclosure**: an oblong plot surrounded by a rubble wall with a corniced coping-stone, 1727. Nearby is **Crarae Lodge**, a largely late Victorian affair which still incorporates the inn of *c*.1810. In Crarae Glen, a wonderful wild woodland garden.

Stretched along the loch shore, Minard has the look of ribbon suburbia. But the old village still retains the characteristic ingredients. Two small churches: **Lochfyneside Free Church**, *c*.1848, a roughcast oblong with a heavy bellcote and a few lancets and **Lochfyneside Church**, 1910, a splendid corrugated iron shed by Speirs & Co. complete with stained glass in an octagonal gable window. **Minard Hall**, 1899, somewhat incongruously built in polychromatic brick. **Minard Primary School** and **Schoolhouse**, 1871, by William Mackenzie, pleasantly asymmetrical with a buttressed chimneystack rising through the façade. And the **Post Office Building**, mid 19th century, symmetrical housing on a hill, gabled at the centre and the wings.

34 **Minard Castle**, 1842-48, John T Rochead
A Victorian aggrandizement of a modest Georgian mansion of 1775. The original house has all but vanished from sight, boxed in by castellated Gothic pretension. It is vigorously articulated. Every parapet is corbelled and crenellated. Almost every corner seems stressed by a tower, all of them square in plan with the exception of a small octagonal shaft rising high at the centre. Almost every window is hooded. Terraced lawns and gardens add to the conceit. Still grander are the lavishly Gothic interiors: arched stone screens, ribbed and bossed plaster vaulting, ceiling panels rich with cusped tracery,

*Minard Castle.*

*Minard Castle entrance hall and staircase.*

delicately moulded doors, heavily moulded chimneypieces. To the west of the castle is a **walled garden**, mid 19ᵗʰ century. North lies the two-storeyed **Stable House**, the early 19ᵗʰ century court of offices, now converted to residential accommodation. A pend enters the cobbled yard on the north side of which, symmetrically placed, are two forestairs.

## LOCHGAIR

A haphazard cluster of fishermen's **cottages**, some probably early 19ᵗʰ century, now a picturesque residential hamlet. Included in the transformation are a few timber buildings which originally provided storage for nets and tackle. **Lochgair Church**, 1867, is no more than a saddle-
35 back roofed roughcast oblong. **Lochgair Hotel**, built as a roadside inn by David Crow, 1855, acquired its attractive conically roofed porch and gable in alterations carried out a century later. At the north end of the village **Lochgair Power Station**, 1961-62, a rather bland building by Ian G Lindsay; inset in the boundary wall is a medieval arch-head, recovered from an island in Loch Glashan during hydro-electric operations on the hills above.

Below *Lochgair Church;* Middle *Lochgair Hotel;* Bottom *RCAHMS drawing of Asknish House.*

36 **Asknish House**, *c.*1780
Five-bay classical mansion, the principal south façade divided in three by tall Tuscan pilasters set on storey height bases. The central zone advances slightly but is unpedimented. The ground-floor entrance repeats the tripartite arrangement of the façade with glazed side-lights framed by pilasters carrying a full entablature. Above this is a Palladian window with fluted

*South elevation*

*Point House.*

Ionic pilasters and at second-floor level a reduced version of the same with a central niche. Set in line of sight from the house and close to the entry to Loch Gair is the now-derelict **Point House** (or Catherine's Castle), late 18th or early 19th century. A small, two-storeyed, harled cube with a slated pyramid roof and some Gothic arching in the walls, it seems to have been erected as a picturesque folly.

The road continues south through **Port Ann** before turning west and then north along the shore of Loch Gilp. Hidden in the trees to the south is **Castleton House**. Begun *c*.1840, it seems to have acquired a gabled and bayed south wing *c*.1875, probably the work of Peddie & Kinnear. But it is the lower extension on the north, 1898 – a roll-moulded doorway link and pedimented gable wing – which is more intriguing; it may be the work of Robert S Lorimer. An inscribed stone panel invokes the gods of the altar and hearth: *pro aris et focis*.

## LOCH GILP

**Kilmory Castle**, 1828-36, Joseph Gordon Davis Like Minard Castle, Kilmory is a massive enlargement of a pre-existent house. The fabric of this earlier house may be embedded in the south front, the consequence of initial extensions carried out 1816-20. These in turn were engulfed by the programme of works begun a dozen years later. Like Minard, too, the style is castellated Gothic, though the transformation is accomplished with much less *élan* and to much less consistent or engulfing effect. Towers are again in evidence: octagonal at the south-west corner, square at the north-west, both corbelled out to crenellated parapets. Between, however, is the seven-bay west range, symmetrical, roughcast and decidedly dull. At its centre a

Although the Campbells of Kilmory began the remodelling of the family mansion at **Kilmory** in 1816, by 1824 the *beautiful estate on Loch Gilp* was being offered for sale at an upset price to meet the demands of creditors. Marriage, however, saved the family inheritance for, in 1826, Eliza Campbell wed Sir John Powlett Orde who bought the estate and began extensive improvements. Three years and three children later, Eliza died. Three years after that, Sir John remarried. Despite his rehabilitation and enlargement of Kilmory and his ubiquitous involvement in local affairs, he was not popular. Legend has it that Sir John refused to enter Lochgilphead; to bypass the town he constructed the Clock Lodge and from it laid a causeway across the tidal flats of the loch. It may be, however, that this expensive undertaking was intended to facilitate the passage of a royal visit allowing Queen Victoria to proceed from Ardrishaig, where she would disembark from the royal barge, directly across Loch Gilp to Kilmory. In the event, the Queen seems never to have stayed at Kilmory.

*Kilmory Castle.*

*Kilmory Castle office extension, 1982.*

four-centre archway leads through to a courtyard formed between the older south wing and a north wing, added, 1860-63. A few years later an east screen wall was built with a central round-arch entry under an ogival gable. From 1974-75 the Castle has served as the centre of local authority administration. This use led to the building of a four-storey office block, 1980-82, by Argyll & Bute District Council, suavely skinned in bronze anti-sun glazing. Later refurbishment converted the carriageway through the west range into a reception hall. On the east side of the car-park is the **court of offices**, *c.*1816, remodelled by Davis, *c.*1830. **Walled garden.**

On the A83, looking across Loch Gilp down the barely visible line of a forgotten causeway is **Clock Lodge**, a symmetrical estate entry with a steep Germanic roof and a central round-arched carriageway fortified by mock portcullises. Possibly the work of J G Davis, *c.*1830.

F A Walker

*Clock Lodge.*

## LOCHGILPHEAD
A small lochside town bright and busy with tourist traffic, its development from the early years of the 19th century has always been related to its geographical position. Situated more or less at the centre of mainland Argyll and, more significantly, at the convergence of routes connecting Inveraray and Central Scotland with Campbeltown in the south and Oban to the north, it became an important road junction and, latterly, the focus of county administration. At first fishing and textiles figured in the local

*Lochgilphead.*

From top *Post Office, Colchester Square; Baptist Church; Lochgilphead Parish Church.*

economy while the proximity of the Crinan Canal proved beneficial. But it was the roads which mattered most. For today's tourist and the town's prosperity they still do.

By 1800 two small villages established at the head of Loch Gilp in the Oakfield and Kilmory estates were linked by the main coast road. **Kilmory Quay** was built, early 19th century, but could not match the success of the deep-water quay down the loch at Ardrishaig. By 1811 the coastal road link had been regularised as Poltalloch Street and Lochnell Street. At right angles, Argyll Street was laid down as the spinal stem of a T-plan, the junction widened and formalised into Colchester Square by 1822. Streets parallel to the main east-west route soon followed. By the end of the century more spacious development was taking place uphill to the north-east as detached villas spread along the contours.

**Colchester Square** struggles to maintain its rightful dignity. An eleven-bay, two-storey, corniced terrace with pilastered shopfronts and lugged or consoled windows above, forms the eastern side. Designed by David Crow, it houses **The Institute** and **Post Office**, 1841. Opposite, **Nos.5-11**, is a range of three, three-bay houses with pilastered doorways. The Square narrows slightly into **Argyll Street**. The scale is predominantly two-storey, though the gable-to-gable street wall is peppered with attic dormers and interrupted by the occasional third storey. The **Stag Hotel**, completed 1938 by Colin Sinclair, is such an intrusion but its conically capped corbelled bow gives a confident flourish to the corner of Lorne Street. Otherwise, the west side is more or less consistent, most houses dating from the 1825-60 period. **Nos.7-13** have decorative ironwork gutter brackets. **No.85** is neatly symmetrical with a pediment gable, chimney and oculus; at the rear a turnpike stair with a sunburst fanlight. On the east, a strongly painted Victorian shopfront at **Nos.10-12**, a much more recent, glazed front under a segmental arch at **No.24**, and, at **Nos.34-36**, two trim and tidy doorpieces. At the corner of Union Street is the **Baptist Church**, 1815, a stern and simple hall, making no concessions to beauty.

41 **Lochgilphead Parish Church**, 1884-85, John Honeyman
A replacement for the Telford church of 1828, a standard two-door design set axially at the head

Opposite page from top *St Margaret's Church; Lochnell Street c.1900; Police Station; Free Church; Masonic Lodge; Left Nos.43-57 Union Street.*

of Argyll Street. Gable-fronted and steepled, Honeyman's Early English Gothic is uncomfortably asymmetrical in this calculated urban context.

**St Margaret's Church**, 1927-29,
Reginald Fairlie (?)
Apsidal T-plan in modest Norman style. Rubble porch with glazed gable by John G Peace, 1987.

**Lochnell Street** runs south-east from Colchester Square. **Dalriada House**, 1887, by Donald Gillies, was built as a hotel but its four Baronial storeys and crenellated corbelled bays are now council offices. Similarly robust and battlemented, the **Court House** and **Police Station**, begun 1848-49 by Thomas Brown but extended in 1899 by Neil Gillies. Then a severe series of latter-day **tenements** from the 1950s by Colin Sinclair. A century older, the **Argyll Hotel**, a plain roughcast wall penetrated by a segmentally arched pend. Next, the bare, belfried gable of the **Free Church**, 1843-44. Across the street, the idiosyncratic roughcast façade of William Todd's **Masonic Lodge**, 1909, a provincial experiment in Glasgow Style *Art Nouveau*, and the contemporary **Coronation Mansions**, *c*.1905, a polychromatic tenement with parapetted canted bays. Round the corner is **Kilmory Guest House**, early 19th century, its original three-bay charm now somewhat cluttered and encumbered. **Nos.1-7 Paterson Street**, *c*.1815, preserve a street-row memory of Kilmory village.

**Union Street** is mostly two-storey, gable-to-gable late Victorian, solid but undistinguished. Much better, however, are **Nos.43-57**, a white harled terrace by Ian G Lindsay & Partners, 1963, minimum means with maximum effect. A tall

gabled hall, the former **Free Church School**, *c*.1850, survives as a reminder of austerer regimes. By contrast, **Lochgilphead Resource Centre** on Whitegates Road, 1990-91, by Strathclyde Regional Council, is a light-hearted,

light-filled cluster of portholed, grid-glazed sheds.

**Argyll & Bute Hospital**, 1862-64, David Cousin
At once intimidating and depressing, **West House**, built as an asylum for the insane (the first to be built following the passing of the Lunacy Act in 1857), gazes blankly onto banked lawns. **East House**, 1881-83, by Kinnear & Peddie, added a second three-storeyed block of equally dismal aspect. The former **Combination Poorhouse**, 1861, by David Crow, is barely better.

**Poltalloch Street** looks south across a grassy foreshore to the loch. Some roughcast **houses**, c.1840, a good, green rubble tenement with canted bays at **Nos.2-4**, then villas. The **Hollies** is castellated, the **Clydesdale Bank** Baronial; both are late 19th century. Simpler, smoother and symmetrical, **Islay Lodge**, early 19th century. A little to the north, on the corner of Lorne Street, a clean-cut **Doctor's Surgery**, 1996, by John Hepburn, lies low under a piended roof of profiled metal.

42 **Christ Church**, 1850-51, John Henderson
A linear and recognizably Episcopal grouping of rectory, belfry, nave and chancel in Decorated Gothic. North organ chapel and vestry added 1888. An earlier proposal for the church prepared by William Butterfield was rejected as too expensive.

**ARDRISHAIG**
The coastal road south from Lochgilphead follows the line of the Crinan Canal (q.v.) for almost 3km. to Ardrishaig. **Oakfield Bridge** is a small steel swing bridge constructed in 1871 by Glasgow engineers P & W MacLellan. The **Bridge-Keeper's Cottage**, c.1800, is three storeys to the road but two to the canal where a simple classical doorway opens to the footpath. The town itself, once alive with Canal commerce, Clyde steamers and the herring fleet, is a disappointment. Among villas on the northern

From top *Lochgilphead Resource Centre; East House, Argyll & Bute Hospital; Clydesdale Bank; Islay Lodge; Doctor's Surgery, Lorne Street; Christ Church; Right Combination Poorhouse, Argyll & Bute Hospital.*

edge of town are **Glendarroch**, mid 19th century, a gabled cottage with hood moulded windows and a verandah on the canal bank and **Seacliff House**, also mid 19th century, a two storey villa with lower wings and a rudely classical doorpiece. The **Royal Hotel**, 1841, may be by William Burn, though its lugged gables are scarcely Jacobean. **Stables and Coachhouse** have been pleasantly converted to residential apartments, their arched cart-entries simply glazed. **Chalmers Street** has lost its east side; now open to the loch, it has little to commend it. The heavily roughcast **Public Hall**, *c.*1912, by William Todd, essays a louche flirtation with *Art Nouveau*. At the **pier**, some sense of the town's *raison d'être* survives. Telford's improvements brought the first steamer in 1817; twenty years later, a curving **breakwater** sheltered the harbour and the debouch of the canal; extensive repairs were effected in the 1930s. The **Canal Office** and a much altered **Pierhead Building** of 1891 remain. **Swing Bridge** carrying the A83 across the canal by engineer L John Groves, 1890.

**Ardrishaig Parish Church**, 1860
Simple Decorated Gothic nave fronted symmetrically by a buttressed tower. Semi-octagonal, castellated transepts and spired steeple added in 1904.

South of the Canal, past the black-and-white **Cliff House**, a former inn of *c.*1850, are several varied villas. **Oakbank**, mid 19th century, has a bargeboarded gable. **Argyll Cottage**, 1856, is lower and couthier. **Achnasgiach**, late 19th century, squares up behind fine iron gates. **Attichuan**, *c.*1840, is plain late Georgian. Spiked with attic gablets, **Ardfinaig**, late 19th century, has a good wooden porch. **Fascadale**, *c.*1863, is Bryce-like Baronial. **Tigh an Ruadha**, on the other hand, is Anglophile; late Victorian Arts and Crafts.

From top *Bridge-Keeper's Cottage; Public Hall; Canal Office and Pierhead Building; Attichuan; Fascadale.*

**SOUTH KNAPDALE**

**INVERNEILL**

A ribbon hamlet on the west shore of Loch Fyne. **Inverneill House** has the look of a tower-house but fails to convince. Built *c.*1890, it is the rump wing of an earlier house, late 18th or early 19th century. In the **walled garden**, somewhat unusually surrounded by a free-flowing rubble wall, are two, cone-roofed, summer-house **pavilions** and vestigial **gatepiers** topped by urns. Nearby in the woods, close to Inverneill Burn, is the **Campbell Mausoleum**, *c.*1883, gabled Gothic with a pointed-arch recess framing a doorway which preserves the mason's name, John Wilson, in the lintel soffit.

*Right Aerial view of Inverneill House and walled garden; Above Inverneill House garden pavilion; Below Stronachullin Lodge; Bottom Erines House.*

43 **Inverneill Church**, *c.*1775

A ruinous roofless T-plan kirk. Three gables have central doors below a circular window set between round-arched openings. It seems probable that the interior was galleried. **Session House** added 1817.

44 **Stronachullin Lodge**, 1894-96, Robert S Lorimer

Harled vernacular Scots with curvilinear eaves dormers. Outbuildings embrace a sheltered courtyard. (see p.95)

**Erines House**, 1912-14, William Todd

A latter-day exercise in idiosyncratic Baronial by

a Lochgilphead architect. Now converted to flats.

## ACHAHOISH

The narrow B8024 crosses Inverneil Burn at **Auchbraad Bridge**, 1846-47, a dramatic segmental-arch span poised on buttressed abutments above a gorge. At the head of Loch Caolisport a branch road continues down the west shore. **South Knapdale Parish Church**, 1775, is a plain harled box; first orientated to a pulpit on the short axis, it was recast in mid 19<sup>th</sup> century with an entrance stair tower erected on the north-east gable. **Lochhead House** is 18<sup>th</sup> century in origin but altered by Robert S Lorimer, 1901. Some 3km. along the loch shore is **St Columba's Chapel**, some rubble walling and a gable from the 13<sup>th</sup> century. Nearby are two **caves** with evidence of Early Christian worship: a rough altar, water basin and cross carvings.

45 **Ellary House**, 1870, David Bryce
Not the most exuberant of Bryce's Scottish-Jacobean mansions. After a fire, Robert S Lorimer rebuilt the interior adding a crenellated entrance tower and a billiard room. Not far south of the house, at Cladh a'Bhile, is an ancient **burial ground** which contains many **stones** and **slabs**, 7<sup>th</sup> and 8<sup>th</sup> century, including one with hexafoil and cross motifs, the most elaborate monument of its kind in western Scotland.

## KILMORY KNAP

46 An early 13<sup>th</sup> century **chapel** still standing to the wallhead. Round-arched windows in the east preserve their sandstone dressings. During partial restoration in 1934 a glazed flat roof was installed below the wallhead in order to protect a remarkable collection of **funerary stones** which includes some Early Christian examples with cross motifs, several **tapered slabs** and **fragments**, 14<sup>th</sup>-16<sup>th</sup> century, and a reconstituted early 16<sup>th</sup> century **cross** showing interlaced ornament. Almost 3m. high, **MacMillan's Cross**, 15<sup>th</sup> century, has a disc-head carved with the crucified Christ flanked by Mary and John.

From top *Ellary House; South Knapdale Parish Church; St Columba's Cave; Early Christian Cross Slab at Cladh a' Bhile Burial Ground.*

## KILBERRY

On higher ground above Loch Caolisport is **Ormsary House**, begun in the late 18<sup>th</sup> century(?), extended a century later and finally given Baronial garb by Charles S S Johnstone, 1905. **Druimdrishaig Farm**, late 18<sup>th</sup> century(?), is a

tidy, two-storey, gabled dwelling; the lofted **steading** built round a U-plan yard with a central pedimented pend entry.

47 **Kilberry Castle**, from late 16th century
Now a Baronial Revival mansion, the old L-plan tower-house of c.1595 is hidden inside several 19th century changes. From 1844 until 1849 the castle was rebuilt as a T-plan house with crowstepped gables by Thomas Brown. In the north-east re-entrant is a round stair tower with witch's hat roof. In 1873, Peddie & Kinnear built a new block alongside the earlier north-south arm of the T, well lit on the west by gabled canted bays and dormers. Across the north side of the house a new kitchen and conservatory were also added. **Kilberry Farm**, c.1845 and 1881, has steading sheds with castellated end pavilions. In a **burial ground**, last used in the 1760s, rubble footings may betray the medieval chapel of St Berach or Berchan. **Mausoleum** to Captain Dugald Campbell, dated 1733, with elaborately carved **mural monument**. Some Early Christian **stones** and a number of fine funerary **slabs** are housed in a small shelter, *open to the public*: those of 14th-16th century date are decoratively carved in Kintyre School or Iona School manner; others, 16th-17th century, are more crudely cut.

**Kilberry Parish Church**, 1821, Alexander Grant
A solid piend-roofed box overlooking the headwaters of Loch Stornoway, architecturally unprepossessing but compelling in its simplicity. Tall round-arched windows originally flanked the pulpit but alterations in 1881 rearranged the seating and added a west porch. Porch bellcote, 1888. Galleried interior no longer reached by forestairs.

**Carse House**, 1828, George Johnstone
Unremarkably Georgian in its three-bay organisation, a small isolated mansion with a surprisingly urban flavour. At the rear a Victorian **laundry** and earlier **coach-house**.

**Gorten Steading**, early 19th century
U-plan court with end pavilions and a pedimented doocot over the central pend entry.

48 **Ardpatrick House**, begun 1769-76
The original five-bay, gabled house looks east over the narrows at the mouth of West Loch Tarbert. It has rusticated quoins and a Gibbsian

doorway hidden by a 19th century porch. The three-light windows on each side of the entrance are unfortunate disruptions, c.1923. To the west is an open central pediment below which the stair landing has been opened to a garden terrace, possibly early 20th century. The north wing may be late 18th century, the mildly Baronial south wing a hundred years later. **Walled garden** and **home farm**.

## DUNMORE
### Kilnaish Burial Ground

The site may be ancient. An 18th century **mausoleum**, surrounded by a high rubble wall with a boldly moulded coping stone and ball finials, contains several **mural panels**.

49 **Dunmore House**, c.1850(?)

What seems to be a tower-house is almost certainly mid-19th century, though there are surely vestiges of an earlier building incorporated in the structure. Burnt out by fire in 1985, the shell still stands with its random openings and mock machicolations intact. On the west, connected to the hollow tower by a parapetted link, 1950s(?), are lower, perhaps also partly pre-Victorian, buildings picturesquely capped with two conically-roofed turrets. **Dunmore Court**, early 19th century, is the former court of offices converted to residential use.

**Achaglachgach House**, c.1870

Large but undemonstratively Baronial mansion with a high cone-topped tower.

50 **CRINAN CANAL**

Wonderfully picturesque and atmospheric canal which links Loch Fyne with the open sea between mainland Argyll and the island of Jura. First envisaged in 1771 when the engineer John Rennie surveyed possible routes from Loch Gilp, it was 1785 before the Parliamentary Commissioners, persuaded of the benefits such a connection would bring to trade in timber, kelp, grain, slate and fish, recommended the formation of a company to fund the project. In 1794 work began. The canal route leaves Ardrishaig, following the shore to the head of Loch Gilp before swinging north-west across country. Holding to the southern edge of Moine Mhor moss, it reaches the silted estuary of the River Add and arrives at Loch Crinan. The distance of 14.5 km. is negotiated through 13 **inland-locks**

From top *Kilberry Parish Church; Ardpatrick House; Carse House; Kilnaish Burial Ground mausoleum; Achaglachgach House.*

Opposite page.
From top *Kilberry Castle; Carved lintel at the entrance to Kilberry Mausoleum; Mausoleum monument; Carved stones in Kilberry shelter.*

*Right top* Dunardry Bridge, Crinan *Canal;* Right bottom *'Linnet' steamship passing the Cairnbaan Hotel c.1923.*

Officially opened in 1801, the **Crinan Canal** was dogged by financial and constructional difficulties for almost two more decades. Only after the intervention of Thomas Telford was the waterway finally in regular and safe operation. Traffic increased with the opening of the Caledonian Canal to the north in 1822. At first a horse-drawn passenger boat plied between Ardrishaig and Crinan linking the steamer services which called at the east and west ends of the maritime short cut. In 1866 the twin-screw *S S Linnet*, built for David Hutcheson & Co., began to transport passengers – though not their luggage, which had to go by road – from the terminal on Loch Fyne to the pier at Crinan where steamers left for Oban and the North. The *Linnet*, which could carry only 270 passengers, provided a summer service for four months only. At the height of the season in July, when holidaymakers from Glasgow and the Clydeside towns thronged the west coast, a relief vessel was needed to help convey the crowds through the locks along the nine-mile trip, a journey of less than two hours. In 1929 the *Linnet* was finally withdrawn from service.

and two **sea-locks**. Constructional difficulties, coupled with delays in finding financial support for the venture, disrupted progress but by 1801 the canal, still in an unfinished condition, was finally opened. It was 1809 before completion was achieved. Even then flooding necessitated a realignment between Oakfield, just west of Lochgilphead, and Cairnbaan. Between 1816 and 1817 Thomas Telford was supervising the repair of locks, replacement of timber bridges with cast-iron, and the extension of the pier at Ardrishaig. Such pier repairs continued intermittently through the 19th century to cater for the changing needs of increased steamer traffic. New sea-locks were constructed 1930-34. From the middle of the 20th century, however, the canal ceased to have any commercial significance and today its value is predominantly as a convenient short-cut for yachtsmen sailing to the outer isles.

## CAIRNBAAN
**Cairnbaan Hotel**, early 19th century, serves both canal and the Oban road. A respectably classical three-bay gabled inn, its 20th century growth lacks the same well mannered dignity. Along the north bank of the canal are two roughcast **cottage rows** with gabled eaves dormers back and front; built in concrete for slate workers, *c.*1876. Cairnbaan has some of the best examples of **cup-and-ring markings**, a strange lapidary legacy casting its spell across more than four millennia.

## BELLANOCH

A linear hamlet beside the canal's berthing basin. Some early 19th century dwellings, a Gothic Revival **school** and **schoolhouse**, and a late Victorian **tenement**   A road north to Kilmartin Glen crosses the iron girders of **Islandadd Bridge**, 1851, by engineer John Gardner.   Uphill, on the Loch Sween road, is **Bellanoch Church**, 1868-69, the simplest of buildings, its use indicated by a few small lancet windows and a porch.   In the forest at Barnluasgan, a cruck-framed **Shelter** has been constructed, 1997, by Stephen Hunter, using traditional methods with green oak timber and larch shingles on the roof.

From top *Islandadd Bridge; Bellanoch Church.*

## CRINAN

A picturesque little road-end village with a distinctly nautical air.   Black lock-gates and the white walls of a few small early 19th century buildings clustered together; among them, **Lockkeepers' Cottages** and the former **Post Office**, a plain piended building with four buttressed chimneys.   **Crinan Hotel**, which began as an inn built by the canal company in 1801, has been altered and rebuilt several times; nonetheless, its hybrid busyness, above all its third-floor roofscape glazed and balconied like a ship's bridge, has an almost maritime zest.   To the west lies Jura.   North across the open waters of Loch Crinan, Duntrune Castle (q.v.) can be seen.   Around the headland at Crinan Harbour are the ruins of a **factory** set up *c.*1850 to distil pyroligneous acid from birchwood.   Beside it, **Harbour House**, an incongruous three-storey tenement, late 19th century.

*Aerial view of the Crinan Hotel and canal.*

## NORTH KNAPDALE

### KILMICHAEL OF INVERLUSSA

At Achnamara there is a **clapper bridge**, *c.*1684. Constructed of two large slabs of schist, it is the last flag bridge in Argyll.

**North Knapdale Parish Church**, 1820, Alexander McDougall

A five-bay piend-roofed box with a central pediment to the south carrying a bellcote. Two tall arched windows to the north indicate a central pulpit but late 19th century changes have recast the interior, creating a longitudinal liturgical axis and removing the original galleries.

51 **Inverlussa House**, 1820, Donald McDougall

Typical, two-storey, three-bay, former manse. A central gable on the west façade and lower piended wings which abut the chimneyed gables add to the *gravitas*.

52 **CASTLE SWEEN**

An ancient, powerfully massed stronghold rising out of a coastal ridge. Begun by Suibhne at the end of the 12th century, it was continued by the MacSweens in the following century, strengthened with a north-west tower by the Stewart Lords of Knapdale in the early 1300s and further enlarged with a north-east wing in the 15th century at the instigation of the Lords of the Isles. Forfeited in 1475, the castle passed into the care of the Earls of Argyll but by the middle of the 17th century it had been abandoned.

The plan is best described as a distorted parallelogram defined by a rubble curtain roughly 2m. thick and buttressed at the corners and mid-points of the walls. The walls are generally around 9m. high but more on the seaward side where the ground drops quickly to the shore. At the centre of the south wall a round-arched entrance leads through a barrel-vaulted passage to the courtyard now devoid of all but a few footings. These indicate the existence of later inner ranges on the east and west, the latter much less evident and more speculative. Rising from the yard over the main portal to the wallhead is a ruinous stair. A west wing, begun in the early 13th century, rose to three storeys perhaps a 100 years later when a cylindrical tower was constructed at the north-west corner. In the 15th century the north-east corner was reinforced by what was in effect an

From top *Inverlussa House; Castle Sween;* Below *RCAHMS ground floor plan of Castle Sween.*

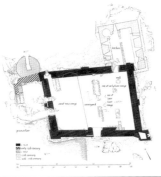

added tower-house. This MacMillan's Tower was rectangular in plan and, although now degraded above first-floor height, retains sufficient evidence at lower levels to show that it housed extensive kitchens. Approached from the land the castle presents a rugged implacable wall of masonry pierced only by the deeply shadowed arched portal. Seen from the shore to the north-west, its towered mass erupts from the rocks with intimidating intensity.

## TAYVALLICH

A safe anchorage on upper Loch Sween, reached by road from Bellanoch or by sea from the Sound of Jura. Three small settlements – Kintallan, Tayvallich and Carsaig – cluster at the narrow isthmus separating the sheltered inlet of Loch a'Bhealaich from Carsaig Bay. **Tayvallich Church**, 1893-94, a bare Gothic box by James Edgar, is the fourth place of worship to be built here since a preaching house was established in the early 18th century. The former manse of the Free Church is at Carsaig, **Tigh na Linne**, *c.*1854, the standard three-bay dwelling to which canted bays have been added. At **Dounie**, some 5 km. up the coast, another of the same, dated 1771: three-bay without the canted bays but with lower flanking wings.

**Scotnish Lodge**, 1912-14, Albert E King
A large freely planned shooting lodge with an angled tower and a dominant roof staked with chimney stacks and peppered with dormers. Hipped planes and gables in abundance.

53 **Taynish House**, from early 18th century
Begun as a five-bay laird's house but swollen by a cylindrical stair drum at the rear and bow-ended additions to the gables in the last years of the 18th century. In the early 1800s another bow was built alongside the north-east end of the house. Harled walls with simple dressed margins. Octagonal Gothick **dairy**, a five-bay **barn** that might be a church, a **summerhouse**, also Gothick, and a **piggery** with arched pens, are all early 19th century. The **walled garden** may be earlier. 2 km. up the loch are the ruins of a **corn-mill**, early 19th century. Remote now, this was once the landing point for cattle coming from Islay, Jura and Colonsay. The drovers' **quay**, 18th century, was strengthened, 1817-20, when the surviving L-plan **jetty**, designed by engineer John Sinclair, was constructed. Across Loch na Cille

From top *Tayvallich c.1900; Taynish House; Taynish House summerhouse; Garden gate detail, Taynish House.*

From top *Keills Parish Church; Sculptured slabs at Keills Parish Church, drawn by A. Gibb, 1867; Kilmichael Glassary Parish Church.*

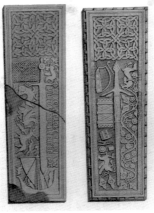

on the tidal island of Danna there is a **lime-kiln** and **storehouse** from the late 18th century, the latter with a segmental brick vault over the ground floor and a forestair to the upper level.

## KEILS

54 **Keills Parish Church**, 12th century
Despite its antiquity and its lonely site the church fails to evoke its past.   Re-roofing and restoration, 1977-78, deadens the spirit.   A new roof keeps out the rain, protecting the collection of carved stones but turning a place of worship into a storage shed.   Not even the revelation of an ancient altar base, the presence of two aumbries and the small round-arched opening in the east gable which retains its original form, can stimulate imagination or aspiration.   The **funerary stones** themselves speak louder.   There are some Early Christian **slabs** with cross and plait motifs, **tapered slabs** of various schools, 13th-16th century, carved with a fascinating variety of imagery, and the wonderful **Keills Cross**, 8th or 9th century, Iona School, 2.25m. high, carved with spiral work, key patterning and animal and human forms, all on one face only.   On the bleak hillside an uncarved replica faces the elements.   *Open to the public.*

## KILMARTIN GLEN

From Cairnbaan on the Crinan Canal the A816 north to Oban skirts the eastern edge of Moine Mhor.   The modern road crosses the River Add at Bridgend.   To the east is the old **bridge**, *built by the shire 1737*; it carries a branch route through Kilmichael Glassary north-east over the hills by Loch Leathan to Loch Awe.

**Kilmichael Glassary Parish Church**, 1872-73
In 1826-28 a *long and narrow* church, 17th or early 18th century, was replaced by a new kirk.   The pyramid-roofed tower of this early 19th century church survives but the four-bay gabled nave behind is later.   Small gabled chancel added by Peter MacGregor Chalmers, 1907.   Busy **graveyard** with **tapered slabs**, 14th-15th century, and some **cross fragments**, 14th-16th century.   Richly carved **tomb-chests**, early 16th century.

Further north, a little to the west of the main road, is **Dunadd Fort**, a rocky outcrop dramatically prominent on the marshy plain.   The remains of rubble ramparts augment its evident potential as a natural fortress.   In use

from Neolithic times, it was ultimately the capital of Dalriada, an important stronghold in the conflict between Scots and Picts. Some unusual **carvings** survive, including a sunken footprint said to be used in the ritual of regal inauguration. At Rhudil there is a three-storey **corn mill**, late 18th century, cleverly converted to a dwelling in the 1980s by Diana MacLaurin. In the hills north-east of Rhudil, **Kilbride Chapel**, 13th century. Roofless and ruinous though partially restored c.1900, its surviving east gable preserves two tall lancets. To the west of the main road, a network of narrow roads traverses the flat lands that stretch to Loch Crinan.

Kilmartin Glen is exceptionally rich in archaeological remains testifying to an intensive human presence in the Neolithic and Bronze Age periods. The oldest burial mound is the **chambered cairn** at Nether Largie South, perhaps 3000 BC, but there are **cairns** scattered over a large area, effectively a linear cemetery stretching north-south along the valley floor. **Cup-and-ring** markings abound. At Ballymeanoch, a circular **henge** with outer banking and inner ditches. There is a **stone circle** at Temple Wood and numerous **standing stones**, notably at Ballymeanoch and Nether Largie. All of this is splendidly interpreted at **Kilmartin House** which, built as the local manse in 1789 and enlarged to the west in 1863-64, is now an award-winning museum of local history and landscape. *Open to the public.*

*Above Sculptured slab at Kilmichael Glassary Parish Church;* Left top *Dunadd Fort;* Left bottom *Sunken footprint at Dunadd Fort.*

**The landscape of Kilmartin Glen** is mysteriously endowed with an exceptional range of monuments dating from prehistoric times. Though there is a dearth of evidence of settlement in the valley, it seems likely from the wealth of cairns, cist burials, standing stones, henges and stone circles that this area, centrally located in Argyll, was somehow set apart for ritual ceremonies associated with the disposal of the dead. The concentration of Neolithic and Bronze Age remains, shaped and constructed over a period of more than two millennia, is remarkable. Several cairns lie in linear sequence along the valley focusing on the chambered cairn at Nether Largie South. Excavations in the area began in the early 19th century since when archaeological interest has been sustained and greatly refined.

## KILMARTIN

**55 Kilmartin Parish Church**, 1834-35, Joseph Gordon Davis

Seen from the south the battlemented west tower makes a fine impact on the skyline but, despite its Perpendicular arches and traceried clearstorey windows, the church is ill at ease with crude crowstepping and changing roof pitches over nave and aisles. Designed by the London-based architect of Kilmory Castle (q.v.) to replace its much rebuilt 16th century predecessor, it was in turn altered, 1899-1900, by James Edgar who removed side galleries and added new lobbies at the aisle ends. There are some good Neoclassical **mural tablets**. In the **burial ground**, entered under a stepped granite **war memorial** arch, 1921, are some Early Christian cross-marked **slabs** and numerous **tapered slabs**, 13th-16th century. The **MacLachlan Monument**, late 17th century, is a mural panel framed by naïve pilasters. Several commemorative **monuments** to the Gow family, improvers of the Poltalloch estate from c.1796. Close to the church, a stone **mausoleum** to Bishop Neil Campbell which may date in part from the 16th century; it serves as a lapidarium.

**56 Kilmartin Castle**, 16th century

Probably built for Neil Campbell, Bishop of Argyll from 1580. A modest country seat, typical of the mid 16th century Marian period. Gabled with circular corner towers east and west. A turnpike stair projects on the north-west wall. Abandoned in the early 19th century it has been restored to residential use in the late 1990s.

The village of Kilmartin has a tight continuity, a brief linear settlement on the curving crest of the road. **Kilmartin Hotel** is a plain three-bay inn, c.1835, with short single-storey wings added in the 1890s by James Edgar. About a kilometre to the south, on a minor road leading to the hidden hamlet of Slockavullin, lies **Kilmartin Primary**

*From top Kilmartin Parish Church; Kilbride Chapel; Rhudil Mill before conversion; Nether Largie South chambered cairn; Kilmartin Castle before restoration.*

*Kilmartin c.1900.*

**School**, designed in village Gothic style as an Episcopal School by Joseph Gordon Davis, 1835, and later extended, *c*.1875. The **Victoria Hall**, 1897, by James Edgar, is gable-fronted like the school but the idiom is Arts and Crafts; half-timbering, mullion-and-transom windows and a parapetted verandah. Gable-fronted too the low wings of **Nether Largie Farm**, a standard three-bay house of *c*.1840.

57 **Carnasserie Castle**, 1565-72 (see p.95)
Built as a residence by John Carsewell, Bishop of the Isles, the high rubble walls of its *main house* stand almost intact, dominating the narrow route north through the hills to Loch Craignish and Lorn. Tower-house and hall-house abut in a linear east-west relationship, the interior of each an open shell save for vaulted basement chambers. A square entrance tower containing a turnpike stair projects at the north-west corner. Both masonry and architectural detail suggest that everything, apart from some changes made to the windows on the south façade in the later 17th century, is the work of the third quarter of the 16th century. There are, however, some signs of earlier building in the tower-house and there may have been some smaller pre-Reformation tower whose dimensions in some way constrained Carsewell's builders. Brought from Stirlingshire, these masons were evidently aware of the latest Renaissance fashions, as the vestigial detailing of a fireplace in the north wall of the tower and the superimposed pilastered aedicule panels over the main entrance doorway indicate. Ruined walls extend from the castle defining what must have been gardens and enclosures to the south and west; an arched gateway is dated 1681.

Just north of Carnasserie the B840 branches north-east to Ford and Loch Awe. **Ford Church**, 1850, is little more than a small hall with a triple lancet in the gable. The **Old Parish Church**, at Kilneuair above the south shore of Loch Awe, is a rubble ruin successively altered and extended from the 14th century until it was superseded in the early 17th century by the kirk at Kilmichael Glassary. There is little to see. Nor is the 13th century, hall-house form of **Fincharn Castle** discernible from its ruinous vestiges nearby on the lochside.

## POLTALLOCH
58 **Poltalloch House**, 1849-53, William Burn

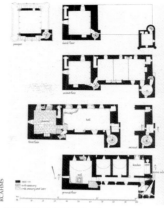

From top *RCAHMS plan of Carnasserie Castle; Carnasserie Castle.*

**The builder of Carnasserie Castle**, John Carsewell, served as Rector of Kilmartin and Chancellor of the Chapel Royal at Stirling in the years immediately preceding the Reformation. Cast in the role of Superintendant of the Isles by the Reformers, he accepted the title of Bishop from Queen Mary. Though he was never in fact consecrated he adopted the title of Bishop of the Isles, much to the displeasure of Presbyterian opinion. In 1567 he was responsible for the first book ever to be published in the Gaelic language, a translation of the Book of Common Order, first printed in Edinburgh in 1564 and known as John Knox's *Liturgy*. The translation is written in *the classical literary register of the language* but also incorporates traces of vernacular Gaelic. Carsewell died in 1572 and is buried at Ardchattan Priory (q.v.).

*Poltalloch House.*

Jacobean mansion-house broadly disposed on a landscaped setting of terraced lawns devised by Burn's *man on the site*, the century's greatest designer of formal gardens, William Andrews Nesfield. Burn's asymmetrical façades, two tall storeys high except on a long low stables wing which is nonetheless dormered and turreted, are generously decorated with curvilinear gables, strapwork ornament, mullion-and-transom windows and a balustraded cornice at the eaves. But the house is a hollow shell, dismantled and stripped when the Malcolm family moved to Duntrune Castle (q.v.) in 1957. Gabled **West and East Lodges**, by William Burn, 1854-55, have decoratively cut bargeboards. East Lodge linked by balustraded walls to finialled **gatepiers** and **bridge**. The home farm is at **Barsloisnach Steading**, 1860-62, a U-plan court with two-storey dwellings terminating the long south front. (see p.95)

*Below St Columba Chapel; Bottom Duntrune Castle.*

59 **St Columba Chapel**, 1852-54, Thomas Cundy
Erected as the private Episcopalian chapel of the Malcolms of Poltalloch. Skew gables to nave, chancel and memorial chapel; simple shafted lancets with buttresses between. The interior has droved ashlar walls and a timber roof with arched bracing to corbelled collar trusses. Three 16th century **choir stalls** of unknown provenance.

60 **Duntrune Castle**, from 15th century; house from *c*.1600; reconstructed in the late 18th century and again, 1833-35, this time by Joseph Gordon Davis. Seat of the Campbells of Duntrune until the Malcolms became lairds in 1796. A castellated curtain enfolds house and courtyard, picturesquely perched on the summit of a rocky knoll on the north shore of Loch Crinan. This classic form, typical of the Gaidhealtachd sea-

edge stronghold, suggests the castle may well be earlier than the 15th century date customarily ascribed to it. The three-storeyed gabled and dormered house, which rises above the wallhead at the southern point of the curtain's arrow-headed pentagonal plan, is clearly 17th century. Pressed into an L-plan arrangement, it is entered in the re-entrant from the inner yard, itself approached by a sinuous path climbing to a portal formed in the late 18th century in the east wall. At the gateway, an armorial panel dated 1851 brought from Poltalloch House when the Malcolms returned to Duntrune. Single- and two-storey ranges on the north. Despite its pronounced sense of enclosure, the castle is intimate and domestic in scale. (see p.96)

*Ardifuir dun.*

To the north, estate **outbuildings** and **cottages**, early 19th century(?) in two parallel rows. **Walled garden,** *c.*1800. A kilometre north-north-west the drystone walling of **Ardifuir dun** has been well preserved.

At Crinan Ferry, 2.5km. south of Barsloisnach Steading, a harled **tacksman's house** of *c.*1710, restored 1976, preserves the solid low-ceilinged scale of a rural world elsewhere overtaken by the improving changes of the 18th century. Nearby, the **Ferry House** inn, late 18th century(?) and an early 19th century **steading**; both converted to residential use. **Ice-house** with turf roof, 1833, provided for local salmon fishers.

*Tacksman's house, Crinan Ferry.*

## LOCH CRAIGNISH

61 **Barbreck House**, 1790 (see p.96)
Built by Major-General John Campbell when the family re-acquired their Barbreck estate earlier lost through forfeiture. A finely judged classical façade, simple in its ornament, elegant in its proportions. Three storeys high and five bays wide, the central three-window zone of the main south-west front is pedimented. An armorial device fills the tympanum with urns set on the

eaves cornice. Pediments and urns are repeated on single storey wings linked right and left by blind arcaded walls, the coping stone of which continues across the house façade as a string course separating the ground floor from the *piano nobile* above. This classical simplicity, plain but potently Palladian, is all the more effective seen across the flat meadowland which distances the house from the passing road, as if set back from the edges of some Veneto canal.

The plan is structurally tripartite, as the chimney stacks indicate, the central bay projecting at the rear to accommodate both the main staircase and a service stair laid alongside. 19th century additions obtrude on this clarity. Low **service buildings** aligned with the rear of the flanking wings return to close a broad U-plan courtyard whose ranges include laundry, cart- and coach-sheds, stables and byre. North-east of the house is a Gothick **folly** and north-west a **walled garden** and pyramid-roofed **mausoleum**; all late 18th century.

### Turnalt House, c.1800

A smaller version of Barbreck House built 2km. up the valley of Barbreck River. The house is only two storeys high and three bays wide but the central pediment and flanking wings are repeated. A Venetian window at first floor recurs in the wings with blind side-lights. North-west of Turnalt is **Kilbride Farm**, a rude gabled dwelling with low eaves and minimal window openings which may date in part from the 17th century.

At the head of the loch the village of **Ardfern** with its sheltered anchorage has become popular with yachtsmen.

### Craignish Parish Church, 1826-27, David McDougall

A hip-roofed oblong in harled rubble with sandstone dressings to round-arched windows. Pediment with block bellcote to the north. Internal staircases east and west rise to galleries. As the original central entrance is blocked, entry is now gained from the door leading to the west stair. The former manse, 1833-34, now known as **Ardfern House**, is also by McDougall. Not surprisingly perhaps, its design echoes the pedimented three-bay facade of the church.

*From top Folly at Barbreck House; Turnalt House; Craignish Parish Church; Ardfern House.*

**Old Parish Church**, early 13<sup>th</sup> century

*Craignish Old Parish Church.*

A rectangular rubble chapel sited further down the loch at Kilmarie. Repaired in the 19<sup>th</sup> and 20<sup>th</sup> centuries, the walls have been stabilised to eaves height and the east gable to the apex. The outer arches of several small windows have been renewed. In the walled **burial enclosure** are two Early Christian **slabs** with incised crosses and several **tapered slabs**, 14<sup>th</sup>-15<sup>th</sup> century.

62 **Craignish Castle**, from late 14<sup>th</sup> or early 15<sup>th</sup> century (see p.96)

Roughcasting cannot conceal the ungainly accumulation of three different phases of building. Beside the original three-storey tower-house only two bays remain of what was a four-bay house of 1837, once gabled and turreted, perhaps by William Burn, perhaps by Joseph Gordon Davis, while a staircase block has been added sometime in the 20<sup>th</sup> century on the north gable of the diminished mansion-house. It is all unfortunate and undignified.

*Craignish Castle.*

Shortly before the A816 reaches the sea south of Asknish Bay, a track branches left to **Craobh Haven marina**. The building of this leisure village, created from 1983, entailed forming a causeway and sea wall to link two small islands to the mainland. The design of the housing at first engaged Gillespie, Kidd & Coia, but not for long. Others followed but the results are unconvincing: kailyard architecture, indiscriminating and sentimental. Everything admirable in the tradition of Scottish vernacular architecture – the severe street walls, its

*Craobh Haven.*

From top *Buidhe Lodge; Lunga House; Stonefield Castle Hotel.*

functional directness, a consequential austerity and restraint of form and material – all this is eschewed in favour of a mawkish couthiness. Johnston Erdal's **Buidhe Lodge**, 1987-88, has nothing to do with the familiar white-walled tradition but its timber framed and boarded walls are unaffected and honest.

**Lunga House**, from 17th century
A gabled agglomeration of varied forms and dates: part battlemented Gothic, part bartizaned Baronial.

63 **Stonefield Castle Hotel**, 1836-40, William Henry Playfair
Impressive and precocious Baronial redolent of William Burn in its free functional planning and quasi-Jacobean details. The south-west entrance, its doorway surmounted by a strapwork pediment, rises to a gable set between two symmetrical turret tubes capped by conical roofs. To the south-east, gables and bays pile up ahead of a roofscape jagged with ridges, dormers, chimney stacks and the main staircase tower soaring to a crenellated parapet. A pusillanimous bedroom block added to the

north-east some time after the Castle became a hotel in 1949 cannot live with such quality, but the more recent dining room, a low glazed insertion at the east corner, retains some uncompromised dignity. The interiors are high ceilinged and richly panelled. Playfair's drawings hang framed on the stair and corridor walls.

The **gardens** are densely packed with exotic azaleas and rhododendrons. **Lodges** and **stables**, duly crowstepped to echo the conceit of the main house, are by Playfair as is the four-arched **viaduct** which carries the drive over a deep gorge. Down on the loch shore is a small harbour with rubble **jetty** and **boathouse**. Scots too, **Barmore Farm**, which retains the name originally given to the Castle, is a single-storeyed steading now in residential use.

*Stonefield Gate Lodge.*

*Tarbert c.1890.*

## TARBERT

The strategic significance of Tarbert's situation is easy to understand. A sheltered natural harbour opening into Loch Fyne coupled with the narrowness of the land bridge across Kintyre from East Loch Tarbert to West Loch Tarbert make it an obvious location for settlement. From early medieval times the site was fortified to command routes north-south and east-west. In the 14th century Robert I reinforced the castle, at the same time raising the tiny castletoun to the status of royal burgh, 1329. The town remained small, its economy negligible until, in the 18th century, herring fishing in Loch Fyne brought modest prosperity; *the village*, recalled one

*Tarbert Castle.*

**Tarbert Castle** figured strongly in James IV's efforts to pacify the western isles. The king was in Tarbert in 1494, 1498 and 1499 and it was probably he who built the tower-house which advances from the south-east curtain wall of the earlier fortress. Archibald, Earl of Argyll, was appointed Keeper of the Castle a few years later but for most of the first half of the 16th century Tarbert was in the hands of a renegade scion of the MacLeans of Duart. In 1600 James VI contemplated a new punitive expedition against the MacDonald Lords of the Isles, but no campaign was undertaken; instead, a bitter clan conflict developed between the Campbells, to whom the king granted Kintyre in 1607, and the MacDonalds. In 1647 Sir Alister MacDonald of Dunaverty laid waste to the whole of Kintyre. Failing to defend Tarbert, he was soon defeated, his forces compelled to retreat south to Dunaverty where a Covenanting army under General David Leslie *put every mother's son of its garrison to the sword.*

Following the Restoration, Tarbert remained a royal castle. But, on the succession of the Catholic monarch James II in 1685, the Protestant Earl of Argyll, in collusion with the English Duke of Monmouth, raised a rebellion. A force of some 1,200 men assembled under Argyll at Tarbert. The revolt quickly failed and Argyll was captured and executed. In 1689, however, his successor resumed the rights forfeited and the office of hereditary Constable of the Castle was restored to Campbell patronage. But, by the middle of the 18th century, following the defeat of the second Jacobite rebellion, the castle was no longer in use as either garrison or residence.

Victorian writer, *has not inaptly been called the capital of herringdom.* Failure to cut a canal across the Kintyre isthmus curtailed development while the importance of fishing declined. Today it is a picturesque place, busy, at least in summer, with the lively bustle brought by tourists and yachtsmen.

64 **Tarbert Castle**, begun 12th century(?)
A lane climbs from Harbour Street to a grassy plateau overlooking the south shore of East Loch Tarbert. The defensive advantages are obvious but the physical evidence of fortification leaves much to the imagination. The signs of building are reduced to turf-covered footings, some rubble remains and the shattered shell of a large, four-storey tower-house, built by James IV, 1494. To the south-west, parallel ridges betray the quadrilateral plan of a courtyard castle, probably 13th century. In the 1320s, a large area north of this first stronghold became a protected outer yard fortified by a perimeter wall with two round towers, still discernible on the north-east flank.

65 **Tarbert Parish Church**, 1885-86, McKissack & Rowan
A splendid crown-and-lantern belfry steeple dominates the scene from the rise of the Campbeltown road. At the base of the crown ribs, finials enliven the skyline, dropping as stepping buttresses angled at each corner of the tower. The splays of two of these buttresses flank a round-arched entrance at the foot of the tower. Behind the steeple, the gabled nave has a single north-west aisle, twice gabled to the road below. Inside, arch-braced trusses support a boarded timber roof painted with Romanesque motifs.

**Tarbert Academy**, 1893
Until recently, a forbidding tower and classroom block cluttered and confused with successive alteration and extension. Now reorganized and refurbished by Crerar & Partners, 1996-99. A new primary department has been added and the group unified by white render, grey roof tiling and careful landscaping.

Life animates the waterfront against the backdrop of a continuous wall of variegated building. Little if any of this is pre-Victorian. At the centre, eschewing any daring colour, is the black and white **Tarbert Hotel**, begun in the early 19th century and later busied with balcony-linked oriels and a glazed ironwork porch. On the north-west side of the loch, some gable-to-gable houses on **Barmore Road** and a rubble cottage or two on **Garvel Road** may date from the 1840s; on the south-east side, below the Castle, a stretch of fishermen's stores with flats above and pend access to the rear, similar in date. Intermittent tenements raise the scale. **Bannockburn Buildings**, 1884, has a peaked gablet at the centre of the street elevation; at the obtuse bend in Harbour Street, a symmetrical three-storey block, c.1880, houses the **Tarbert Information Centre** behind original shopfronts; **Ardencorrach**, too, late 19th century, retains its shopfront; in Castle Street, an unexpected ashlar façade at **Braeside**, c.1890. Severe **Templar Hall**, 1872, eaves-on to the quayside street. Much of the rest is undistinguished, the attractiveness of the harbour saved perhaps by quayside activity, the occasional highlight, like the fascia and first-floor window joinery of **Caladh**, c.1880. Some brave splashes of colour and a bold seaside *insouciance* that barely manages to avoid kiss-me-quick *kitsch*.

Pier Road runs east round the southern shore of East Loch Tarbert to the Portavadie ferry and a little beyond. There are some good late Victorian villas with decorative bargeboarded gables: **Rockfield**, **Rosemount** and **Queensgate**, all c.1885. The contemporary **Columba Hotel,** three-storeyed and piended, has a narrow central bay topped with a lampshade roof. Uphill, looking out to Loch Fyne, **Sealladh Mor** and its neighbour, two latter-day black-houses, designed in the 1970s by Peter Speakman.

*From top Queensgate; Columba Hotel.*

### THE WEST COAST ROUTE
Leaving Tarbert, the main road south to Campbeltown, the A83, passes **An Tairbeart Heritage Centre**, a neat if unprepossessing overgrown timber shed completed in 1995 to showcase West Highland life. Further on, at the head of West Loch Tarbert, is **West Loch Hotel**, an 18th century coaching inn with added gabled dormers. Behind the hotel, a small residential enclave, attractively casual and township-like in layout. The old pier is disused now, the ferry connection for Islay leaving from Kennacraig some 5km. down the loch.

## CLACHAN

An estate village. The local mansion-house, now **Balinakill Hotel**, was given a Baronial gloss in extensive enlargements, *c*.1870, though the older dwelling was later demolished in the 1960s. There is an estate **farmhouse**, a U-plan **steading** with three crowstepped façade gables and a delightful **walled garden**. The **Lodge**, now isolated by the A83 beside the quadrant **walls** and **gatepiers** which once marked the entrance to the estate, seems overburdened by Baronial detail. In the village, a few **cottage rows** built for estate workers and a gabled Georgian **manse**, 1827, by Edward Stewart.

*Kilcalmonell Parish Church.*

66 **Kilcalmonell Parish Church**, 1760; enlarged 1828 Harled kirk gabled east and west with two tall windows with Gothic sashes on the south wall. North porch added 1879. Galleried interior with internal stairs on the gables. Pedimented and pilastered back panel to oak pulpit in south wall. In the graveyard, an Early Christian **slab**, several **tapered slabs**, 14th-16th century, and war memorial **gateway** by Edinburgh's City Architect, Ebenezer MacRae, 1921-22.

*Kilcalmonell Free Church.*

67 **Kilcalmonell Free Church**, 1878, John Burnet(?) Gable-fronted with decorative bargeboarding and wide bracketted eaves. A pagoda belfry at the apex hints at the Italianate towered villa though this allusion to a rustic domestic classicism is compromised by the inevitable symmetry of the plan. Converted to residential use.

**Ronachan House**, late 19th century; rebuilt and enlarged 1897 Asymmetrical ashlar mansion looking south-west to the Sound of Gigha. Bay, porch and dormer windows capped with copper. **North Lodge**, late 19th century; a gabled L-plan with square-pillared porch. Courtyard **steading** with a conically roofed tower at the north-west corner.

## TAYINLOAN

Crossing-point to the island of Gigha. The village itself is unremarkable, though a few cottages may date from mid 18th century. To the north are two early 19th century houses: **Ballure House**, *c*.1805, and **Gortinanane**. Both are plain, three-bay, piended dwellings, the former modestly ennobled by a central pedimented projection with pilastered doorpiece. South of the village, a much grander house.

*Ballure House.*

68 **Killean House**, from 1875, John Burnet; completed by J J Burnet
Baronial pile in fawn sandstone, built for the shipping magnate James Macalister Hall as a replacement for an earlier house of *c*.1840. Impressively endowed with the style's familiar formal features - and some not so familiar. On the west, a canted bay corbels into a crowstepped gable; a round, north-east corner of arched windows rises to a conical roof ringed with gabled eaves dormers; linking south to the service wings is a five-storey tower roofed by a steep pyramid. Interior apartments, opening from a central top-lit hall, decorated with a cooler classical reserve. The **Home Farm**, by J J Burnet, *c*.1895(?), extends its long façade parallel to the A83, a pyramid-roofed pavilion marking the pend access to the yard behind. Also by the
69 roadside, **Killean Cottages** and **Mission Hall**, *c*.1895, three rubble buildings more English than Scots with casement windows, wide eaves, verandahs and steep tiled roofs; their playful Arts and Crafts charm may come from Burnet or, perhaps, H E Clifford.

70 **Killean Old Parish Church**, from 12th century
Overgrown ruin. The roofless oblong nave is the oldest part, extended east in the 13th century when a new chancel was created. A double-light, round-arched window in the east gable has dog-tooth ornament on the outside. The 15th century north aisle, which has a pointed barrel-vault, was used as a burial aisle by the MacDonalds of Largie. In the walled graveyard are some carved **tapered slabs**, 14th-15th century, and a number of 18th century **headstones** with vocational imagery.

*Top left Killean House; Above from top Killean Cottages; Killean Old Parish Church; Tombstone at Killean Old Parish Church; Killean Parish Church.*

71 **Killean Parish Church**, A' Chleit, 1787-91
The classic classical Presbyterian kirk here set

close to the shore. An oblong plan with piended roof. At the centre of the south-east front is a pedimented projection with blind arched windows and portholes, a pedimented and pilastered door and a tall birdcage belfry, 1879, perched at the apex. The galleried interior, which is supported on timber columns and has a timber goalpost frame carrying the projecting laird's loft, has been unbalanced by the closing off of the north-west side. Adjacent is **Killean School**, 1861, by Robert Weir, given round-arched windows to match those of the church.

### GIGHA

A small attenuated island with a ragged shoreline lying off the west coast of Kintyre. The hamlet of **Ardminish** is reached by ferry from the mainland at Tayinloan. There are a few simple houses, a 72 harled **manse**, 1816, and **Gigha Hotel**, which dates from *c.*1790 and is much enhanced by the vernacular elegance of Morris & Steedman's bedroom wing extensions, 1977-78. Less than 2km. north-west of the village at Port an Duin is a ruined rubble meal **mill** with an overshot wheel originally powered by water running in a cast-iron lade from an artificial loch.

From top *Gigha Hotel; Gigha Manse; Port an Duin mill; Right Gigha Old Parish Church.*

**Gigha Old Parish Church**, 13th century(?) Polychromatic sandstone remains of St Catan's Chapel. In the east gable, a tall round-arched window, a reconstruction of an earlier pointed-arch opening. The walled burial enclosure contains several **slabs**, 14th-15th century, carved with swords, scrolls and animals and one with the effigy of a warrior. A granite pillar, the so-called **Ogham Stone**, 7th century, bears a still problematical inscription. Just south of the church a gated Gothic Revival portal opens to a small burial enclosure: the **Scarlett Mausoleum** commemorating the island laird James Scarlett and his wife, both of whom died in the 1880s.

**Gigha and Cara Parish Church**, 1923-24, John Jeffrey Waddell
Random rubble Romanesque with a gabled

chancel and saddle-back belfry shaft. The font is medieval, an irregular octagon of schist originally in the Old Parish Church (see above).

*Achamore House.*

73 **Achamore House**, 1882-84; rebuilt *c*.1900, John Honeyman

Honeyman's first project, which recast and extended an earlier 18th century house, was a sprawling Baronial mansion rising to three and four storeys and liberally peppered with bartizans, eaves dormers and bowed or bayed windows. The walls were harled with ornament confined to dressed stone mouldings, carved dormer pediments and a vertical frontispiece carried up from the main entrance doorway through three storeys. A disastrous fire in 1896 forced a radical reconstruction which, though the building's footprint remained the same, reduced its height to its present two storeys. Crowstepped gables were retained or rebuilt and a single witch's hat roof survived but the house's Baronial character was much muted – perhaps for the better. Another cone roof appears over the porch of the estate factor's cottage, **Achamore Lodge**, 1895, doubtless also by Honeyman. **Achamore Farm**, however, is early 19th century, a long harled steading with forestairs rising to gabletted loft entries. Woodland walks and **walled gardens** luxuriant with rhododendrons and exotic trees and shrubs are the estate's principal glory; developed by Sir James Horlick, who bought the island in 1944, they are now in the care of the National Trust for Scotland.

**The Gardens of Achamore House** are for many the highlight of a visit to the island of Gigha. The 50 acre display is at its best in late spring when banks of deciduous and evergreen azaleas and rhododendrons begin to replace a carpet of daffodils. Developed by Sir James Horlick, who purchased the island in 1944, the collection of exotic shrubs is extensive and magnificent. Rare species and hybrids splash wonderful colour along the woodland walks. There is a walled garden divided into two zones: in the north, some rare conifers and the estate greenhouses; in the south, vegetables, soft fruit and flowers. A pond garden is surrounded by colourful herbaceous plants. Mature trees, variegated in foliage and blossom, add to the beauty of the planned landscape.

*Achamore Farm.*

From top *Cara Chapel; Cara House;*
Right *Glenbarr Abbey (Barr House).*

Off the south end of Gigha is the tiny
uninhabited island of Cara. **Cara Chapel**, 15th
century, is a deserted oblong cell with both gables
still standing. **Cara House**, *c.*1733, a five-bay
tacksman's dwelling, abused by later alterations,
abandoned to conspicuous loneliness.

### GLENBARR

Swinging away from the coast, the A83 passes
**Glencreggan House**. Built in the 18th century,
but rebuilt, *c.*1905, after a fire, the five-bay front
has a splendid porch of Ionic pilasters flanked by
tripartite windows. The old road then dips
through the valley of the Barr Water. **Glenbarr**
village is a short straight street of cottages, ridges
stepping with the slope.

74 **Glenbarr Abbey** (Barr House), *c.*1815, James
   Gillespie Graham(?)
Nothing more than whimsy justifies the abbatial
allusion. This is a simple three-bay house of
mid-18th century provenance cased in a Gothick
cassock. Tracery and lancets, crocketted finials
and crenellated parapets are all in evidence
testifying to the caprice of Colonel Matthew
Macalister and his architect. In 1844 the
romantic sanctification continued with coach-
house and other offices stepping down the
hillside behind the earlier mansion. Interiors too
are gothicised.

After Glenbarr the road reverts to the coast. The
**Macalister burial ground**, which lies between the
road and the sea, dates from the 17th century, but
the present walled enclosure accented by obelisk
pinnacles must be late 18th or early 19th century.
At Bellochantuy, the church of 1825, a sister kirk
for Killean Parish Church at A'Chleit, has gone,
tragically demolished in the 1970s as part of road
improvements. The local inn of 1808, now
known as **Drumore**, has, however, survived as a
private house, though its oddly unbalanced
three-bay front suggests some lingering
inebriation. **Putechan Lodge Hotel**, remodelled
and extended in the 1980s, is smart and

*Drumore*

sophisticated with a glazed verandah and inset bedroom balconies enjoying the view west.

From top *Tangy Mill*; *Kilchenzie Old Parish Church*; *Claonaig Church*; *St Brendan's Church.*

## KILCHENZIE

75 **Tangy Mill**, *c.*1820.
A three-storey L-plan mill which continued in production until 1961. The whinstone structure has been restored and adapted as a lettable holiday home by the Landmark Trust. Cast iron overshot wheel and most of the surviving machinery have been retained.

**Kilchenzie Old Parish Church** (St Kenneth's Chapel), from 12th century
Little remains; an eroded gable and barely enough to discern two oblong cells. The arrangement is similar to that at Killean Old Parish Church with a short nave to the west, 12th century, and a chancel in the east, 13th century. Several carved **tapered slabs**, 15th century, lie within the ruined walls.

## THE EAST COAST ROUTE

Close to the Kennacraig ferry terminal a single track road crosses Kintyre to reach **Claonaig** on the east coast. At **Claonaig Church**, a harled hall no longer in religious use but recognizably devotional by its pointed-arch windows and birdcage bellcote, the route south dips to bridge the Claonaig Water. Before the bridge, a branch road continues past the ferry point for Lochranza in Arran (see *Ayrshire & Arran* in this series) and follows the shore to Skipness.

## SKIPNESS

A road-end village strung out along Skipness Bay. There are some rubble cottages, a **school**, 1868, with a bargeboarded gable, a **village hall** with a pointed-arch entrance that betrays its origin as the Free Church, 1892. Services are still held in **St Brendan's Church**, 1896-97, by Bertram Vaughan Johnson, a simple lancet-lit nave built in coursed rubble with red sandstone dressings. Beside the church a small bridge crosses Skipness River into Skipness estate.

6 **Skipness House**, 1878-81, John Honeyman Honeyman's new mansion for Robert Chellas Graham was dominated by a four-storey Baronial tower with bold bartizan corners which rose above lower rambling wings. In 1969 a fire destroyed much of this romantic conceit and, though the house was reconstructed in 1972, cut

*Right Skipness House during construction, 1881.*

*Skipness House Lodge.*

down and recast it is ill at ease. Something of Honeyman's scholarly detailing, if no longer his compositional skill, can still be seen in the crowstepping and eaves dormers that have survived and in a round stair tower capped with the familiarly Scottish slated cone. At the entrance to the estate grounds is **Skipness House Lodge**, a mini Windsor composition of castellated drum and tubular chimney.

*Skipness Castle.*

77 **Skipness Castle**, from the 13th century
The flat site has no natural defensive advantages but the location, commanding the sea routes north through the Sounds of Kilbrannan and Bute, has evident strategic importance. The earliest structure, built in the first half of the 13th century, perhaps as part of Alexander II's pacification programme, is an oblong hall-house, three surviving walls of which are assimilated by later building on the north side of the present courtyard. A rectangular chapel of contemporary date appears to have existed some distance south of the hall-house. Vestiges of this early church, including some splayed window ingoes, have been incorporated into the castle's south wall. At the end of the 13th century, or perhaps a little later, these two separate structures were unified by a battlemented masonry curtain, over 2m. thick and still in places c.10m. high, that rises from a battered base. The large enclosure created is rectangular with a

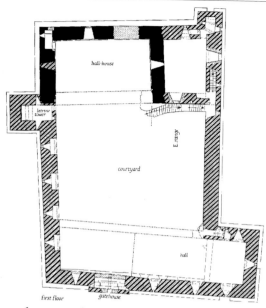

RCAHMS

*RCAHMS first floor plan of Skipness Castle.*

gatehouse on the south, towers at the north-east and south-east corners, and a smaller latrine tower projecting from the west wall. Considerable evidence of these features remains but, as a consequence of demolitions carried out at the end of the 18th century, there is little trace of the ranges of buildings which filled the east and south sides of the yard, the latter superseding the old chapel when a new church was built some distance south-east of the castle closer to the shore (see below). In 1502 the castle passed into the ownership of the Campbells who, in the early years of the 16th century, set about raising the south-east tower to its present four storeys. Later, sometime before 1600, the forestair climbing from the yard to first-floor level was built and the corbelled rounds, parapet walk and upper works of the tower-house completed.

The castle was abandoned at the end of the 17th century. In the following century it functioned as a farm. Various alteration were made including the removal of the east and south ranges and the conversion of the latrine tower into a doocot. A new round-arched entry was cut in the north wall and, although the original pointed-arch gate with its vaulted portcullis chamber above still exists in the south wall.

*Kilbrannan Chapel (St Brendan's Chapel).*

78 **Kilbrannan Chapel** (St Brendan's Chapel), late 13th or early 14th century

After 700 years walls and gables are still standing. The plan is a very elongated rectangle which was originally divided into nave and chancel by a timber screen. Lancets are narrow with weathered dressed surrounds and splayed ingoes. There is a bifurcated window in the east gable and moulded pointed-arch doorways north and south. Facing the shore on the south wall are two **burial enclosures**, both commemorating members of the Campbell family: one is a classical aedicule wall monument with Tuscan half-columns, entablature and pediment; the other stylistically similar but pushed out from the wall as a sheltering porch. In the graveyard, a few carved **tapered slabs**, 14th-16th century, and many interesting 18th century **headstones**.

*Cour House.*

79 **Cour House**, 1921-22, Oliver Hill

This astonishing dwelling, canopied under a mountainous roofscape of Purbeck slates, lies on a hillside falling gently above the shore. Strange beehive-shaped roofs swell at the corners of an L-shaped plan, the south-east arm of which, stepping down the slope in great glazed bays, seems imbued with Elizabethan nostalgia. And yet, although there is no overt Scottishness, Cour is in thrall to the *genius loci* for the widespread planes of the roof, the layered terraces, long eaves lines, grids of metal casements gathered in horizontal groups, and the textured masonry of the local grey-green whin all combine to bond the house to its site. (see p.129)

## GROGPORT

**Grogport Church**, 1897, is a small skew-gabled hall now residential and scarcely worth a glance unless perhaps to note a sandstone panel carved with open Bible and knotted rope. The former manse, **Grogport House**, early 19th century, is three-bay gabled standard; it preserves its 12-pane sashes and has a later porch crested with ironwork.

## CARRADALE

A working fishing village with a tight, if not entirely picturesque, little harbour. Its attractive coastal setting, a nearby sandy beach and pleasant woodland walks have made it popular with holidaymakers able to tolerate the ubiquitous midges. On a rocky knoll not far south of the harbour the masonry traces of **Airds Castle**, a vaguely determined curtain wall enclosure of equally vague medieval date, add to the rural charm. More recent residential building undoubtedly does not. There are two schools: one, gable-fronted in red sandstone, the **School Board School** of 1890; the other, **Carradale Primary School**, one of several clusters of monopitch classrooms built by Strathclyde Regional Council in Argyll in the 1980s. There are two churches, both undistinguished Gothic. **Kiloran Church**, 1887, by H E Clifford, rises to a tapering belfry on the north gable; at Bridgend, **Saddell Parish Church**, *c.*1900, has a wheel window and lancets.

*Carradale House.*

80 **Carradale House**, 1844, David Bryce
Harled Baronial jagged with gables and bartizans of the type prior to Billings' *The Baronial and Ecclesiastical Antiquities of Scotland*. Bryce employs the elements known from the work done by his partner William Burn on several Scottish houses of the 16th and 17th century. Among such details is the square bartizan from Pinkie. Bryce's much favoured gable corbelled over a canted bay also appears. (see p.129)

81 **Torrisdale Castle**, 1815, James Gillespie Graham
A castellated Gothic mansion situated less than 2km. south of Dippen Bridge. The original dwelling, recognizable as a core to which flanking wings have been added, is essentially the 18th century country-house plan given Gothic garb. On the west façade, symmetry reigns. Hood moulded windows and traceried glazing

*Torrisdale Castle.*

have simply been preferred to classical fenestration, while behind a crenellated parapet the familiar piended roof can be seen. But there is a critical departure; at the north-east corner a taller octagonal tower intrudes a single lop-sided accent on the skyline. In the first decade of the 20th century H E Clifford added the north and south wings more or less, it seems, along lines originally envisaged by Gillespie Graham. Clifford's interiors are freely eclectic, introducing both classical and *Art Nouveau* decorative elements. Gillespie Graham's Perpendicular Gothic panelling is austere by comparison. Symmetrical **gatehouse** (The Arch) with a pointed archway under a crenellated attic. U-plan **stables** castellated and gabled. **South Gate Lodge** in harled Gothic with screen walls linking to **bridge**, dated 1840.

## SADDELL

82 **Saddell Abbey**, from *c.*1160

*Saddell Abbey.*

A Cistercian house, founded by Somerled, Lord of Kintyre, or his son Reginald, and now almost, but not quite, invisible. Vestigial fragments of walling and a few tell-tale lines of grassy footings are the clues to reconstruct a picture of the church's cruciform plan; nave and presbytery extended almost 42m. and were crossed by transepts north and south. Some low walls around the east end are 12th century but much reconstructed, while part of the 13th century gable in the north transept still stands. To the south all that remains of the claustral buildings is part of the 12th century refectory undercroft. Burials have taken place in and around these ruins. Carved **tapered slabs** depict clerics, mailed figures, animals real and fantastical, swords, ships, etc. **Mural monument**, late 18th century; pedimented entablature carried on widely spaced fluted pilaster.

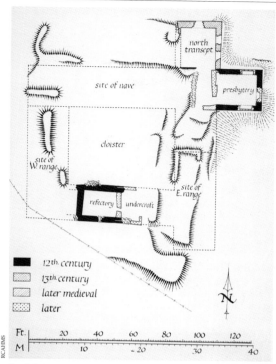

*RCAHMS Saddell Abbey site plan.*

Map legend:
- 12th century
- 13th century
- later medieval
- later

N

Ft. 20 40 60 80 100 120
M 10 20 30 40

**83 Saddell Castle**, 1508-10

A tower-house, oblong in plan, rising to four storeys and garret. The original building was burnt out in 1558. Major reconstruction begun in 1650 by William Ralston, a plantation laird who had settled in Kintyre and leased the castle from the Marquess of Argyll. Repaired and remodelled internally in the late 19th century and much more radically, 1975-77, by Stewart Tod for the Landmark Trust who have adapted the castle to holiday home. The exterior remains substantially as it was in late medieval times. Distinctive chequer pattern corbelling under the parapet. Lower offices, 18th century, form an L-

*Saddell Castle.*

plan court on the west and south. Some later outbuildings.

**Saddell House**, 1774
A two-storey mansion-house with attics and sunk basement, built by the Campbells of Glensaddell to replace Saddell Castle as the family home. The north-west front is pedimented with an asymmetrical porch added in the late 19<sup>th</sup> century. A central, semi-octagonal bay projects to the south-east. Interior remodelled after a fire in 1900.

Top right *Saddell House;* Above right *Kilchousland Old Parish Church;* Above *Headstone at Kilchousland Old Parish Church.*

Further south is **Kilchousland Old Parish Church**, a roofless oblong ruin begun in the 12<sup>th</sup> century but elongated in the 16<sup>th</sup>. The west gable and north and south walls survive. In the surrounding graveyard, a collection of 18<sup>th</sup> century **headstones** intricately carved with vocational symbolism and trade insignia.

## CAMPBELTOWN

Campbeltown is something of a surprise. At the
end of the long drive down the Kintyre peninsula
it is suddenly and intensely urban. Far from
urbane, and beset by the tawdriness that comes
in the wake of economic blight, it nevertheless
retains a robust built inheritance from better
days: tenement ranges that have few peers
elsewhere in Scotland, a library and museum of
exceptional architectural distinction, a quaint
little Picture House (amongst the earliest in
Britain and still viable), and a succession of fine
villas strung along the north and south shores of
Campbeltown Loch – all signs of the Victorian
and Edwardian prosperity brought from Central
Scotland by fast and frequent steamer links.
While steamer services have operated from time
to time to Northern Ireland, the long road
journey north remains the only route to Glasgow.

Until the 17th century there was nothing, or
almost nothing, here. A few cottages clustered at
the head of Campbeltown Loch; a few vessels
sheltering behind Davaar Island and The
Doirlinn sand spit. In 1609, however, an Act of

Campbeltown c.1900.

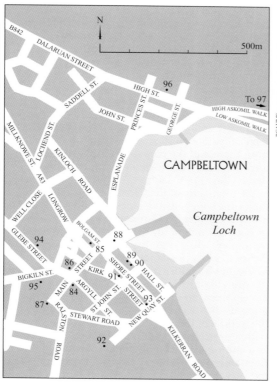

*Campbeltown, etching by Frank Bott, 1867.* Argyll and Bute Council Museum Service

Parliament gave the 7th Earl of Argyll authority *to plant a burgh*. Argyll built a small castle (only its memory survives on Castlehill) and invited *Lowland men and trafficking burgesses* from Bute and the Cumbraes to establish themselves in Campbeltoune, as the new *town* came to be known. By mid century, this policy of plantation received added stimulus from an influx of Covenanting émigré lairds driven from their farms in Renfrewshire and Ayrshire. In 1700 it was made a royal burgh, but the settlement remained small, little more than one main street, then called the High Street, which ran downhill from the site of the House of Lochhead (the fortified family home of the Campbells had been demolished in the later years of the 17th century) to the town jetty at the Old Quay Head. From this spine some narrow lanes began to push north-west towards Campbeltown Water, the original alignment of several still preserved in the town plan. To the south-east, the building of the Parish Church close to the shore in 1642-43, the first stone-built kirk in the town, had encouraged the growth of Kirk Street and Shore Street and development in this direction was given further impetus by the construction of the New Quay in the middle of the 18th century. Now furnished with a protected harbour between the two piers and a third jetty at Dalintober, it seemed that the town might grow apace. A plan drawn up by the surveyor George Langlands in 1801 clearly indicates the intention to regularise expansion south along Argyll Street and north around the head of the loch absorbing the village of Dalintober as a suburb of the town. Within a generation this was duly accomplished, though not on the basis of established economic conditions, for while the town remained a market focus for local farming, the herring fishery thrived for a few more years and the modest amount of mining carried on had received a boost from the cutting of a canal from Drumlemble to Campbeltown Loch in 1783, it was as a result of two new factors that growth was assured. At the conclusion of the Napoleonic Wars changes in excise regulations made the commercial production of whisky an attractive proposition. Distilleries sprang up all over the town; between 30 and 40 in the course of the 19th century. Moreover, although the fishing industry declined, the town's dependence on the sea increased with the coming of the steamer and regular trade and passenger links with the Clyde coast. The relative ease of communication between Glasgow and the community at the southern tip of the Kintyre peninsula sustained Campbeltown's modest prosperity through the 19th century. (see p.129)

In late Victorian years, a significant level of local patronage developed, sufficiently attractive, indeed, to persuade some of Glasgow's finest architects to take train and boat south to discuss the design of those public and private buildings which remain the town's unexpectedly rich architectural legacy. So convenient were these steamer links that, in contrast with Lochgilphead, Dunoon or Oban, no local architect found it profitable to set up business in the town; local builders and tradesmen were, of course, active but in the 50 years preceding the outbreak of the First World War virtually every major building erected in Campbeltown, public or private, had been designed in a Glasgow office. James Boucher, John Burnet, his son John James Burnet, Frank Burnet & Boston, Henry E Clifford (who, by virtue of marriage, came closest to being a local man), Campbell Douglas & Sellars, William F MacGibbon, James Monro and Thomas Lennox Watson were all involved in such long-distance commissions.

84 **Main Street** is generous in width, running back from the Campbeltown Cross, a disc-headed shaft stranded on an island roundabout at the

Among several Glasgow architects who contributed to the townscape of Campbeltown, **Henry Edward Clifford** (1852-1932) had both a professional and a personal relationship with the town. Born in Trinidad, he returned with his widowed mother and siblings to Scotland in 1859. In 1867 he became an apprentice in the Glasgow office of John Burnet, studying in the evenings at Glasgow School of Art. Leaving Burnet in 1878, he established his own practice, surviving in part by teaching at the School of Art. In 1885 he prepared a design for St Kieran's Church and parsonage, the first of a series of commissions carried out in and around Campbeltown. Towards the end of the century, Clifford's work in Glasgow also prospered, though success in the competition for the design of the city's Royal Infirmary did not lead to the award of the commission. In 1904 he was married in Longrow Church, Campbeltown, and later, during World War I, seems to have lived in the town. Retiring from practice on medical advice in 1923, he and his wife moved to Surrey. He is buried in Kilkerran Cemetery.

*Main Street.*

*Courtesy of St Andrew's University Library (Valentine Collection)*

*Nick Haynes*

*RCAHMS*

*RCAHMS*

Old Quay. To the south-west, where the ground rises, Castlehill Church closes the view. The street itself might be medieval, but it is probably not earlier than the 17th century; the Cross, genuinely medieval but relocated more than once, is an uneasy transplant; the pedimented church, evidently 18th century, now no more than a shell for flatted accommodation. Yet these deceptions scarcely matter. The street preserves a sense of urban space and scale. This has much to do with a number of dignified if plain tenements, among them **MacLean Place** on the corner of Bolgam Street and **Nos.16-20**, survivors of town improvements made *c.*1820, **Nos.58-62**, 1813, three-storeys with piended dormers, and **Fleming's Land**, a seven-bay block built uphill on the opposite side of the street at much the same time and later restored by T L Watson in 1909. At the junction with Lorne Street, ogee-capped dome and flanking chimney stack mark the octgonal corner of **The Club**, 1896-98, by H E Clifford. From here to the Old Quay Head, shops animate the scene. Hotels, too, figure in the street wall.

The **White Hart Hotel** may be early 19th century in origin, but another corbelled octagon corner capped with a slated ogee dome betrays the extensive alterations carried out by Sydney Mitchell, 1897-1907. The **Argyll Arms**, an ashlar façade with two canted oriels at first floor level, *c.*1900, fronts its much earlier more vernacular incarnation in Cross Street where the adjacent and not dissimilar **Commercial Inn** is dated 1774. A few more late 18th and early 19th century buildings compressed along **Cross Street**, **Union Street** and **Burnside Street** mark this as the oldest part of town. On **Bolgam Street**, a pend entry leads to an inner courtyard from which steps climb to the former **Court House and Gaol**,

From top *Main Street, c.1950; Nos.16-20 Main Street; Nos. 58-62 Main Street; The White Hart Hotel.*

85

18th century, remodelled 1852-53, and now derelict. Filling the corner of Main Street and Cross Street is Campbeltown's Town House, the historic heart of the place, its civic significance signposted above the rooftops with steepled confidence.

86 **Town House**, 1758-60, John Douglas
A replacement for the original tolbooth and a sign of municipal ambition. Skew gables with Gibbsian quoins, a hefty eaves cornice and round-arched windows accented by chunky keystones. At first floor the windows are elongated to light the town-hall, which was recast with a coffered segmental ceiling in 1866. Symmetrically placed on the street front, the steeple (designed and built by John Brown of Inveraray in 1778) projects in a half-octagon to mark the original entrance; above eaves height it rises in two stages to a spire pierced with louvred belfry openings and circular recesses. Campbell Douglas, who carried out the 1866 alterations, added the matching bay to the south-west; armorial sculpture by William Mossman.

**Sheriff Court House**, Castlehill, 1869-71, David Cousin
The work of an Edinburgh designer in a town dominated by Glasgow architects. A symmetrical composition, in scale more mansion-house than court-house, in style eclectic. Crowstepped gables and some rough polychromatic masonry seem quasi-Baronial, but the central belfry tower has a steeply pitched Frenchified roof and an ecclesiastical Gothic entrance.

87 **Castlehill Church**, 1778-80, George Haswell
The site is that chosen by the Earl of Argyll for his House of Lochhead, built c.1610 and demolished before the end of the century. The north-east façade, austerely classical, oversees the secular scene on Main Street; five bays, pedimented at the centre, carrying urns and a tall bellcote positioned obliquely on its apex plinth. Converted to residential use as Castlehill Mansions, 1986.

88 **Campbeltown Cross**, Old Quay Head, c.1380
Medieval memorial cross of Loch Sween schist, richly carved with saints, animals and interlaced foliage. Latin dedication to Ivor MacEachern and his son Andrew, both parsons, the former at

From top *Former Court House and Gaol; Town House; Sheriff Court House; Castlehill Church.*

*Campbeltown Cross.*

Kilkivan near Machrihanish where the cross may first have been raised. Moved to become the town's mercat cross, it stood in front of the Town House from the early 17th century until the 1940s.

Despite its axial response to Castlehill Church at the opposite end of Main Street, the Cross is ungraciously sited on a roundabout island at **Old Quay Head**. Nor do its neighbours do much to enhance or toughen the townscape at the pier. On a corbelled corner bow, the **Royal Hotel**, by James Monro, 1907 (rebuilt after war damage) offers an ogee dome. But across the street the brutal flank of **Woolworth's** makes a grim, gatepost entry to Main Street, while the **Christian Institute**, designed by an off-form H E Clifford, 1885-87, is intimidating and confrontational. It leads, however, into **Hall Street**, a short esplanade incongruously aggrandized to dual carriageway status but with three seaward-looking buildings of real architectural quality.

**Royal Avenue Mansions**, 1900, Frank Burnet & Boston
Tenement range in polychromatic sandstone busy

Top and Above *Inveraray Castle;* Right *Tapestry Drawing Room.*

Top *Auchindrain township;* Above
*Carloonan Doocot;* Middle *Thatched
building at Auchindrain township;*
Bottom *Powdermills Cottages, Furnace.*

Top *Poltalloch House by William Burn,
1849;* Above *Stronachullin Lodge
entrance;* Middle *Stained glass window
commemorating William Sim 1895,
Cumlodden Parish Church;* Bottom
*Carnasserie Castle.*

Top *Duntrune Castle;* Middle *Barbreck House;* Bottom *Interior of Craignish Castle.*

with gables and dormers in a clever composition that isn't as symmetrical as it at first seems.

89 **Picture House**, 1912-13, Albert W Gardner
A toytown cinema, alive with idiosyncratic seaside invention and without the Art Deco geometries or Mayan *gravitas* of later Thirties Modernism. The interior, remodelled in 1934-35 and again in 1988, retains some original fragments.

90 **Public Library and Museum**, 1897-99, J J Burnet
More polychromatic sandstone: Scots Renaissance freely interpreted with inventive Mannerist detail. A series of carved panels representing the town's arts and crafts enriches the Hall Street elevation. Marking the corner with St John Street is an octagonal Reading Room and an ogee-domed lantern rising over the entrance foyer. Along St John Street, canted bays with mullion and transom windows light the Library which leads to the top-lit Museum. This L-plan arrangement creates an inner garden edged by a cloister-like loggia. The interior is lavishly detailed with panelled walls, carved chimneypieces, decorative plasterwork and, over the foyer, an open timber roof. (see p.130)

From top *Picture House; Public Library and Museum; The Manse.*

Hall Street continues to the **New Quay** without distinction. At the pierhead is the smart new **Ferry Terminal** for Ballycastle; designed by John Wilson Associates, 1995-97, it is low-key and nicely undemonstrative. Alongside, a segmental canopy roof carried by four masts, a gesture to nautical structures by engineers Montgomery-Smith & Partners. The two buildings do not quite gell. But this is of little import compared to the aggressive impact made by high barrier railings marching down the pier, the brutal accompaniment, it seems, of travel to and from Northern Ireland.

Behind Hall Street, three more or less parallel links connect New Quay Street and Main Street. Two of these date from the period of the plantation town. **Shore Street**, which backed onto the harbour until 19th century reclamation consigned it to disregard behind Hall Street, has little to offer. **Kirk Street** is better with several early 19th century town houses including **The Manse**, 1835, by David Hamilton, and **No.70**, both with good columned porches. Three bifurcated windows in a rubble wall light the

91 interior of the **Highland Parish Church Halls** recast by H E Clifford in 1904 from vestiges of the church built in 1706 to house the town's English-speaking immigrant community. Clifford ends the street wall with a strange tower-house corner. On **Argyll Street**, which appears for the first time as part of the ordered rectilineal expansion proposed in Langlands' plan of 1801, these same three-bay, late Georgian, mansions recur; at **No.31, Barochan House**, four bays over three tweak the rule. **Barochan Place** provides flatted accommodation for a more urban late Victorian life-style, and it does it with style! A long polychromatic masonry wall of varied bays, aedicules, gables and dormers by T L Watson, 1907, perhaps the best tenement of all. **St Kiaran's Church** is by Ronald Walker, 1891; its straightforward Gothic with a triple lancet in the street gable preferred to earlier proposals by William Butterfield, 1849, and H E Clifford, 1885.

*Highland Parish Church.*

92 **Highland Parish Church**, New Quay Street, 1803-08, George Dempster
Built by the town's Gaelic-speaking congregation, who originally occupied a church erected closer to the shore in the 1640s, this was a calculated response to the Lowlanders' Castlehill Church. Like the latter it is classical in setting and design. A five-bay pedimented façade, widened by stair tower wings and axially heightened by a pinnacled belfry (added by John Baird in 1833, but rebuilt 1884-85), it looks down New Quay Street to the pier, a distinct if quieter echo of the townscape strategy on Main Street.

*Court Hill.*

New Quay Street is rigorously straight from church to pier. Another of Campbeltown's
93 splendid tenements, **Craigdhu Mansions**, by J J Burnet, 1896-97, fills the block between Shore Street and Kirk Street with rough and folksy Baronial in ochre and red sandstone. Diagonally opposite to the east is **Pensioners Row**, an early 19th century L-plan development of dormered cottages, rehabilitated 1994-95.

**Kilkerran Road** marches with the lochside to the south-east, a succession of varied villas looking across Quarry Green to the sea. Several are early 19th century: **Court Hill** and **South Park** standard three-bay Georgian; **Stronvaar** is five-bay with a recessed porch below a Venetian window; **East Cliff**, 1825, but rebuilt by H E Clifford in 1896, has balustraded bows and a verandah wing.

*Stronvaar.*

Also by Clifford, **Redholme**, 1896, in free asymmetric Tudor. Finally, the **Lifeboat House**, 1898, gabled Arts and Crafts, its polychromatic sandstone walls battered and buttressed along the flanks.

*Limecraigs House.*

**Limecraigs House**, early 18th century
A five-bay, two-storey, piend-roofed laird's house probably built for Elizabeth Tollemache, widow of the 1st Duke of Argyll. It originally stood in planted grounds with a forecourt flanked by symmetrical outbuildings. Now much abused by alteration and encroachment it remains important as one of the earliest classical houses in Argyll.

**Kilkerran Cemetery**
A raised knoll just south of the graveyard's Gothic Revival gates marks the site of Kilkerran Old Parish Church, dedicated to St Ciaran in the 13th century. Some fragments of medieval **burial slabs** and the reconstructed shaft of a 15th century **cross** survive. There are many carved **monuments** and **headstones** from the 18th and 19th centuries and a few with late 17th century dates. The **McEacharn Monument**, dated 1715, is a tall armorially crested aedicule set between elongated fluted pilasters, the unlettered **McDowall Monument**, 1791, a steep pyramidal obelisk on a rough classical plinth, worn and weathered to sublime ruggedness. A low **mural monument** with a plain block pediment marks the grave of architect H E Clifford (1852-1932).

The road continues round the edge of the loch, past a pier in the lee of Davaar Island, and on to Kildalloig Bay. On the north side of the island is **Davaar Lighthouse**, 1854, a short tube tower with the usual single-storey keepers' houses. Not far south on the coastal road, **Kildalloig**

From top *Headstone at Kilkerran Cemetery; McDowall Monument, Kilkerran Cemetery.*

**House** sits back on higher ground, wide and white-harled with a classical doorpiece and a roofscape punctuated by piended eaves-dormers; an impressive house crafted with quasi-Lorimer skill.

Back in the town centre it was not until 1908-09 that urban surgery lanced through the lanes and wynds crushed between Main Street and the Witch Burn to link with the extended line of Longrow entering the town from the north-west. Polychromatic three-storey walls of tenement flats and shops on **Longrow South**, by T L Watson, formalise this entry in parallel ranges modelled with shallow bays. Though confidently straight, Longrow itself is much less grand, its earlier tenements unremarkable. The **Clydesdale Bank**, late 19th century, muscles in with some welcome Victorian Gothic.

94 **Lorn and Lowland Church**, Longrow, 1869-72, John Burnet

Burnet's strange design (a *Rundbogenstil* nightmare?) gets breathing space between Longrow and Glebe Street but the generous forecourt only serves to exaggerate an uncharacteristic ungainliness. Pedimented gables emerge in T-plan arrangement from an amphitheatre core. A high square steeple, top-heavy with an open beehive spire of arched ribs plated on a deep cornice, punches down into the north-east gable on the entrance stem of the T.

95 **Lorne Street Church**, Lorne Street, 1867-68, James Boucher

Not quite Butterfield's *streaky bacon* Gothic but a close-run thing. A gabled façade with tall apex bellcote and pinnacled buttresses banded in polychromatic stone. The same red and ochre stripes track across quoins and jambs. Originally the Gaelic Free Church; from 1995 a community museum presenting local culture and history. **Hall** at the rear by H E Clifford, 1889.

*From top Lorn and Lowland Church; Lorne Street Church; Springbank Distillery.*

Longrow skirts an area of distillery decline. Many warehouses are derelict but, grouped around a courtyard, the three-storey rubble buildings of **Springbank Distillery**, 1828, are still in operation. **Millknowe Road** continues north-west. On the left, **Nos.83-103**, a long range of flatted workers' housing, by Robert Weir & Son, 1878; roughcast with a central run of gabled dormers. On the right, **Nos.90-120**, two-storey terraces of local authority houses, 1951, with bold arched entrances. At the edge of town, an elegantly plain mansion-house with columned porch: **Drumore House**, *c.*1820, altered *c.*1875.

Dalaruan Street runs back east into the village suburb of Dalintober. **High Street** retains some sense of its early 19th century character, both industrial and residential. **Glen Scotia Distillery** bulks large: 11 bays of three-storeyed roughcast with two hoist dormers at the eaves.

**The distilling of whisky** has been a preoccupation of Campbeltown's inhabitants, probably from the foundation of the town in the 17th century. The first documented evidence of the industry does not, however, occur until 1706 when the Town Council Minutes refer to *Distillers in the Burgh.* In 1792 the First Statistical Account recorded 22 distillers in the town producing around 20,000 gallons of *uisge bheatha.* But, by the end of the century, the imposition of harsh licensing duties reduced profits to such an extent that legal production virtually ceased until the end of the Napoleonic Wars. A reduction of duty in 1823 gave a new impetus to the industry and by 1860 there were 20 distilleries in independent production. This number remained more or less constant until 1920 when a rapid contraction set in. By 1925 there were 12, by 1930 only three. Today, though the ruinous evidence of several plants can still be found, the Springbank Distillery, founded in 1828, and the Glen Scotia Distillery, founded 1832, are the only active survivors.

96 **Springfield House**, *c.*1815, originally a sea-captain's residence, is a skew-gabled mansion with tripartite windows, urns on the parapet and a splendid flying stair rising to a columned porch. On North Shore Street, **Sandbank**, *c.*1820, is a plainer version of the same, once gracious, life-style. Around Kinloch Park, council housing on **Prince's Street**, **John Street** and **Parliament Place,** by James Thomson & Son, 1936-39, is unambiguously, if crudely, Scots.

From top *Drumore House; Glen Scotia Distillery;*
Top left *Springfield House;* Below left *Parliament Place.*

**War Memorial**, Esplanade, 1923, A N Paterson A high masonry obelisk on a splayed and buttressed base. A competition winner, axially sited at the head of Campbeltown Loch.

Above *War Memorial*; Right *Bellgrove*.

**Low Askomill Walk** runs by the loch shore as far as Trench Point. A chain of south-facing houses enjoys the view across the water. In a group of five early 19th century three-bay mansions, **Rockbank** is best with pedimented and pilastered tripartite windows. Gardens are elevated above the road; at **Rosemount**, 1810, behind a rubble wall as powerful as a castellar curtain. Eclectic preferences prevail. **Hawthorne** and **Belmount** are both late 19th century; Italianate and Baronial respectively. **Beach Hill**, perhaps 50 years earlier, flirts with Gothic. **Craigard**, 1882, is towered with round-arch windows and a two-storey bow; altogether Thomsonesque. **High Askomill Walk,** the B842, climbs slowly with the contours of the hillside, the views across Campbeltown Loch below even better. **Ardgowan**, *c*.1840, is neat gabled Georgian. Double-height bows swell out from **Airdaluinn**, late 19th century, and **Auchinlee**, *c*.1885, the latter dramatized by a heavy entrance tower. At **Rothmar**, 1897-98, J J Burnet adopts the town's familiar polychromatic sandstone in a design full of eclectic classical grandeur. **Bellgrove**, *c*.1820, on the other hand, has an understated almost Palladian simplicity.

### MACHRIHANISH

From Campbeltown it is less than 8km. across the Kintyre peninsula to the Atlantic. A row of semi-detached **miners' cottages**, 19th century, line the road at Drumlemble. A little to the west is the ruinous shell of **Kilkivan Old Parish Church**, possibly 13th century, an oblong rubble chapel with a pointed-arch door surviving in the north wall. Further on, **West Trodigal**, a tidy farmhouse, *c*.1840(?), with a yard behind enclosed symmetrically by lower piended wings.

Machrihanish itself is a linear hamlet, little more than a hotel and a handful of villas all looking north on to Machrihanish Bay and the 5km. of sand dunes across which stretches one of the finest links golf courses in the country. Since the course was first laid out in 1876, golf has sustained the village. Redolent of better busier days, **Machrihanish Hotel**, 1898, by Sydney Mitchell & Wilson, is a large black-and-white affair with half-timbered gables and dormered attics. Several contemporary villas, white-walled, too, but with red-tiled roofs, are the work of H E Clifford; **Dunlossit** and **Swallowholme** are characteristically playful concoctions of canted bays and ogee-domed corners. (see p.130)

98

**The Links of Machrihanish** stretch along the Atlantic coast at the southern end of the Kintyre peninsula. Exposed to the full fury of the western gales, the sands undulate in grassy hillocks and dunes – a landscape *specifically designed by the Almighty for playing golf*. In 1876 the Kintyre Golf Club (now Machrihanish Golf Club) was founded. Improvements were made three years later by Open Championship winner Tom Morris of St Andrews and in 1914 the course was again altered and upgraded by another Championship winner, J H Taylor. Today's links course, which attracts golfers from all over the world, is the result of further improvements carried out by Sir Guy Campbell during and after the Second World War.

*George Washington Wilson Collection, University of Aberdeen*

**Lossit House**, 1824-30; enlarged *c*.1890 by Sydney Mitchell & Wilson
Sited uphill south of the village, an early 19th century ashlar house aggrandized by later pedimented flanks and a central *porte-cochère* tower.

*RCAHMS*

Above *Swallowholme;* Left *Machrihanish Hotel, c.1895.*

## SOUTHEND

From Stewarton, some 2km. west of Campbeltown, the B842 heads south. **Kilchrist Castle** is a harled tower-house, romantic but rather dull early 19th century make-believe. **Oatfield House** is similar in date, or perhaps a little earlier, but without such stylistic nostalgia, though a garden folly has been contrived from medieval fragments spirited here from restorations carried out at Dunblane Cathedral, 1893. Halfway to Southend the medieval vestiges of **Killellan Chapel** are all but invisible in the turf.

*Michael Davis*

*Lossit House.*

Founded by the Duke of Argyll in 1797, the village of **Southend** (then known as Newton Argyll) came later than the parish church. But settlement at this southern tip of Kintyre has ancient roots. Legend associates the place with the missionary activity of St Columba in the 6th century while some form of fortified redoubt is recorded in the 8th century.

From top *Southend Parish Church; St Columba Church.*

**St Columba's Footprints** are carved into the rock above the medieval chapel dedicated to the saint. There are two footprints; one known to have been cut by a stonemason in 1856, the other of considerable antiquity. It is possible that the latter was used in the inauguration of the kings of ancient Dalriada (as at Dunadd not far north of the Crinan Canal). The association with St Columba, who sailed from Ireland to Iona in 563 and landed in Kintyre, is long established and to some extent substantiated by excavations in the nearby Keil Caves which confirmed habitation there dating from the Dalriadic period. Vestigial traces of a rectangular building just to the west of the carved footprints could be those of an Early Christian place of worship.

**Southend Parish Church**, 1773-74, James Stirling
Skew-gabled kirk, harled and heavily quoined. At the centre of the south wall is a high blind porthole recess set between two tall pointed-arch windows flanked in turn by superimposed lintelled windows lighting above and below the U-plan gallery within. Additions made on the west, north and east in the 1970s comprise architectural austerity. Nestling against the hillsode near Keil Point, **St Columba's Chapel**, seems to be embedded in the rural landscape, a roofless rubble ruin part late 13$^{th}$ century, part late medieval or post-Reformation. In the graveyard are several carved **tapered slabs**, 14$^{th}$-16$^{th}$ century, and later **headstones** bearing heraldic devices and the symbols of various local crafts and occupations.

Forgotten on the off-shore island of Sanda, the equally ruinous **St Ninian's Chapel**, also late medieval.

**St Columba Church**, 1889-90, Robert Hay
Now redundant, the church boasts a classical front, inventive if rather incongruously urban in its rural setting.

100 **Dunaverty Castle,** rebuilt 1539-42, dismantled 1685
An ancient fortress, known to have been besieged by Sealbach, King of Dalriada, in 712, its configuration may well have followed the classic pattern of the Gaidhealtachd stronghold wrapping a high rubble curtain around the summit of the natural dun on which it stood. Demolished in 1685 after the forfeiture of the Earl of Argyll, it is today reduced to fragmentary stretches of masonry hidden in headland rock pushing precipitously into the sea.

Fragments, too, are all that survive of **Keil House**, 1872-75, a few walls recalling the palatial Tudor mansion by Campbell Douglas & Sellars. Even **Keil Hotel**, 1938-39, by J Austen Laird, though its white walls still stand as a reminder of inter-war seaside style, has been abandoned.

Above *Keil Hotel;* Right *Keil House, c.1895.*

On the fringes of the village and beyond there are some fine farm buildings. **Machribeg**, 1843, and **Blasthill**, early 19<sup>th</sup> century, are both three-bay houses with low symmetrical wings. At **Machrimore Mill**, 1839 (disused since 1960), the cast-iron overshot wheel still has some of its wooden blades in place.

**Macharioch House**, 1873-77, George Devey
A rambling country house some 4km. east of Southend. Devey's rebuilding is picturesque with a plethora of gables, tall chimneys and mullioned windows. A four-storey turreted tower and a buttressed drum-shaped **Lodge** with a slated cone roof add castellar accents.

**Lephenstrath House**, 18<sup>th</sup> century
A plain five-bay dwelling with added canted bays.

*Macharioch House Lodge.*

*Carskiey House.*

**Carskiey House**, 1904-09, Rennison & Scott
A wide two-storey dwelling with a curvilinear gable centrepiece on the north-west entrance front. Harled walls and crowstepped gables give the design a marked but reserved Scottish flavour. In the garden, symmetrically located on the south-east side of the house, are two identical **doocots**, one is late 18<sup>th</sup> or early 19<sup>th</sup> century, a relic of an earlier mansion, the other a later matching copy.

**Mull of Kintyre Lighthouse**, 1786-88, Robert Kay
Remotely and dramatically located above the cliffs at the extreme south-west point of the peninsula. A low domed cylinder with an encircling corbelled walk. Later flat-roofed **Keepers' Houses** and ancillary buildings, 1857 and 1883, crowd around the light with little deference.

*Mull of Kintyre Lighthouse.*

**BRIDGE OF ORCHY**
From Tyndrum the A82 runs north *en route* to Fort William. On the opposite side of the valley are the railway line and the military road laid by Major William Caulfield in the 1750s, now the West Highland Way. Pressed together at Bridge of Orchy, river, road and railway run in parallel. The **bridge**, *c*.1751, by Caulfield, is impressive: hump-backed with a segmental arch rubble span of almost 19m. The **hotel**, a 1954 rebuild, is enlivened by a corner octagon. More daring, the modern vernacular of the **Way In Bunkhouse**, a slated shed with oversailing eaves reached across a bouldered sheugh; by Stephen & Maxwell, 1987. Uphill is the **railway station**, 1894, by James Miller, a tile-hung, timber-framed structure, typical for the West Highland line.

*Right Bridge of Orchy; Above Achallader Castle.*

Hidden in a forest not far south of Dalmally is the site of **the lost village of the MacNabs**, who for generations practised as swordsmiths from the smithy at Barr a Chastealain. From the early 15th century, when Duncan MacNab first set up as a blacksmith, the family produced swords, arrows, spears, pistols, armour, tools, jewellery and brooches as well as shoes for cattle and horses. Duncan's work at Kilchurn Castle seems to have made his name known well beyond Argyll, for there is a tradition that he travelled to Italy and may have met the Venetian swordmaster Andrea Ferrara. The family skill was passed down the centuries until following the collapse of the Jacobite rebellions in the 18th century a period of peace diminished the need for weaponry.

At the west end of Loch Tulla on the old road is **Inveroran Hotel**, a plain three-bay droving inn dated *c*.1708, extended 1855. At the east end of 104 the loch, **Achallader Castle**, a blasted, one-room-and-stair tower; a hunting lodge built by Sir Duncan Campbell in the late 16th century but now reduced to a ragged stand of shattered rubble.

*Glenorchy Church.*

**DALMALLY**
105 **Glenorchy Church**, 1808-11, James Elliot
A white Gothick octagon and square tower elevated on a grassy knoll above the river. Buttresses at the angles of the pyramid-roofed church and crenellated tower are topped with obelisk finials. In the surrounding **burial ground** are several **tapered slabs**, 14th-15th century, carved with interlacing, floral ornament and figural images. Provincially Palladian piend-roofed **manse**, 1804-05, by John Stevenson, with balanced Venetian windows.

**Dalmally Bridge**, 1780-81, by Lewis (Ludovick?) Piccard, crosses the Orchy in three segmental arch spans. Piccard was also resposible for **Dalmally Hotel**; in its original form, a three-bay,

The Gaelic poet **Duncan Ban Macintyre** (1724-1812) is commemorated in a circular peristyle of rough-hewn Appin stone elevated on Dunach Hill close to the old military road climbing south-west from Dalmally. Macintyre's poetry draws on his experience of nature as a forester and gamekeeper in Argyll and Perthshire. His poems are full of evocative descriptions of the flora and fauna of the Highland landscape. In *Moladh Beinn Dobhrain* (In Praise of Ben Doran), for example, his praise for the beauty of the deer which live on the mountain comes from his close observation and knowledge of the countryside of his birth. In his best known poem to Mairi Bhan Og, the daughter of the innkeeper at Inveroran whom he married, it is nature that provides the metaphors with which he describes his love.

three-storey inn, enlarged by a west wing, 1841-44, but now a vast affair with mansard bedrooms and a colossal *porte-cochère* by Crerar & Partners, 1995. Among several eaves-dormered houses in the village, some with decorative bargeboards, is the charming **Old School and Schoolhouse**, late 19th century.

106 **Macintyre Monument**, 1859-60, John T Rochead
A memorial to the Gaelic bard Duncan Ban Macintyre, primitive but powerful on a summit skyline south-west of the village. A twelve-pier henge of granite blocks rising from a three-step circular stylobate set on a massive square base.

**McLaren Monument**, late 19th century(?), Sydney Mitchell & Wilson
Close to the old road at Stronmilchan, a high Celtic cross finely carved by William Beveridge. In memory of Duncan McLaren, Lord Provost of Edinburgh, 1859-60, and MP for the city.

From top *Dalmally Bridge; Macintyre Monument; Fraoch Eilean Castle.*

**LOCH AWE**
107 **Fraoch Eilean Castle**, 13th century
An island hall-house built by the Macnaughtons on royal authority. Ruinous walls reveal little, though it seems likely that the oblong plan rose no more than two storeys. Long derelict, it was reinhabited by the Campbells of Inverawe in the 16th century; theirs is the degraded three-storey gabled dwelling built into the east end of the hall-house.

Thomas Pennant on his first *Tour in Scotland* in 1769 was much impressed by the scenery around Loch Awe. *This water is*, he wrote, *prettily varied with isles, some so small as merely to peep above the surface; yet even these are tufted with trees; some are large enough to afford hay and pasturage; and in one, called* Inch-hail, *are the remains of a convent. On* Fraoch-Elan, *the Hesperides of the Highlands, are the ruins of a castle. The fair* Mego *longed for the delicious fruit of the isle, guarded by a dreadful serpent: the hero* Fraoch *goes to gather it, and is destroyed by the monster. This tale is sung in the* Erse *ballads, and is translated and published in the manner of* Fingal.

*Cladich Parish Church.*

*Upper Sonachan House.*

Steamers plied the waters of Loch Awe for almost 100 years. The S.S. *Eva* arrived in 1861 and by the turn of the century there were three vessels linking Ford at the south-west end of the loch with Lochawe station at the north end. Travellers from Glasgow to Oban could reach Ford by coach from Ardrishaig where the Clyde steamers called, cruise the length of the loch and then continue their journey by train or coach through the Pass of Brander to Oban. Hotels on the loch were connected by steam launch. The last passenger vessel, the *Countess of Breadalbane*, was withdrawn from service in 1952. In 1985, however, the railway station at Lochawe was reopened. Three years later, cruising was reintroduced when the reconditioned steam launch *Lady Rowena*, built on Lake Windermere in 1826, was brought to the loch.

Less than 2km. west of Dalmally a road diverts left to follow the south-east shore of Loch Awe. It leads to **Cladich**, once a weaving hamlet. **Cladich Steading**, 19th century, is a gated U-plan court with piended ranges. A few cottages are packed close to the bridge over Cladich River; one of them, 1792, was once the **inn**. The former **Cladich Parish Church**, a humble hall of 1773, reconstructed in 1845 and again in 1896, is now in residential use. The medieval **Old Parish Church** survives on Inishail island as low walls and footings. In its **burial ground**, an Early Christian **cross-slab**, some **tapered slabs**, 14th-16th century, and a carved **altar frontal** from the 16th century.

Further down the loch is the old ferry point of **Port Sonachan**. Six black-and-white bays of **Port Sonachan Hotel** are recognizably those of the mid-18th century inn, though there have been many additions since, the latest being the conservatory foyer and offices added in 1991. The original **stables** block across the road converted to bedrooms and bar by Tom Grant, 1991. **Sonachan House**, *c.*1850, enlarged 1875, is dull Baronial with a three-storey west tower; now flatted. **Upper Sonachan House** is pleasantly if modestly and distantly classical, a mid-18th century laird's dwelling which originally faced south onto the old road. Sometime after the middle of the 19th century this relationship was reversed and gable-fronted wings added north and south.

**St James Ardbrecknish Church**, 1891
A tiny Episcopal church complete with nave, chancel, porch and chapel. Lancet Gothic. Along the road is **Port Sonachan Church**, one of a number of corrugated iron kirks which appeared in Argyll in the late Victorian years.

108 **Ardbrecknish House**
A complex accumulation of gables, the sequence of which is almost impossible to disentangle. The saddleback south-west tower may be medieval. The three-bay house to the north may be 17th century; certainly 18th. Baronialized accretion began *c.*1857 when the house was used as a shooting lodge. More of the same followed towards the end of the century. Most of this later work is in rubble and sandstone, the early work being rendered. A flatted subdivision was carried out, 1979-82, by Donald Wilson whose

white, Y-plan **Hill House**, 1990-91, (it shares no more than harling with its Helensburgh namesake) sits on a nearby knoll looking out on the loch.

Left *Innis Chonnell Castle, c.1890;*
Above *Innis Chonnell Castle.*

109 **Innis Chonnell Castle**, 13th century
Far down the loch, on an island overgrown with vegetation, are the gaunt and massive ruins of a Campbell stronghold long favoured by the Earls of Argyll as a reliable prison. The island has an hour-glass plan. To the east are the traces of the outer bailey; to the west, the inner bailey and the castle itself, a square curtain buttressed, it seems likely, by angle towers, one of which survives. North and south of the narrow neck of land between, were landing places. Within the walls are vaulted chambers forming the cellars of a west range with a hall above and a four-storeyed block in the south-east corner, all added in the 15th century. At the same time, the main curtain was raised to parapet walks still surviving on the north, west and south.

Left *Kilchurn Castle;*
Above *Kilchurn Castle, c.1880.*

10 **Kilchurn Castle**, from mid 15th century
Rising out of the marshes on a peninsular site at the headwaters of Loch Awe, this is the calendar-

**A simple monument located at Lochawe station** commemorates the victory won on the shore of Loch Awe by Robert the Bruce in the spring of 1308. Bruce was then opposed both by the English and by a powerful faction of Scottish nobles including John of Lorn, bitterly resentful of the king's killing of his cousin the Red Comyn. Bruce moved his forces west along Loch Awe towards the Pass of Brander where Lorn's 2,000 men were entrenched commanding the narrow route through to the coast. It seems likely that the trap was not set in the Pass itself but to the east, probably somewhere between the Falls of Cruachan and Innis Chonain. Forewarned, Bruce committed part of his army to the high wooded ridges of Ben Cruachan while the remainder marched into the Pass. Lorn launched his attack only to see his men come under a hail of arrows from above, and the defending forces were swept from the Pass.

*Right Loch Awe Hotel, c.1890; below Tower of Glenstrae.*

conscious castle *par excellence.* Begun by Sir Colin Campbell, 1st of Glenorchy, as an orthodox tower-house, the laich hall was added on the south-west side of the barmkin before the end of the 15th century. Various repairs and additions were carried out through the 16th and 17th centuries until, *c.*1690-98, extensive alterations and enlargement were undertaken for the Earl of Breadalbane at the direction of the mason, Andrew Christie. A four-storey barracks block was created on the north-west and angle towers added to the curtain. Dated evidence of some of these later works can be found: a lintel with armorial carving and motto over the north-east door to the tower-house, 1693; another in the tower's west turnpike, 1691. Kilchurn was garrisoned at the time of the second Jacobite rebellion but in less than a generation had been abandoned. Since 1976 the fabric has been consolidated. Seen across the loch or haughlands the ruinous walls are an irresistible romantic attraction. (see p.130)

*George Washington Wilson Collection, University of Aberdeen*

The hamlet of **Loch Awe** is scarcely more than a halt on the railway line. But the wooded lochside landscape is a delight. **Loch Awe Hotel**, 1880-81, by John Young, is an immense Baronial legacy of the Earl of Breadalbane's desire to make the most of Victorian tourism. Young extended its granite crowstepping and turrets with a north-east wing, 1891-93. Several large houses nearby do, however, maintain a Baronial respectability: **St Conan's Tower**, *c.*1895, has an onion-topped gazebo six storeys up; the less exuberant **Tower of Glenstrae**, 1895-97, by John Lownie, is attractively asymmetrical and possesses a Glasgow Style interior in what was the dining room; **Carraig Thura**, 1904, by George P K Young, is bulky and bay-windowed with slated cones at the corners.

*Philip Graham*

Left *Interior of St Conan's Kirk;* Top *St Conan's Kirk;* Above *Lead roof detail of Cloister Garth.*

**111 St Conan's Kirk**, 1881-86, 1918-30, Walter Douglas Campbell

An astonishing little lochside church ambitiously and liberally eclectic, yet engaging and endearing. It began in the 1880s on a gabled cruciform plan with a square tower over the north porch. This tower with its pointed-arch west doorway remains recognizable, as does the traceried wheel window in the west gable. In 1907 Campbell recast the north wall and extended the chancel to the east in a five-sided parapetted apse lit by round-arched windows, at the same time taking advantage of the fall of the ground to the loch to construct an undercroft and crypt. Although he died before its completion, Campbell's complex design for the south side of the church was realised by his sister Helen between 1918 and 1927. This entailed the addition of the Bruce Chapel, a small saddleback tower obliquely set at the transept, some flying buttresses arcing down to a terrace banked above the shore, another small tower, a third tower inexplicably Saxon in derivation, and, finally, St Bride's Chapel arranged in an unconventional reversal of the church's liturgical axis, and, beyond it, St Conval's Chapel, built over the burial vault of Walter and Helen Campbell. Both chapels lie parallel to the south aisle of the

**The designer of St Conan's Kirk,** Walter Douglas Campbell, the young brother of the First Lord Blythswood, lived with his sister Helen and his mother at Innis Chonain on Loch Awe. From there the journey to the nearest church at Dalmally meant a longish coach drive, something Campbell's mother found tiring and tiresome. The small church, which was completed between 1881 and 1886 (the nave and part of the chancel of the present building), seems only to have whetted his artistic appetite for greater things and in 1907 Campbell began to transform St Conan's into a much grander place of worship. Work stopped with his death in 1914 but his sister, Helen, continued building following her brother's plans. She died in 1927 with the work still in train and the family trustees ensured completion. An avid collector of varied *objets d'art*, Campbell's design is essentially eclectic, and the suggestion that he wished to incorporate every aspect of architectural style evident in Scotland may well be true.

original church from which they are reached.
Linked west is an intimate Cloister Garth.
Efforts have been made to improve the
landscaping and setting of the church, for too
long unkempt and neglected.

The interior is of granite and sandstone with
dark stained timber trusses above. Rough
granite makes a fearsome crypt. In the church
itself the granite masonry is less severe, softened
by the fall of light and the carefully cut capitals
and mouldings of the upper chancel and side
chapels. Furnishings vary in style and quality:
canopied Gothic **choir stalls** of Spanish chestnut
and the Celtic latticework of the **organ screen** are
notable.

112 **Cruachan Power Station**, 1959-65, James
Williamson & Partners
By the lochside 3.8km. west of St Conan's Kirk is
the North of Scotland Hydro Electric **Visitor
Centre**, by James Shearer & Annand, a low flat-
roofed office slab, clad in exposed aggregate
precast concrete panels. From here a tunnel,
1.1km. long, bores into the mountain to reach the
vast machine hall, 38m. high. High above this
feat of engineering are the dammed waters of
**Cruachan Reservoir**.

*Bridge of Awe.*

Pressed through the Pass of Brander, road and
railway cross the River Awe. The old three-arch
**Bridge of Awe**, 1778-79, by Lewis (Ludovick?)
Piccard, is in ruins. Clad in rubble, the single
segmental arch of the new concrete road **bridge**,
1937-38, by Sir Frank Mears, looks perilously thin
at the apex. At Taynuilt (see below) a minor road
cuts south through Glen Nant to Loch Awe. It
passes **Ichrachan House**, *c*.1908, by Robert S
Lorimer, a little severe and graceless on its hilltop
site. **Kilchrenan Inn**, early 19th century and
**Taychreggan Inn**, now largely 20th century, have
historic cores that date from the 1700s or earlier;
both retain vernacular scale, though the drovers
who once passed this way would scarcely
recognize the latter's sophistication. Hard by the
loch edge as its name suggests, the

uncompromisingly box-frame form of **Tigh na Uisge**, 1961, by Morris & Steedman, makes no concessions to the past.

113 **Kilchrenan Parish Church**, 1771
A white skew-gabled oblong which has lost some of its 18th century integrity. At the centre of the symmetrical arrangement of round-arched windows and recesses on the south wall is a walled forestair rising to a blank wall. This was the original access to one of three galleries, the others reached by similar forestairs at the north-west and north-east corners. In 1904 James Edgar realigned worship to the east, retaining only the west gallery. A new west door was also formed, while fragments of dogtooth ornament, which probably derive from the church's medieval predecessor, were incorporated into the gables. In the graveyard, built against the south wall of the church, is the Campbell of Sonachan **burial enclosure**, 1779. Nearby, the **McIntyre Monument**, an early 19th century plinth-and-obelisk exercise in Neoclassical design.

Left *Kilchrenan Parish Church;*
Above *McIntyre Monument.*

Far down the loch south-west from Kilchrenan is a still smaller and simpler gable-ended kirk. **Dalavich Church**, *c.*1771, has four round-arched windows to the south, one of them converted to a door when James Edgar rearranged the interior in 1898. Dalavich itself is a forestry village with a settlement of timber-framed and lined **chalets** and a smart **community hall** roofed with scissor trusses, 1980-81, by Hird & Brooks.

*Hayfield House Steading before conversion.*

On the dead-end road that leads north-east from Kilchrenan is the ruined pedimented shell of **Hayfield House**, mid 18th century, and its

Right *Ardanaiseig House*; Below
*Taynuilt Hotel.*

The bishopric of Argyll, founded in 1222, had its first **church at Killespickerill** or Muckairn, Taynuilt; *the smallest of our cathedrals, fifty-six feet long by thirty feet broad, perhaps the humblest in Britain.* Not many years later, *c.*1236, the see was moved to Lismore. A second church, built at the beginning of the 16th century survives in ruins close to the present kirk. In 1637 the parishes of Muckairn and Ardchattan were united and for most of the next 200 years or so worshippers met in the church at Killespickerill (by then known as Gillespickerall). When Parliament voted a considerable sum from its Peace Fund, set up at the conclusion of the Napoleonic Wars to finance the construction of a series of new Parliamentary kirks and manses, Muckairn manse benefited from this government money; but it was General Campbell of Lochnell who paid for the church itself, a fact which may explain why the design of the building departs somewhat from that of the standard Parliamentary model.

courtyard **steading**, early 19th century, converted to residential use by John Peace in the 1980s. At road-end, William Burn's modestly Jacobean 114 **Ardanaiseig House**, 1833-34, enjoys the prospect of the loch across tranquil terraced lawns.

## TAYNUILT

The village stretches from the main road north to Loch Etive and the mouth of the River Awe. 115 **Taynuilt Hotel** has an 18th century core but its gabletted dormers and pedimented porch are early 19th century. Several rubble **cottages** surviving from the early 1800s are scattered around the village at Ichrachan, Kirkton, Brochroy and on the road to Airds Bay. The old **Public School**, *c.*1895, extended 1912-13 by G Woulfe Brenan, has classroom gables with tripartite windows; now abandoned it has been superseded by **Taynuilt Primary School**, *c.*1990, a colourful assemblage of monopitch roofs and gridded glazing by Strathclyde Regional Council. Timber-framed **Railway Station**, dated 1879, with a glazed canopy on decorative iron brackets over the platform. The **Church of the Visitation**, 1901-02, and the former **Muckairn Free Church**, 1860, are both gabled oblongs; the former lancet Gothic, the latter preserving its vaguely Italianate tower but traduced by conversion.

116 **Muckairn Parish Church**, 1828-29
Evidently a variant of Telford's Parliamentary Church design; skew gables, symmetrical north and south elevations and four-centre arch windows. As with so many kirks, the original orientation to a pulpit on the long south wall has been altered in late Victorian times, 1887(?). West gallery remains above west entrance. A **sheila-na-gig** stone, possibly 13th century, and another ancient stone, *a grinning ecclesiastic* who may have served as a skew putt, have been incorporated high in the south wall. Both may have come from the late medieval **Parish Church of Killespickerill**, now no more than some ivy-

*Muckairn Parish Church.*

Above *RCAHMS drawing of Bonawe Ironworks; Left Bonawe Ironworks furnace.*

hidden masonry in the graveyard. The **manse**, 1829, by William Thomson, is the standard T-plan model with a three-bay doorless front.

**17 Bonawe Ironworks, from 1752**
Impressive remains of the industrial settlement established here by a Cumbrian company in the middle of the 18th century. Importing iron ore by sea and drawing on plentiful local timber and water power, the works continued in operation until 1876. The high, battered walls of the charcoal-burning **blast furnace**, built on a sloping site to facilitate the production process, survive. Its square, granite rubble structure rises almost 9m. to the wallhead At the upper level a piended roof covering the bridgehouse leans against the broad chimney stack. Below are the openings for blast input and slag removal. On the east was the millwheel (no longer extant) driven by water brought by lade and aqueduct from the River Awe. Uphill to the south are the restored rubble **charcoal sheds** and **ore shed**, mid to late 18th century, all built into the slope to permit the delivery of material at the higher level. Collar and tie roof trusses; king-posts in the east charcoal shed. (see p.130) *Open to the public. Guidebook available.*

Nearby are several rows of workers' housing: a **cottage row**, c.1755, two-storey **tenement**, late 18th century, an **overseer's house**, also two-storey,

**Commercial production of cast iron** in Britain was well under way from the late 16th century. Works at Glen Kinglass on the east shore of Loch Etive were in production from c.1722 to c.1738. In 1752 Sir Duncan Campbell of Lochnell, proprietor of the lands at Glen Kinglass, entered into an agreement with the firm of Richard Ford & Co. of Furness granting timber rights and leasing land for a new blast furnace at Bonawe. Further access to wood for charcoal was obtained from the Earl of Breadalbane. In 1753 construction, and perhaps smelting, started at Bonawe. At peak output the furnace could produce almost two tons of pig iron per day. There was no forge, most pigs being shipped to Furness, the Severn and Wales. Production fell in the 19th century as the industry moved closer to the coal seams and in 1876 Bonawe ironworks finally closed.

and, abutting this to form an L-plan, another **tenement**, early 19th century, with forestair access to the upper flats. All are still in residential use. **Bonawe House**, mid 18th century, was built for the ironworks manager; a five-bay, three-storey mansion with a fine timber doorpiece of fluted pilasters, it was flatted *c*.1980. At Airds Bay on the lochside, iron ore arrived and pig iron, bark, kelp and salmon were dispatched from **Kelly's Quay**, late 18th century, a long turf-covered rubble jetty, reinforced with concrete, *c*.1962.

*Bonawe House.*

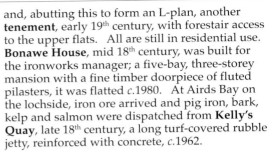

118 **Inverawe House**, from 16th century (?)
A substantial white-harled mansion on the east bank of the River Awe. Busy with gables, its successive alterations are difficult to discern and attribute. The central tower may be medieval in origin though its Baronial turrets and crowsteps are Victorian, probably part of the remodelling carried out by Charles Wilson, 1850-52. At the north end of the east façade is a three-bay house, evidently 18th century. Its doorway is subservient to a larger entrance to the left which has moulded architraves with a scrolled panel above. Further remodelling took place 1913-14 when Robert S Lorimer refurbished the interior. In 1953-54, Leslie C Norton removed the north wing and altered the west side of the tower by removing a gable and reducing the corner rounds. At the road end is **Inverawe Power Station**, a huge pink granite shed, *c*.1960, by Shearer & Annand and engineers James Williamson & Partners.

*Inverawe House.*

From Taynuilt a narrow minor road cuts across country to Kilmore (q.v.). *En route* it passes **Lonan House**, formerly Barguillean House, where Robert S Lorimer has created slate-hung bays and a recessed arched porch, 1906-08. At Strontoiller there are the ruins of a **township** and a cruck-framed **byre**, late 18th or early 19th century.

*Connel Bridge.*

## CONNEL

The A85 passes **Achnacloich**, 1885, a Baronial mansion by John Starforth with all the usual trimmings, including a Pinkie bartizan. By the lochside, **Dunfuinary**, late 19th century, maintains this romantic Scots idiom. Yet nothing is more dramatic on the Oban road than the suddenly seen engineering architecture of **Connel Bridge** (see p.131) crossing the Loch Etive narrows at the Falls of Lora. Its daring span of triangulated steel, 1902-03, by engineer Sir J Wolfe Barry, is the second largest cantilevered bridge in Britain. Built to carry the Caledonian Railway north, since 1966 it has served as a road crossing only. The village, however, is gathered cosily around the older bridge over the Lustragan Burn.

**Village Hall** with hip-gabled roof, 1994-95, by Crerar & Partners. There are three churches. **Connel Free Church**, 1893, is modest Gothic with a vestry apse. **St Mary the Virgin**, 1903, is more basic still; corrugated iron with the suggestion of half-timbering. Both are no longer used for worship.

**St Oran Church**, 1887-88, David Mackintosh The name hints at an Iona link and indeed the gable-ended cruciform arrangement with central tower seems modelled on Iona Abbey. This

Below *Dunstaffnage Mains Farm;*
Below right *Dunstaffnage Castle.*

tower, however, is excessively bulky, out of balance with the more modest ambitions of the rest of the plan. Gothic tracery in the chancel and transepts; quatrefoils in the hooded tower windows. The church is richly endowed with stained glass.

### DUNBEG

A cluster of local authority housing at the head of Dunstaffnage Bay. **Dunstaffnage Mains Farm**, late 18th century(?) preserves its white rural dignity with some difficulty. On the south side of the bay is another farm now adapted as part of a yachting **marina**; on the north side, a low, flat-roofed office block, **Dunstaffnage Marine Laboratory**, 1962-63, by Crerar & Partners, and a magnificent medieval castle.

The building of **Dunstaffnage Castle** is usually ascribed to Duncan, Lord of Lorn, though his son and successor, Ewan, may also have had a hand in the construction. It was a stronghold of the MacDougall clan who held sway over much of the western seaboard including the islands of Lismore, Mull, Coll and Tiree. In 1309 Dunstaffnage fell to Robert the Bruce who subsequently placed the fortress in the charge of the Campbells. In 1388, however, the Lordship of Lorn was given to the Stewarts. For a few brief years in the 1460s the MacDougalls reasserted their control but by 1470 the castle was back in Campbell hands where, with a few interruptions during the wars of the 17th century, it has remained. In the early years of the 20th century a dispute arose between the hereditary keeper of Dunstaffnage and the Duke of Argyll as to which Campbell exercised the right of ownership. In 1912 the Court of Session ruled that the castle belonged to the Duke as Lord of Lorn but that the keeper or Captain retained the right of residence. In 1958 the then Duke and Captain agreed to pass the guardianship of the castle to the state.

121 **Dunstaffnage Castle**, from the 13th century Strategically sited on a promontory at the mouth of Loch Etive to command the Firth of Lorn and the route east through the Pass of Brander to Central Scotland, the high masonry curtain impresses with its evident impregnability. The walls rise from a rocky base erupting through trimmed lawns. All but devoid of openings, they surround an irregular quadrangle, imperceptibly swelling into corner towers. All this is the work of the founder, Duncan, Lord of Lorn. More than 200 years later, the castle passed to the 1st Earl of Argyll and it remained in Campbell hands until state care begin in 1958. The bulging gatehouse was formed in the late 15th or early 16th century, though it has been altered several times since. The long straight-flight forestair which climbs to the round-arched entrance portal set in a pointed-arch recess is no earlier than the late 18th century. The upper gatehouse rises independently behind the bowed frontal structure below; much may be late 16th century but the garret gables, dormers

and turret probably date from 1903-04 restoration. Within the *enceinte* there is nothing left of the east range which probably contained the hall at first floor level. On the north-west is the shell of a dwelling built, 1725, on the footings of the original kitchens. A modern timber stair gives access to the parapet walk on the west.

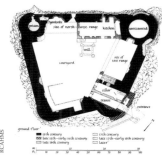

RCAHMS ground floor plan of Dunstaffnage Castle.

### 122 Dunstaffnage Chapel, c.1240

A long, beautifully built, rectangular chamber standing to the wallhead. Coupled windows on each side of the chancel were chamfered, rebated and had dog-tooth carving, though only those to the north retain their round-arched heads. The mouldings of the east window have been cut down to the sill. A timber screen once divided the chancel from the nave. The walled **Campbell Burial Aisle**, added to the east gable, 1740, is entered through a gated opening flanked by Ionic pilasters carrying entablature and small pediment. Inside are numerous commemorative **slabs** and **stones**.

Left *Campbell Burial Aisle;* Above *Dunstaffnage Chapel.*

Two kilometres south-west of Dunbeg the road passes **Pennyfuir Cemetery**, Oban's burial place. Among a wealth of funerary sculpture, the best of which is located around a central mound, are a tall Celtic **cross** to David Hutcheson, d.1880, pioneer of steamship services to the islands, a **monument** with a female figure and incised artist's palette and brushes, to the Oban painter Alexander Gray, d.1916, a granite **pyramid** to Arthur Gregorson, d.1873, and another granite **monument** with a gorge cornice, raised in memory of William Chambers, d.1929. A kilometre more and the road drops into Oban Bay (see below).

## BENDERLOCH AND APPIN

### BENDERLOCH

Connel Bridge takes the A828 over the Falls of
Lora and north into Benderloch. At Ledaig there
is an **Old School and Schoolhouse**, early 19<sup>th</sup>
century, two storeys, with a semi-hexagonal front,
a piended roof and tall chimney stacks. In
Benderloch itself, some pleasant sheltered
123 housing, unpretentiously rural in scale; **Ford
Spence Court** by Argyll & Bute District Council,
1990-91. The former **United Free Church**, 1911-
12, by Hippolyte Blanc, was converted to a
dwelling, Lake Falconer, 1938-39, preserving its
Decorated Gothic windows and low-towered
entrance porch. Monopitch classrooms of
**Lochnell Primary School**, 1991-92, have the
gridded glazing and stepping sills much
favoured by Strathclyde Regional Council
architects.

**St Modan Church**, 1904-05, G Woulfe Brenan
A small church which yet manages to assimilate
nave, apse, transept, porch and belfry spire in
Norman style.

*Lochnell House.*

124 **Lochnell House**, from late 17<sup>th</sup> century
Three conjoined houses facing Benderloch over
Ardmucknish Bay comprise the seat of the
Campbells of Lochnell. The rump of a late 17<sup>th</sup>
century house, now a service wing; a three-bay,
three-storey Georgian mansion of 1737-39,
perhaps by John Douglas; and a castellated L-
plan block of 1816-28 which united its two
predecessors, though not without unfortunate
encroachment on the existing classical façade.
The first is solid and plain, farmhouse-fast in
vernacular dignity. The second decidedly more
up-market: a five-bay front with pedimented
centrepiece carrying urns, perhaps the design of

*Lochnell House.*

John Baxter, or possibly John Douglas. Despite
its arrogant attack on the Georgian restraint and
balance of its neighbour, the towered and
turreted asymmetry of the third, by Archibald
Elliot, achieves a measure of castellar conviction,
when seen rising behind the walled forecourt on
the north-west. The U-plan **stable court** is early
19th century. **Walled garden** with rustic rubble
**folly**. **Lady Margaret's Tower**, dated 1754, is a
square rubble structure rising to a domed
caphouse and crenellated viewing gallery.

### ARDCHATTAN

To the east, some 6km. along the north shore of
Loch Etive, another church, the vestiges of its
predecessor, a shattered medieval chapel and the
125 complex ruins of a still older priory. **Ardchattan
Church**, 1836, scarcely beautiful but arresting,
faces the loch with a broad crowstepped gable
supporting a domed and pinnacled belfry.
Parochial Gothic with a genuinely Presbyterian
interior that preserves its double pulpit and long
communion table. Beyond the Priory are the
footings of the **Old Parish Church**, 1731-32, and
**Ardchattan Point**, the former manse, 1773-74.
On the hill above, gable, walls and graveslabs of
a late medieval **chapel** dedicated to St Modan or
St Baedan.

*Ardchattan Church.*

126 **Ardchattan Priory**, begun *c.*1230
A Valliscaulian foundation; church and
conventual buildings much altered and much
reduced. Degraded walling indicates a
cruciform church plan the chancel of which was
greatly extended, late 15th - early 16th century.
With secularisation the refectory range became
the Commendator's dwelling, the choir and
transepts were adapted for reformed services and
two burial aisles were built. In the 18th century a
parish church was erected (see above) and much
of the Priory abandoned as a quarry for masonry.
The house remained in occupation and, in the

Founded in 1230 by Duncan MacDougall, an ancestor of the Lords of Lorn, **Ardchattan Priory** followed the Benedictine observance practised by the Valliscaulians of Burgundy. There were only two other similar foundations in Scotland – at Pluscarden in Morayshire and Beauly in Inverness-shire. Life was austere for the Rule and entailed silence, wearing hair shirts, sleeping fully clothed, abstinence from meat, etc. Worship took place seven times in every day. The number of monks never rose above 30. King Robert the Bruce held a royal council at Ardchattan in 1308 after his victory over John of Lorn and the MacDougalls at the Pass of Brander. John Carsewell, a leading cleric of the Reformed Church who from 1565 adopted the contentious title of Bishop of the Isles, is believed to be buried near the west wall of the Priory. The last Prior, Alexander Campbell, was appointed in 1580. Twenty years later, on the death of the last monk, Campbell was granted the Priory lands and rights by James VI and became the first Laird of Ardchattan.

middle years of the 19th century, was much altered and extended across the footings of the former cloister and nave by Charles Wilson. This modestly Jacobean residence, known as **Ardchattan House**, contains a charming reminder of its ecclesiastical provenance: the small vaulted pulpit room opening through a pointed-arch arcade from what was once the east end of the Priory's refectory.

### BARCALDINE

127 **Barcaldine Castle**, 1601-09

An L-plan tower-house, country seat of Sir Duncan Campbell, 7th of Glenorchy. Abandoned in 1724 when the family built Barcaldine House (q.v.); restored 1897-1911 by Alexander Buttar. The walls are harled with small randomly spaced openings, each of the three crowstepped gables has a corbelled corner round with a slated cone roof, and, in the re-entrant, there is a cylindrical stair tower also conically capped. The result is a delight.

Top right *Ardchattan Priory;* Above *Barcaldine Castle.*

The **Ferry House** at South Shian is a simple inn of *c.*1840, with a rubble **slipway**, probably early 19th century. Further north, past Balure, a narrow, steel lattice-truss **bridge**, *c.*1900, crosses to the

128 island demesne of the **Isle of Eriska Hotel**. Built as a towered and castellated country house by Hippolyte Blanc, 1884, in a polychromatic Baronial idiom, it is suitably secretive in location and sentimental and allusive in style to satisfy the romantic imaginings of a rich elitist clientèle.

129 **Barcaldine House**, from *c.*1724

The original mansion begun in the 1720s and extended 1733 has gone but its three-storey successor, *c.*1759, remains as the west end of the rather messy grouping of alterations and extensions which have accumulated over the years. Proposals by James Gillespie Graham, 1813-14 and 1821, remained on paper, though his **court of offices**, 1815, was built. A Jacobethan

Left *Barcaldine House;* Below from top *Glenure; Appin Post Office; Kinlochlaich House.*

library appeared, 1831, a low bedroom wing to the west, 1838. Parapetted entrance block added at the beginning of the 20th century.

## APPIN

The road north to Appin must round the head of Loch Creran. It passes **Druimavuic**, a plain laird's house, *c.*1768, extended south (evidently) sometime in the 19th century. In the valley of the River Creran are two small churches, both in the simplest Gothic and both now in residential use: **St Mary's Church**, 1879, episcopal nave-and-chancel with a parsonage attached; and **Elleric Church**, 1887-88, by David Mackintosh, with a pyramid-capped open-cage bellcote. Cantilevered from the valley hillside on concrete beams, **Invercreran Country House Hotel**, built as a dwelling by Charles Cochrane, 1968-70 and converted 1984, presents itself boldly in a convex curve of bedrooms with terrace above. Further up the glen is another 18th century laird's house, **Glenure**, 1740-41, with a kitchen wing of 1751; *the best-preserved example of its class* in Lorn. Back on the Loch Creran road are **Inver Boathouse**, late 19th century (?), a castellated octagon topped with a glazed pyramid-roofed room in a domestic conversion by Paul Bradley, 1992-93, and **Cnoc Lodge**, an early 20th century (?) structure built in concrete, with a steep dormered roof and just the hint of *wannabe* distinction as a latter-day tower-house.

In Appin village the **Post Office** is a piended house with chimneyed gables. Beside it, a **cottage** (once a byre) and another single-storey **house**, both with corrugated iron roofs. All three are late 18th or early 19th century. The gabled **School and Schoolhouse**, *c.*1880, are equally simple. **Appin Parish Church**, 1889, is also a modest affair, undemonstratively Gothic.

130 **Kinlochlaich House**, from the 18th century Gothic, too, if grander and more Georgian than Victorian. Around 1820 the original house, the

**The Appin Murder** was the shooting of Colin Campbell of Glenure, factor for the forfeited Jacobite estates of the Camerons of Callart and Mamore and the Ardsheal Stewarts, in May 1752. Anxious to prevent any disturbances that the killing might provoke among Jacobite sympathisers, the authorities pursued intensive enquiries which led to the prosecution of James Stewart, half-brother of the exiled leader of the Ardsheal Stewarts. It seems likely that *James of the Glens*, as he was known, was indeed deeply involved in the conspiracy. He was tried at Inveraray and hanged. The name of the actual killer, however, has remained a mystery. One candidate was Alan Breck Stewart, an army deserter in the service of the French who later figured in Robert Louis Stevenson's *Kidnapped*, but Camerons, Maclarens and several of the Appin Stewarts have also been accused. There is a tradition that local families pass on the name of the murderer from generation to generation.

The Wordsworths spent the evening of Friday September 2nd, 1803, at Portnacroish at *an indifferent inn by the side of the loch.* The view, however, more than made up for the rudimentary accommodation. Dorothy wrote: *Ordered a fowl for dinner, had a fire lighted, and went a few steps from the door up the road, and turning aside into a field stood at the top of a low eminence, from which, looking down the loch to the sea through a long vista of hills and mountains, we beheld one of the most delightful prospects . . . A covering of clouds rested on the long range of the hills of Morven, mists floated very near to the water . . . and were slowly shifting about: yet the sky was clear, and the sea, from the reflection of the sky, of an ethereal or sapphire blue . . . green islands lay on the calm water, islands far greener, for so it seemed, than the grass of other places . . . The view was endless, and though not so wide, had something of the intricacy of the islands and water of Loch Lomond . . . Immediately below us, on an island a few yards from the shore, stood an old keep or fortress [Castle Stalker]; . . . We sate a long time upon the hill . . .*

standard three-bay model, was extended by the addition of a taller wing of public rooms, fronted by a buttressed entrance gable with a hooded round-arched window criss-crossed by intersecting astragals. Some windows are pointed, some lintelled; most have hood mouldings and Gothic glazing bars. Could this be the work of James Gillespie Graham? Close by is the roofless ruin of the **Old Parish Church**, 1749, enlarged from oblong to T-plan in the late 19th century; a segmental-arched door and a forestair survive.

## PORTNACROISH
Here, as at Appin, there are vernacular survivors. Gable-to-gable along the A828 are **Post Cottage**, **Forge Cottage**, the **Old Inn** and a low rubble **barn**, a white wall of late 18th and early 19th century date.

### Church of the Holy Cross, 1815
An Episcopalian church first arranged in the Presbyterian manner with the altar at the centre of the south wall and galleries west and east. In 1887 the layout was recast with the altar in the east. Later still worship reverted to its original orientation. Three pointed-arch windows in the south front, all with later cusped sashes. Above the central window is a small gable and cross finial.

131 **Appin House**, from early 18th century
The seat of the Stewarts of Appin on an ancient site. A classical house, possibly pedimented, was masked in 1831 by a new front with a balustraded parapet. The house was largely demolished in the 1960s but retained its south-east wing with projecting bay, balustraded eaves and angle turrets. This is now the principal apartment of a modern dwelling by the David Newman Partnership. Some high harled walls to the north-east recall (just) the grandeur of the original conception.

From top *Appin Old Parish Church; Church of the Holy Cross; Appin House, 1961.*

132**Castle Stalker**, from *c*.1540-42

A wonderfully picturesque oblong tower islanded at the mouth of Loch Laich. Erected by the Stewarts of Appin at the behest of James V. By the early 17th century it was in Campbell ownership and in 1631 was reconstructed at the upper levels and reroofed. In 1686 it was in Stewart hands again but was once more lost, this time in forfeiture for Jacobite allegiance. Roofless by 1840, it returned to the Stewarts in the 20th century and in 1965 a programme of restoration was set in train.

The castle is reached by boat. There is an entrance at ground floor level leading to vaulted cellars. But the principal approach to the tower is against the north-east wall by a powerfully sculptural forestair begun in the late 17th or early 18th century and completed during repairs undertaken in 1909. This entrance leads to the lower hall. The oblong tower rises to a third floor gabled garret with parapet walks, a cone-roofed angle round and a gabled cap-house. This skyline silhouette is full of geometric activity, all the more architecturally effective for the contrast with the crisp rubble walls (originally harled) dropping into reflected planes in the sea below. (see p.2 and 131)

## PORT APPIN

Overlooking the jetty from which the crossing to Lismore can be made is the **Old Ferry House**, early 19th century. Its two, bow-fronted cottages with boathouse between have now been converted to a restaurant. The **Pierhouse Hotel**, 1993-94, has a slated pyramid roof and barrel dormers. **Airds Hotel** is a dormered roadside inn, 19th century, now much enlarged.

*Old Ferry House.*

133 **Airds House**, 1738-39

Grandly Palladian - a pedimented three-storey centre with quadrant arms linking to lower wings which are also pedimented – but minimally enriched. The walls are harled with dressed margins. In the ashlar pediment, however, there is some armorial carving and on the skyline three

*Airds House.*

urns. Gibbsian doors at the quadrant centres, now converted to windows. The **Home Farm**, early 19th century, has hip-roofed ranges and a gabled centre. **Airds Lodge**, early 19th century, known as the *threepenny bit* because of its half-hexagon form.

**Drumneil House**, 1850
Three-gabled front with a central canted bay. U-plan **coachhouse**, 1830. **Walled garden**.

*Gardener's House, Arduaine Gardens.*

Philip Graham

## LOCH MELFORT

Continuing north from Loch Craignish (see above), the A816 crosses a short saddle at Arduaine Point to reach the south shore of Loch Melfort. Since 1962 **Arduaine Gardens** have been in the care of the National Trust for Scotland. *Open to the public.* Hidden in the trees and rhododendrons is the **Gardener's House**, 1992-93, by Page & Park; good modern vernacular.

The lure of good sailing and the beauty of the landscape have prompted the building of several good quality houses in the 1980s. Above the south shore is the pyramid-roofed octagon of **Kames Bay**. On Loch na Cille, **Maelstroma** and **Coille Daraich** are less assertive but crisp and white. Best of all a group of rubble and cedar holiday homes at **Melfort Pier** carefully integrated with the pier and moorings at Fearnach Bay. It is another older story on the less accessible north side of Loch Melfort. At the hamlet of **Ardanstur** a few early 19th century cottages survive by conversion. Further west is **Kilchoan House**, gabled Victorian, and **Degnish**, a lonely three-bay dwelling, dated 1786.

## 134 Melfort Village

In 1838 a gunpowder-works was established in the valley of the River Oude. Water, canalized in a lade, powered four mills; three grinding and one mixing. Various other structures associated with manufacture or storage were built. An explosion in 1867 halted production and in 1874 the estate was sold. More than a century later, 1983-89, a number of the original rubble buildings together with the early 19th century, U-plan court of offices, that once served the original Melfort House, have been transformed into a holiday village of flats, offices, a restaurant

*Melfort Village, gunpowder-works, 1972.*

RCAHMS

and, in the former powder store, a swimming pool. Within the walled garden a semi-circle of pitched roof cottages with stepping ridges has been built by the David Newman Partnership, 1987-98.

135 **Melfort House**, 1962-64, Leslie Grahame MacDougall (see p.131)
An anachronistic successor to an earlier house, this symmetrical, almost Cape Dutch mansion, seems somehow miscast in time and place. Balconied bow front to the south-west; hip-roofed to the north-east between flat roofed flanks. Nearby is the original **home farm**, early 19th century, a simple three-bay two-storey house with a piended bellcast roof.

The main road north cuts inland at the head of Loch na Cill. To the east is **Glenmore**, a symmetrical, hip-roofed house, mid 19th century, enlarged with dormers and flanking wings, 1935-36, by Dick Peddie, Todd & Jamieson. In Kilmelford, **Culfail Hotel** is a high two storeys with a consoled pedimented doorway. It, too, has been extended; to the north, by J Fraser Sim, c.1880.

*Culfail Hotel.*

### Kilmelford Parish Church, 1890
A small narrow kirk with a birdcage bellcote and an eight-spoke wheel window in the west gable front. It is possible that the oblong plan may be based on the footings of the late medieval church of St Maelrubha.

*Rarey House.*

### KILNINVER
Crossing the River Euchar a road branches south-west to the islands of Seil and Luing (see below). At Barnacarry Farm, a ruined **township**, c.1790. The main road to Oban turns left along the south shore of Loch Feochan. In the village are a few, probably early 19th century, **cottages**, trim, white, and splendidly fundamental in form. South of the village, on the west bank of the river, is **Rarey House**, 1743, a single-storey tacksman's dwelling, later extended to two storeys in an L-plan wing.

136 **Kilninver Parish Church**, 1891-92
A gable-ended oblong reconstructed on the foundations of the church of 1792. Round-arched windows with a triple light in the east gable.

*Kilninver Parish Church.*

From top *Glenfeochan House; Kilmore Old Parish Church; Kilmore House; Lerags House.*

## KILMORE

**137 Glenfeochan House**, 1875, John Starforth
A rather Tudor house with a south-east tower capped with a slated cone and an ogee-roofed turret to add Baronial credibility. Woodland **garden** and **arboretum**.

**138 Kilmore Old Parish Church**, 15th or 16th century
Roofless ruinous oblong stabilised in 1876. The original nave seems to have been lit by a window in the west gable, the chancel by windows on all three sides. Socket holes for galleries introduced after the Reformation can still be seen. The three pointed-arch windows on the south, gallery forestairs and porch/vestry were built 1838. Under a semicircular arch on the south side of the chancel, a late medieval **tomb-recess**. In the **burial enclosure**, four **tapered slabs**, Loch Awe school, 14th-15th century. Worship now takes place in **Kilmore and Oban Church**, a simple hall by J Fraser Sim, 1875-76, with lancets and a quatrefoil in the gable.

**Kilmore House**, 1828, John Thom
A wide-fronted, three-bay house built as the manse. Pedimented centre to the north-east; full-height, segmental bay at the centre of the south-west elevation.

About 3km. out of Kilmore, not much short of Oban, a dead-end road branches south-west back to Loch Feochan. **Kilbride Old Parish Church** is ruinous but stabilised like Kilmore in 1876. The masonry walls built to a simple oblong plan are largely those of the *meeting house* kirk of 1706, though these in turn seem to have been built on the site of the medieval church of St Bridget. Elliptical window arches introduced in a rebuilding of 1842-43. In the **graveyard** are several **tapered slabs**, 14th-15th century, most Loch Awe school but two Iona school including one similar to a slab laid in the floor of St Oran's Chapel, Iona. **MacDougall Burial Aisle**, 1786, with armorial panel over elliptical arch in the west gable. Outside the churchyard stands a tall, re-assembled, disc-headed **cross**, carved with the figure of Christ with outstretched arms, dated 1516 and inscribed with the name of the donor, Alexander Campbell of Lerags. Beyond the church is **Lerags House**, 1822-23, a plain three-bay house with a piended bellcast roof.

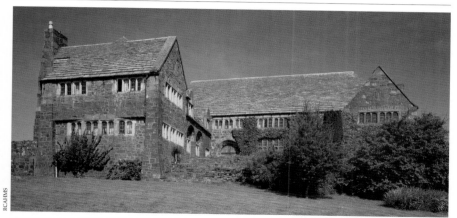

Top *Cour House*; Above *Carradale House entrance*; Middle *Cour House main stair*; Bottom *'View of Main Street on a Fair Day', Campbeltown*, by A MacKinnon, 1886.

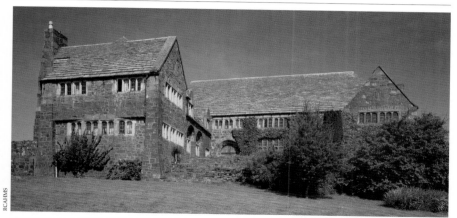RCAHMS

RCAHMS

RCAHMS

Argyll and Bute Council Museum Service

Top *Kilchurn Castle;* Middle
*Swallowholme, Machrihanish;* Above
*Furnace at Bonawe Ironworks;* Right
*Campbeltown Library and Museum.*

Top *Connel Bridge;* Middle *Painting of Castle Stalker by J Williams;* Left *Melfort House by Leslie Grahame MacDougall, 1962;* Above *Gylen Castle oriel window.*

M. Anne Dick

RCAHMS

Top *Torosay Castle, Statue Walk;*
Bottom *Duart Castle, Mull.*

# SEIL

## CLACHAN

139 **Ardmaddy Castle**, 1737

Palladian pretension masks a medieval origin for the *piano nobile* rises on the basal storey of a late 15th century tower-house. The plan has, however, been extended by the addition of two one-room wings on the north-east side of the original oblong. In the recess between is a pedimented Ionic portico, a little cramped but surprisingly delicate. An archway carries a linking passage to a north-west wing added 1790-91. Further mid Victorian additions in Jacobethan style have been largely demolished save for a pinnacled octagonal turret in the west. Late 19th century accommodation closes the group on the north. Roughcast **court of offices**, 1837-39, irregular and heavy-handed, by James Gillespie Graham. At the end of a long **walled garden** is a small but ruggedly Neoclassical rubble **bridge**, mid 18th century. No less enchanting, the Gothick screen-wall of a **boat house**, 1790, in the cliffs of Ardmaddy Bay 1km. south.

140 **Clachan Bridge**, 1791, John Stevenson

A masterpiece of masonry construction crossing the Atlantic (or, to be less hyperbolic, Clachan Sound) in a single segmental arch of 22m. Blind circular recesses and pyramid-topped markers along the parapets added perhaps at the suggestion of Robert Mylne. **Tigh-an-Truish Inn** marks the crossing on the island side. Begun in the 18th century, its low scale, serrated with five eaves dormers, seems still suited to its shoreside site. But beyond, there is something incongruously suburban about the ribbon development lining the west side of the Sound.

**Ardencaple House**, late 18th century

Well set two-storey laird's house compromised by later additions and alterations. Turnpike stair at the rear. To the east, vestigial footings of **Ardfad Castle**, a hall-house of the late 16th or early 17th century.

## BALVICAR

Developed as a slate-quarrying port on the east coast. Four rows of two-room **workers' cottages**, early 19th century, survive amidst post-industrial detritus. More recent **housing rows** by Kinghorn Mee, 1991-92, and Douglas Guest

*From top Ardmaddy Castle portico; Court of offices, Ardmaddy Castle; Clachan Bridge; Workers' cottages in Balvicar.*

Associates, 1993-94, exert some sympathetic discipline. Slate rubble **quay**, late 18$^{th}$ or early 19$^{th}$ century. Outside the village, **Acha** and **Achnacroish Cottage**, both probably early 19$^{th}$ century, have a rude rural beauty. A short low length of rubble walling with an arched tomb recess dated 1685 is all that remains of the medieval **Kilbrandon Old Parish Church**.

*Ellenabeich and Easdale Island.*

*Workers' cottages in Ellenabeich.*

### ELLENABEICH AND EASDALE

More slate quarrying. Here on the west coast was the centre of an industry that prospered from the early 18$^{th}$ century until, following a catastrophic flooding of the seams in 1881, production ebbed to nothing by the time of the First World War. Yet the past is everywhere present. Walls, paths, piers and roofs; man-made banks of quarry waste and a black landscape of screes and cliffs. The small harbours on each side of Easdale Sound, each with **jetties** of vertically laid slate, *c.*1826, have been repaired.

141 The early 19$^{th}$ century **workers' cottages**, laid out in Ellenabeich in neat parallel rows of white walls and black roofs, have found new life as holiday homes. There are no such streets on Easdale where the same houses sit on the grass gathered around an open square. Pyramid-roofed **Drill Hall** built in slate rubble. And a strange ancient-and-modern **house** of concrete and slate by Julian Wickham, 1987-92.

## CUAN

Ferry hamlet at the south end of Seil linked
across Cuan Sound to Luing. *En route* to the
ferry there are three churches. **Kilbrandon
United Free Church**, 1908-09, now derelict, is a
corrugated iron and timber hall with an
octagonal window in the rear gable. Worship
142 continues at **Kilbrandon and Kilchattan Parish
Church**, 1864-66, by Alexander McIntyre, a
simple Gothic hall distinguished by an octagonal
ogee-domed temple-belfry over the west gable.
Inside, the dark rubble masonry of stripped walls
heightens the effect of Douglas Strachan's stained
glass. The manse, **Kilbrandon House**, 1827, lies
a short distance east. In the village, opposite the
ferry jetty, is the **Old Parish Church**, 1735, a T-
plan kirk long since in secular use.

## LUING

### CULLIPOOL

Slate again. Quarrying was carried out along the
north-west coast of Luing and on the tiny, off-
shore island of Belnahua. There are the usual
short streets of early 19<sup>th</sup> century **workers'
cottages**. The episcopal **St Peter's Church**, 1894,
is now a dwelling.

The only church still functioning as a place of
worship is, appropriately, in the centre of the
island. **Kilchattan Church**, built near Achafolla
in 1936, is, however, no more than a harled hall
signposted by a small cross at the gable apex.
Down the road is **Luing Primary School**, 1877, a
short symmetrical front with gabled classrooms
each end. Nearby, a ruined L-plan **mill**; now
used as a cowshed, it still retains its original
outshot iron wheel.

### TOBERONOCHY

Yet more slate. More rows of **workers' cottages**,
early 19<sup>th</sup> century, this time in more casual
arrangement. Another slate **jetty** of vertically set
masonry. But agriculture, too, was, and remains,
important. There is a remarkably extensive
range of byres, barns, sheds, and dwellings at
**Kilchattan Farm**, laid out by Hugh Birrell of
Largo, 1853-55. To the west, **Ardlarach Farm**,
*built by / Patrick McDougall / 1787* as a three-bay
house but extended to an L-plan early in the 19<sup>th</sup>
century.

From top *Cottages in Cullipool;
Tombstone at Kilchattan Church;
Achafolla Mill; Workers' cottages in
Toberonochy; Ardlarach Farm.*

*Gravestone at Toberonochy Old Parish Church.*

143 **Toberonochy Old Parish Church,** perhaps 12th century

Roofless ruined walls reveal a narrow and probably long oblong plan. Here and there the outer faces of stones are cut with crosses, geometrical shapes and West Highland galleys. The **burial enclosure** houses many stones with attractive and interesting inscriptions and motifs. Two panels incorporated into the west wall recall the latter-day Covenanting zeal of one Alexander Campbell, died 1829.

Right *Oban Bay, c.1880;* Below *Aerial view of Oban, c.1930.*

## OBAN

Winding down the short slow descent into Oban the sense of arrival succumbs imperceptibly to the lure of departure. A hilly amphitheatre embraces the harbour; the town is a safe haven. But across the bay, beyond the sheltering shield of Kerrera, lie the open sea and the islands. Oban is the gateway to the Hebrides.

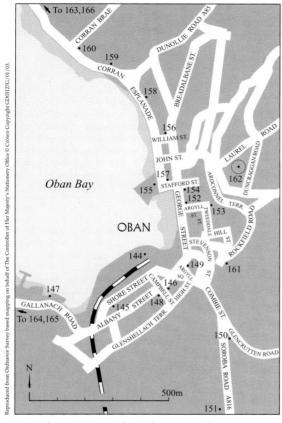

Until the middle of the 18th century there was little settlement; no more than a few fermtouns in the glens running down to the coast. A survey carried out for the Duke of Argyll in 1758 induced the transfer of the Customs House from Fort William to Oban (it was demolished in 1880 to make way for the railway) and this in turn occasioned some planned development in what became the Shore Street/High Street area of the town. Even so, landing from Mull in October 1773, Johnson and Boswell had nothing of interest to remark beyond the fact that they were able to find *a tolerable inn*. Their visit did,

*View over the bay to McCaig's Tower.*

RCAHMS

however, mark the beginning of tourism, an industry which would over the next two centuries progressively supplant the importance of fishing and farming in the local economy. In 1791 plans prepared by the surveyor George Langlands led to the layout of new streets north of the Customs House and pier across the Black Lynn Burn. Confined by Oban Bay on the west and steeply rising ground to the east, the plan was no more than a narrow grid elongated along the parallel lines of George Street, clearly intended, as in so many other Scottish towns of the time, to be the principal thoroughfare, and Tweeddale Street behind. This new town, hinged at Argyll Square to the older settlement on Shore Street, continued to expand northwards while a new line of growth opened up along Combie Street to the south. Significantly, by 1816, a new South Pier had been built to cope with the steamboat service which now linked the town to Glasgow.

**The first steamship to arrive at Oban** was probably the *Ann and Jean* which reached the town via the Crinan Canal in 1816. The *Comet* negotiated the Canal in 1819 but later sank off Craignish, though no lives were lost. In 1821 the second *Comet* was sailing between Glasgow and Fort William, but it, too, was to sink – this time, in 1825, 63 lives were lost near Gourock. By this time the enterprising Stevenson family of Oban were running steamers on the Glasgow route and north through the Caledonian Canal to Inverness. Competition intensified with several companies involved but by 1835 most paddle-steamers carried the livery of the Thomson & MacConnell Co. In 1840 an amalgamation with G & J Burns took place. Many notable personalities made the trip to Oban and the Isles, keen to experience the romantic scenery of the west coast; among them the composer Mendelssohn in 1829, the artist Turner in 1831 and the poet Wordsworth in 1833.

In 1832 Oban became a parliamentary burgh. Its population had reached almost 1,500. It had a distillery, a tannery, a mill, a school and, catering for the growing tourist trade, several inns. Steamer links to the islands multiplied and a North Pier was built at the end of Stafford Street. By mid century, tourists were pouring into town attracted both by Queen Victoria's declared admiration for the natural beauty of the bay and by the romantic spell of the islands that lay in the mists beyond. Hotels sprang up all along the esplanade while the town continued to expand with leafy, villa-lined streets clinging to the contours on Oban Hill and Pulpit Hill. The arrival of the railway in 1880 intensified development. In the late 1880s and 1890s, courthouse, police station and municipal buildings gave Albany Street some civic significance, all appropriately close to the old High Street if a little distanced from the new bustle of George

Street. By the end of the century, Oban was the principal town on Scotland's Atlantic coast, its status visibly crowned by the arcaded grandeur of McCaig's Tower, a vast granite ring set on the hill above the harbour. Dignified and impressive, this strange folly, so much a landmark of the western seaboard, is yet no more than a hollow shell, left unfinished in 1900. Townscape seems thus faintly tinged with irony, for there is, indeed, a slightly sad, unfulfilled air about Oban. Throughout the 20th century the tourists continued to come and the town continued to expand. Housing estates spread out at Glencruitten, Soroba and Corran Brae. But the fashionable promise of Victorian and Edwardian times remains unrealized. Here and there overcome by tawdriness, the town struggles to maintain, let alone augment, its considerable legacy of seaside building. Yet there are treasures still: two cathedrals, several splendid if ageing hotels, a magnificent esplanade tenement. And there is the setting! Hills, harbour and horizon; *en route* to land or sea, no finer traveller's town in all Scotland.

*Left The railway station in 1976;* Below from top *New railway station; Pierhead buildings; Lismore House.*

Life focuses on the **Railway Pier**, built to accommodate the terminal station of the Callander & Oban Railway which swept into town, 1879-80. Travellers and trippers stroll along the curving quay. Ferries, large and small, come and go. Fishing smacks pack three- or four-deep, waiting for better weather. The occasional train pulls in from the south. What is missing is an architecture to honour this activity. The **ferry offices** are utilitarian; the tiny **railway station**, built in ochre brick by British Rail, 1987-88, no more than a tidy box; the **pierhead buildings**, a patently commercial development of the early 1990s, blockwork cubes with slated pyramid roofs. Only the last measure up in scale, if not quite in quality. But there is no integration, no celebration, nothing to match the late Victorian station buildings which for 100

144

years or so housed the needs of the rail and sea traveller in a nine-bayed hall of ironwork frame-and-panel construction, arrival and departure gathered under one lattice-trussed roof. The building of **Lismore House** in the mid 1990s has helped; its four flatted storeys, liberally and nautically enhanced by railed balconies, give **Station Square** a proper sense of enclosure.

Across the railway tracks from the station is **Shore Street**, the oldest part of town. The 145 brightly painted **Claredon Hotel** is late 19th century with a vigorously Mannerist façade but **Cawdor Place**, an early 19th century row of terrace houses only recently shorn of a stout Greek Doric porch, preserves an earlier reserve. Albany Street is Victorian, more civic than residential. The **Municipal Buildings** by Alexander Shairp, 1897-98, are decidedly Italianate if excessively fussy in detail. Across the street, symbols carved in the tympana of the first floor windows betray the **Masonic Lodge**, 1889-90, by John C Hay.

146 **Sheriff Courthouse**, 1886-88, Ross & Mackintosh Italianate again, but calmer and grander with a *piano nobile* of five round-arched windows and a parapetted cornice.

Also on Albany Street is the **Post Office**, 1908-10, designed and crisply detailed by W T Oldrieve of H M Office of Works in an asymmetrical 17th century Scots style. Abstemious by comparison, **Cameron House**, 1960-62, continues the street in a flat red sandstone façade, respectable but bleak. Beyond the **Employment Exchange** and, on Drimvargie Road, the fortress-like **Telephone Exchange**, 1938, by John Wilson Paterson of H M Office of Works, residential buildings return.

Right *Sheriff Courthouse;*
From top *Claredon Hotel; Municipal Buildings; Detail of Masonic Lodge; Post Office; Detail of Post Office.*

There are two notable tenements: **Cawdor Terrace**, 1903-04, Baronial with corbelled corners, and the heavily quoined **Alma Crescent**, c.1880, which curves downhill to Gallanach Road and the town's oldest quay, the **South Pier**. Adapted for steamboats as early as the second decade of the 19<sup>th</sup> century, the pier is still in service. The 147 **Piermaster's House**, early 19<sup>th</sup> century, a white-painted piended cottage with slightly Gothick cone-roofed drums at the corners, survives as the local Lifeboat Station.

**High Street** fails to live up to its name. It is, however, strongly walled with **tenements**, mid and late 19<sup>th</sup> century. Harled and crowstepped, the former **Industrial School**, 1861, is now, appropriately enough, residential. Then, marching up the slope past Campbell Street, the 148 white walls of **Drimvargie Terrace**, 1993-96, by Andrew Merrylees Associates, flatted housing imaginatively varied in height and fenestration under piended roofs.

Shore Street and Albany Street converge on **Argyll Square**. In the gushet is the former **St Columba's Church**, 1888, by J Fraser Sim. Lancet-lit gable and tower (truncated 1977) face the traffic; behind the nave, **halls** added by Alexander Shairp, 1892. At **Nos.17-19**, a good classical range, 1883-84, by Ross & Mackintosh, and across the Square, domed on the corner, the 149 five-storeyed **Royal Hotel**, 1880, probably by the same architects. Mercat cross **fountain** by Alexander Shairp, 1904. From the bridge over the Black Lynn burn, **Combie Street** runs south: on the left, late 19<sup>th</sup> century three-storeyed **tenements**, plain but decent; on the right, commercial tawdriness.

150 **Oban Parish Church**, 1893-94, Alexander Shairp Six-bay Norman nave fronted by a slender ashlar steeple and broach spire which dominate the vista down Crombie Road. Squat obelisk finials on the gable buttresses and porches. In the tower stair is a dated stone tablet saved from the bell-turret of the church's predecessor, a Chapel of Ease erected in 1821.

Further south on **Soroba Road** there is less sense of urban enclosure. Neither the yellow brick Toytown offices of **Lorn Medical Centre**, c.1990, nor the brown brick housing of **Dunmar Court**, 1991-92, by Crerar & Partners, get things right:

From top *Cameron House; Telephone Exchange; Piermaster's House; Drimvargie Terrace; Former St Columba's Church.*

From top *Oban High School; Argyll Mansions; Social Work Offices.*

**Visitors to Oban** required only two things – a room for the night and a steamer timetable – according to Alexander Smith in his book, *A Summer in Skye*, published in 1865. *The tourist,* he wrote, *no more thinks of spending a week in Oban than he thinks of spending a week in a railway station.* Oban certainly deserved its popular description as the *Charing Cross of the Highlands,* a staging post for those *en route* to the Western Isles, but Smith's views were more than a little unfair to the town itself. Its hilly setting had a picturesque if not wild beauty, the prospects west were a delight, and the hotels well appointed. And the visitors kept coming. In 1851 the ex-queen of France sailed into the bay looking for accommodation: the old Caledonian Hotel put 27 rooms at her disposal while the Duchess of Orleans took 17 at the New Inn. Other notable visitors in the second half of the 19th century included Garibaldi, Bismarck, Disraeli, Gladstone, Livingstone and Stanley.

both sacrifice scale. A plain, white-roughcast tenement, **Nos.9-11**, mid 20th century(?), with no architectural pretension whatsoever, knows the 151 score better. **Social Work Offices**, 1988-90, by Strathclyde Regional Council, are streetwise too and unexpectedly exciting in a spatial interplay of cut-away form and exposed structure, though the L-plan **Lorn Resource Centre** behind is an altogether calmer affair. Across the street is **Oban High School**, reincarnated *c.*1995-2002 by Argyll and Bute Council: banded polychromatic brick wrapped around five storeys of gloomily refurbished 1950s curtain-walled classrooms. At the glazed gabled entrance, an open-framed *porte-cochère* and the belvedere from the original school building of 1890-1908, now mounted on a granite cairn.

**George Street** is Oban's High Street. Busy with shops and traffic, it is for much of its length open to the bay. By the early years of the 20th century, hotels crowded together along the southern stretch of the street, enjoying the sea view. Built to catch the railway and steamer trade, the Station Hotel, now the **Caledonian Hotel**, 1880-81, probably by Alexander Shairp, is energetic urban sculpture, a pile of bays, gables and busy roofscapes accumulated over the 30 years or so before the First World War. It pushes north in a wedge of flat-roofed **shops** carrying fine finialled ironwork; added by Shairp, 1884. Packed along the east side of the street are the former **Queen's Hotel**, 1891, a Queen Anne façade with seven gables and a narrow, off-pavement loggia, the pilastered **Palace Hotel**, 1905, by Gardner & Miller, and the mildly Baronial **King's Arms**, 1888, by Kinnear & Peddie. What follows is pusillanimous in scale and quality, ill deserving its harbour prospect. But across Argyll Street dignity returns.

152 **Argyll Mansions**, 1905-07, Leiper & McNab
A magnificent, urban-scaled, polychromatic tenement powerfully modelled with gables and bays to George Street, a canted battlemented corner and four tall chimney slabs ranged down Argyll Street. The detailing of masonry and joinery is impeccable. Ironwork balconies on consoles overlook the harbour from first and second floors. Framed by hefty, pink granite columns lugged below the cornice fascia and again at mezzanine level, the original shopfront bays survive barely modified. The plan – three

generous flats at the principal levels – appears contrived to facilitate conversion to a hotel. The building remains, however, in residential use; perhaps the most salubrious sea-view flats in Scotland.

**Argyll Street** has three-storey tenements, mid 19th century, on the north side. At **No.9** a roughcast, bow-fronted slot by Leiper & McNab, 1906. Raised on a balustraded terrace at the end of the street is the pilastered and pedimented façade of
153 the **Congregational Church**, 1880. In **Tweeddale Street**, more tenements, including the **Woodside Hotel**, *c.*1800, seven bays long with two arched pends. Back on George Street, beside Argyll Mansions, an unremarkable, two-storey, three-bay building, probably early 19th century, has been radically altered at shop level, but the plain upper storey retains the original low-scale, domestic character of George Street.

154 **Oban Distillery**, from *c.*1800
Dark, grey granite malt barns and warehousing with black-painted dressings and white pointing. Cast-iron structure with timber floors. Three-bay offices with a tripartite window in a central corbelled bay; by Alexander Shairp (?).

**Stafford Street** faces south across what was once George Square to the harbour. **Nos 15-19**, dated 1880, have good classical symmetry with tripartite windows left and right. Also symmetrical, **The Oban Hotel** is an early 19th century gable with a Doric door, pilastered and pedimented.

155 **Columba Hotel**, 1902
Red sandstone Glasgow Style with tall chimney stacks and domed corner bows, reminiscent of Argyll Mansions if not quite so assured. The earlier portion of the hotel, 1885, by J Fraser Sim, is in grey Cruachan granite; more severe in character but enlivened by black lace balcony ironwork. Conveniently close for custom is the **North Pier**, repeatedly improved and enlarged

From top *No. 9 Argyll Street; Congregational Church; Woodside Hotel; Oban Distillery;* Left *View of the North Pier and Columba Hotel.*

143

From top *Nos. 102-112 George Street; No. 120 George Street; Cathedral of St John the Divine.*

through the 19th century. Rebuilt in concrete in the 1920s when the metal-domed **Pier Buildings** were built in brick by Burgh Surveyor, David Galloway, 1927.

Beyond Stafford Street, **George Street** continues north, very much the commercial back-bone of the town. Two of the four shops at **Nos.97-101**, oddly named John Square, survive in their original 1865 form. Opposite are two three-bay units, **Nos.94-100**, *c.*1870(?), with bipartite windows in the upper storeys. At John Street, a corner turret, then corbelled canted bays carried on robust brackets; **Nos.102-112**, 1888. **No.120** is a busy gable façade, dated 1901; red sandstone Edwardian Baroque, or almost, with an *Art Nouveau* frieze. On the west side, a succession of strong tenements: **Nos.107-117**, 1897, with a dentilled cornice running over the shops, **Nos.119-121**, 1894, and, past the Episcopal Cathedral, the curving wall of **Albany Terrace**, also late 19th century.

156 **Cathedral of St John the Divine**, 1863-1968
Ungainly, even ugly, but somehow egregiously intriguing. The unresolved Gothic exterior has little to contribute to the townscape other than the enigma of its own intrinsic confusion. The puzzle has three parts. First, the original parish church in Decorated Gothic, 1863-64, built by David Thomson, continuing the commission begun by Charles Wilson; this is now the middle zone of the cathedral with gables in the west and east. Then came a five-bay Gothic aisle and lower hall added by Thomson & Turnbull in 1882 along the south side of the church. Entered from the porch at the corner of George Street and William Street, the 1882 aisle has become a narthex now separated from the church by a glazed screen installed in 1968 when the arcaded wall between aisle and church was removed. In 1908 James Chalmers won a limited competition for a new and larger building. Work began in Romanesque style but was halted in 1910 with only the sanctuary, choir and one transept bay completed on the north side of the existing church. In 1920 the church was inaugurated as a cathedral. Successive proposals to complete the building all came to nothing – in 1928, Harold O Tarbolton; in 1958, Ian Lindsay & Partners; in 1982, Simpson & Brown – and instead a series of structural engineering interventions linked the 19th and 20th century work into the present

strangely inspirational interior. Hidden steelwork permits the removal of the north wall of Thomson's original church, exposed raking steel shores support the thrust from Chalmers' incomplete crossing, while light washes over the pink sandstone of the sanctuary from the high glazed roof. Gothic **reredos** in gilded and stained oak, by James Chalmers, 1910. **Altar** with Iona marble retable, 1910.

From the North Pier, **Corran Esplanade** curves slowly with the shoreline round the bay. It is a parade of varying quality. The street wall starts in white: crowstepped gables, a single cone-topped bartizan and a plain three-storey
157 tenement tied together as the **Argyll Hotel**, early to mid 19th century. The **Regent Hotel**, too, is an amalgam: part Baronial, by Alexander Shairp, 1890, but mostly Thirties Moderne by James Taylor, 1936. Were it white it would be stunning, cream seems a too cautious compromise with its streamlined sea-front style. The **Oban Times Building** is ashlar, by J Fraser Sim, 1883, with corbelled canted bays rising to a pedimented parapet. White again, **Alexandra Place**, a plain but dignified mid 19th century tenement range. Then, suave enough for Brighton beach, the almost imperceptibly concave façade of The
158 **Great Western Hotel** by Charles Wilson, 1863-65. Impaired by later extension and reconstruction, its classical calm still commands the promenade.

**Victoria Crescent**, late 19th century, steps back from the sea in an incomplete arc. The main road swings north-east climbing uphill out of town. But the esplanade continues along the shore. **Corran Halls** by Crerar & Partners, 1963-
159 65, are aggressively horizontal. But **Christ's Church**, Dunollie (now Kilmore and Oban Parish Church), though no less boldly white, is gentler in form and spirit. Leslie Grahame MacDougall's design, scaled down from Ragnar Ostberg's Town Hall in Stockholm, has a copper roof and a square tower with a copper-capped columned octagon on top. It shines against the

From top *Oban Times Building; Corran Halls; Former Christ's Church, Dunollie (now Kilmore and Oban Parish Church);* Left *Regent Hotel.*

In 1871 the **Argyllshire Gathering**, a social assemblage of *gentlemen landowners, their brothers and sons*, met in Oban under the permanent presidency of the Marquess of Lorn. Two years later it was linked with the first **Oban Highland Games**. Twenty years later in 1892 An Comunn Gaidhealach (The Highland Association) held the first national **Mod** in Oban. Modelled on the Welsh Eisteddfod, this annual festival of song, dance, literature and drama has continued to involve those, young and old, in the Highlands and Islands and beyond who cherish Gaelic culture. Fittingly, in 1992, the Centenary Mod took place in Oban.

trees behind. But the most dramatic silhouette lies a little to the west past the busy roofscape of the **Alexandra Hotel**, begun in 1871 but much altered and extended since.

*St Columba Cathedral.*

160 **St Columba Cathedral**, 1930-53, Sir Giles Gilbert Scott

Built to replace the town's remarkably well appointed *tin cathedral*, a prefabricated structure clad in corrugated iron provided for Oban's Roman Catholic worshippers by the 3rd Marquess of Bute in 1886. The tall belfry tower striped with equal elongated lancets dominates the skyline on the north side of Oban Bay. Behind are the slated roof planes and pink granite walls of the nave-and-aisles cathedral church lit by lancets. The conception is simple and powerful, untrammelled by trivial detail. Within, the same austerity moulds the mood. From a stone-flagged floor, thick piers rise into the darkness of a simple trussed roof. In the tower, the lofty baptistery. In the chancel, against a gaunt wall of blue-grey granite, the canopied timber **reredos** in fretted and finialled Gothic, designed by Scott and carved by Donald Gilbert.

Past the cathedral, the Esplanade becomes a ribbon of late Victorian mansions, several converted to hotel use. There are good scrolled bargeboards at **Glencairn** and **Kilchrenan House**, 1883; convex gables at the **Queen's Hotel**; three-storey gabled bays at **Corriemar** and **Glenburnie**, 1897; a filigree iron balcony at **Seaforth**; and at **Barriemore**, 1895, more attractive bargeboards. Finally comes the town's **war memorial**, a bouldered cairn by James S Richardson, 1919-23, with a sculptured group of kilted soldiers carved by Alexander Carrick.

*Glencairn and Kilchrenan House.*

Upper Oban – and there is much that is uphill – is predominantly residential. Terraces, villas and mansions line the leafy contoured streets. Severe and barely Gothic, **Rockfield Primary School**, begun by Alexander MacQueen in 1876 but extended 1894 and 1902 by Alexander Shairp, sits on the lower slopes halfway up Hill Street. At 161 the head of Star Brae, the **Free High Church**, designed by the Edinburgh architect David Cousin in 1846 is, not surprisingly, rather more positively Gothic. On a higher escarpment still, are the ruinous vestiges of Oban's **Hydropathic**, a hotel that never was. Begun in 1881 on a magnificent site with views across the Bay below, the project ran out of money, the building was soon quarried and in 1908 demolition removed all but a few last traces.

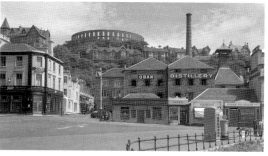

From top *Queen's Hotel; Oban War Memorial*. Left *McCaig's Tower, c.1960.*

162 **McCaig's Tower**, 1895-1900

No building is more memorably associated with Oban and the Western Isles. A hilltop Colosseum, its two tiers of superimposed pointed arches cut through a grey granite ring, it sits like a lithic coronet crowning the top of the town. In fact its intention is not civic but personal. Planned as a family Walhalla by local banker, art critic and philosopher John Stuart McCaig, it, too, ran out of money; a high central tower was never built. Today the arcaded ring encloses a pleasant quiet garden with magnificent views over the bay. Folly or not, seen from the bay, it ranks among the great icons of Scottish architecture.

Downhill to the north the town's leisure centre stretches along Dalriach Road: bowling greens, tennis courts and **Oban Pool**, a long uninspiring shed reinvigorated with a bold bow-trussed roof added by Crerar & Partners, 1997-98.

163 **Dunollie Castle**, from 15th century

To the north, perched above the road to Ganavan sands, another hilltop monument; more ruinous,

**McCaig's Tower** was constructed on Oban's Battery Hill between 1895 and 1900: a *stone lime wall* of Bonawe granite 190 feet in diameter. Beyond an expressed wish to provide employment for local stone masons out of work in the winter months, the precise intentions of the promoter, John Stuart McCaig of Muckairn and Soroba, have never been wholly clear, although he is known to have envisaged a high central tower with museum, art gallery and small chapel. His will instructed that a series of bronze statues of members of the McCaig family should be added to the building but this wish remained unfulfilled. McCaig (1823-1902) had been born in Lismore but came to Oban in the 1830s. He first joined his brother Duncan in a local draper's business but soon the brothers' commercial interests were diversifying and prospering. They established a tobacco manufactory, built gasworks, became bank agents, bought up property. The memorial tablet set in the wall of McCaig's Tower describes John as *Art Critic and Philosophical Essayist and Banker.*

From top *Dunollie Castle; Dunollie House; The Manor House; Gallanach; Gallanach, stair.*

and all but engulfed by the hungry advance of virulent vegetation. A Gaidhealtachd castle, the seat of the MacDougalls of Lorn, it commanded the narrow channel between the mainland and Kerrera; a site so strategically significant its fortification must have an ancient origin. There is little moulded detail to the roofless square tower, now barely discernible through the green, but two mural stairs survive in its four-storey walls. The courtyard wall, penetrated by a restored gateway, is later, probably 16th century. Nearby is the castle's successor, **Dunollie House**, part of which, the east range, may date from the 17th century. North range, 1746-47; wings west and south, *c.*1834-35. Restored by Leslie Grahame MacDougall; all plain and without architectural pretension.

On the fringes of the town are several houses of modest distinction. To the south on Gallanach 164 Road, **The Manor House** may have begun life in the late 18th century as the estate house of the Duke of Argyll: a two-storey block of coursed whin with flanking piended wings. Cast iron lamp standards at the entrance door. Almost 2km. south along the coast road is **Kilbowie House**, 1888; built as a Baronial residence, its red sandstone is animated with crowstep gables, battlements, bartizans, cable moulding, mock cannon and a bastion-buttressed terrace overlooking the Sound of Kerrera. Richly panelled interiors survive but the house's large conservatory is in disrepair. Adapted to administrative use and compromised by a flat-roofed system-built Residential Education Centre in offensive proximity.

165 **Gallanach**, 1814-17, William Burn
A castellated Gothic mansion some 5km. south of Oban. Symmetrical with a sunk basement and a turreted frontispiece and round angle-towers. Three-storey addition by Sir J J Burnet, *c.*1903, ups the scale at the rear but retains the medieval cast.

East of town is **Glencruitten House**, 1897, a modestly Baronial roughcast residence raised to distinction by the addition of an east wing by Lorimer & Matthew, 1927-28. This crowstepped wing, which contains a library at first floor, has tall pedimented eaves dormers and a splendid canted bay in the east gable. To the north, close 166 to the shore, **Ganavan House**, 1888, by William

Leiper; half-timbered, tile-hung, Arts and Crafts hidden in a secret garden.

## KERRERA AND LISMORE

### KERRERA
167 **Gylen Castle**, 1582

*Ganavan House.*

A wonderfully romantic stand of masonry looking south to the Garvellachs. Built by the MacDougalls, it was burnt out and abandoned in 1647 following a siege by Covenanting troops. The surviving shell, built to an L-plan arrangement which is remarkably small (effectively two squares, 6m. square and 4m. square respectively) yet dramatic in its impact. Perched on a rocky promontory and approached along a narrow ridge from the north-east, it stands erect and commanding. The walls are more or less intact for a full four storeys; only at

Clearly seen from Oban, a tall obelisk monument, erected 1883, stands above Ardantrive Bay on Kerrera island. It honours David Hutcheson, died 1880, who with his brother Alexander and David MacBrayne formed the company largely responsible for the development of **steamer services in the Western Isles**. Responding to the growing Victorian tourist trade and conscious of the profits to be made from passenger and goods transport up and down the west coast, their fleet became the indispensable economic life-line of Hebridean travel and trade. In 1878 the Hutchesons retired and David MacBrayne became the sole owner. He increased the fleet, passing on the company to his two sons. The company continues today in the Caledonian MacBrayne firm which exercises a near monopoly of all ferry services in the Inner and Outer Hebrides and in the Clyde estuary.

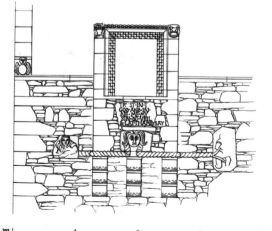

Left from top *Gylen Castle; RCAHMS drawing of oriel window at Gylen Castle.*

Legend maintains that the Irish missionaries **Columba and Moluag**, arriving in Loch Linnhe in 562, vied with each other to be the first to land on the island of *lios mor* (meaning *great garden* or *enclosure*) for both recognized the island as a potential base from which to launch their evangelising project. Seeing Columba's coracle approach the coast ahead of him, Moluag cut off a finger and threw it to the land in order that he should be the first ashore: *My flesh and blood have first possession of the island, and I bless it in the name of the Lord.* Moluag seems to have established some form of religious community, though knowledge of his life and work is decidedly hazy. What is believed to have been his pastoral staff, the *bachuil mor*, survives and can be seen by appointment at Bachuil House on the island.

In 1803 the Roman Catholic church founded **a Highland College on Lismore**. Two years earlier Bishop John Chisholm had been instrumental in purchasing the farm at Kilcheran with this in mind; *Lismore . . . agrees with us very well . . . we never had more or so much liberty to applying to learning and spiritual matters in any other place.* The farm supplied the college with milk and meal but Chisholm counted on the local production of lime to finance the venture. In this he and his successor bishops were disappointed; local industry failed to prosper while the educational standards of the College, denied good teachers and books, remained poor. Sir Walter Scott, sailing past Lismore in 1814, noted that *a Catholic bishop, Chisholm, has established a seminary of young men intended for priests, and . . . a valuable lime work. Reports speak well of the lime but indifferently of the students.* By 1828, the students, of whom there had never been more than 11 boys, had been moved to the Lowlands prior to their going to the newly founded Blairs College in Aberdeenshire.

Right *Kilcheran House;*
Below *An Sailean lime-kilns.*

the gabled skyline has the masonry crumbled. Yet even here, contrasting with the gaunt stone below, there are those *crustaceous projections on top* which Nikolaus Pevsner contended are so essentially Scots – crowstepping, corbelling, bulbous rounds, and a unique oriel window in a billet moulding frame and carved below the sill with a cautionary inscription, female head and cable. Consolidation by Martin Hadlington, from 1993. (see p.131)

## LISMORE

Lying long and narrow in Loch Linnhe, Lismore is reached by ferry from Oban or Port Appin. Settlement on the island is scattered with a few dwellings clustered at Achnacroish pier and inland at Clachan. At **Bachuil House**, Clachan, a characteristically plain 18th century dwelling used as the island's Baptist Chapel from 1860 until 1890, what is held to be the crozier of the 6th century St Moluag is kept. There are early 19th century **lime-kilns** and **workers' cottages** built to establish local industry at Port Kilcheran, An Sailean and Port Ramsay. The last are the best preserved; a shoreside row of two-roomed dwellings now adapted as holiday homes. The kilns at Kilcheran were founded in 1803 by Bishop John Chisholm of the Roman Catholic seminary which had been set up at **Kilcheran House** a year earlier. The original house, late 18th century, was extended *c*.1815; duplicated to the north with a gabled chapel between.

**Achadun Castle**, from 13th century
Seat of the Bishops of Argyll, the castle remained in their hands until the early 16th century when the episcopal seat was transferred to Saddell (q.v.). Thereafter it fell into ruin. The remains of the curtain wall enclosing a square courtyard form an irregular skyline on a ridge above Achadun Bay, with some affinity to Castle Sween.

168 **Castle Coeffin**, perhaps 13th century
A MacDougall fortress now so degraded that

RCAHMS

Above *Achadun Castle;*
Left *Castle Coeffin.*

RCAHMS

interpretation of the plan is difficult. The earliest
structure seems to be an oblong feasting-house
but this was certainly altered in late medieval
times when the inner court was created to the
north-east.

**Tirefour Castle**, near Clachan, is a **broch** dating
from the end of the first millennium BC. The
walls, enclosing an inner space 12.2m in
diameter, stand to just over 3m. At Loch Fiart
there is a second **broch**, slightly larger in internal
diameter but much less well preserved.

169 **Cathedral of St Moluag and Parish Church,**
from 13th century
Chosen as the centre of the medieval episcopal
see, Lismore merited a cathedral church. But the
remote setting and a continued lack of funds
produced no towering monument. The narrow
plan, no more than an elongated oblong of nave
and choir, extended only 40m., its width *c.*7.5m.
At the Reformation, the choir served as the local
parish church while the nave collapsed into ruin.
In 1749 a radical reconstruction introduced

round-arched windows to the south, inserted galleries and orientated worship to the pulpit located on the long south wall. Further changes occurred in 1900 when the pulpit moved to the west wall. Round-arched windows were formed in the north wall, a single east gallery was retained and a new roof constructed. A few memories of the medieval church have survived these vicissitudes; vestiges of north and south doorways, the pulpitum arch in the west gable, the triple-arched sedilia and the pointed-arch piscina. In the graveyard are several burial **slabs**, 14th-16th century, and a splendidly carved **tomb-chest lid**, early 16th century. A number of white marble funerary **tablets**, 18th century, have been built into the east wall of the church.

**Eilean Musdile Lighthouse**, 1833, Robert Stevenson
A white tower, some 31m. from high-water to parapet walk. Flat-roofed **keepers' houses** are symmetrically planned around its base. A rubble **bridge** links the island to Lismore in a single segmental-arch span.

### MULL
The largest of the Inner Hebridean islands. The landscape is wonderfully varied: mountainous around Ben More, which reaches 966m.; soft and sylvan across the narrow neck of land between Salen and Gruline; wild and exposed along the rock-riven Atlantic coast. Separated from the mainland by the narrow Sound of Mull which affords a sheltered route to the outer isles, Mull is linked to Oban by car ferry. Craignure has superseded Tobermory as the most convenient landfall, though it is little more than a roll-on roll-off pier.

## CRAIGNURE

A hamlet grown to staging-post status at the car ferry pier. There are two small hotels: **Bayview Hotel**, 1831, a two-storey-and-basement manse converted to tourist service and **Craignure Inn**, always an inn, its low symmetrical core and even lower flanking wings clearly 18th century.

### Craignure (Torosay) Church, 1783

A white kirk with a varied selection of windows set in segmental-arch openings, evidently the result of repeated alterations carried out through the 19th century. Forestairs, mirrored at each end of the south elevation, give access through first-floor porches to a galleried interior.

*Craignure (Torosay) Church.*

*Left* Torosay Castle; *Above* Staircase and summer house, Torosay Castle.

170 **Torosay Castle**, 1856-58, David Bryce (see p.132)
Known first as Achnacroish House, this is vintage Bryce: a crowstepped gable bulging with two cone-topped double-height angle oriels; another rising on corbelling over a canted bay. The house looks south, dining room, library and drawing room raised to *piano nobile* elevation over a **terraced garden**. Three levels, with balustraded walls, staircases and summer houses almost certainly the work of Robert S Lorimer, 1897-1906, fall towards the sea adding greatly to Bryce's Baronial conceit. Lined along the **Statue Walk** are 19 Venetian figures sculpted in the manner of Antonio Bonazzo (1698-1765). There is an 18th century **walled garden** and a **Japanese garden** laid out in the 1980s.

171 **Duart Castle**, from the 13th century
Majestically sited on the rocky elbow of Mull, Duart surveys the seaways entering the Sound of Mull and Loch Linnhe from the Firth of Lorn,

*Duart Castle; Below Duart Point Lighthouse.*

**Duart Point Lighthouse** stands above the rocky east shore of Mull a kilometre south of Duart Castle. Completed in 1900 it was raised in memory of the novelist William Black whose admirers put up the money with the proviso that the architect should be William Leiper. The Commissioners of Northern Lighthouses agreed and the light took shape as a low baronial tower, circular in plan with castellated parapet and a small, conically capped, turnpike stair rising alongside. Were it not located on a cliff-top site to fulfil its maritime purpose, it might well have doubled as a gatehouse to the castle nearby.

testimony still to the military might of Gaidhealtachd culture. Built by the MacDougalls of Lorn, it passed to the MacDonald Lords of the Isles before becoming a MacLean stronghold at the end of the 14th century. Campbells held it from 1674, but in 1911 it returned to MacLean ownership. An extensive programme of restoration then began under John J Burnet. (see p.132)

A massive curtain wall, raised on an almost square plan in the 13th century but now the result of successive rebuildings, surrounds inner complexity. Entrance is gained at the south-west where a gate-house once stood. Across the courtyard is the late 14th century tower-house, largely remodelled by Burnet. From the hall at first-floor level, Burnet's Sea Room, a glazed link with superb views across the Sound, connects with the north-east range. This retains some 16th century walling but is again much restored: most of the windows and eaves dormers are early 20th century as is the courtyard wall, rebuilt as reconstructed by Sir Allan MacLean in 1673. There is also a south-east range, mid 16th century, which originally contained an upper hall carried on four vaulted cellars; this, too, was much altered by 20th century reconstruction.

### LOCHDONHEAD
An arc of cottages drawn around the head of the loch, a T-plan **school**, begun *c.*1845, and **Torosay Free Church**, a gabled hall of 1852. Across **Auchnacraig Bridge**, 1790, the old droving road skirts the west side of the loch to reach **Grass**

**Point Ferryhouse**, a late 18th century inn, restored 1946-48. From here cattle and drovers crossed to Kerrera and Oban.

Further west on the Iona route, at Strathcoil, another minor road branches south across the River Lussa heading for Loch Spelve, Loch Uisg and Loch Buie.

172 **Kinlochspelve Church**, 1828, William Thomson A T-plan Telford kirk standing in bleak isolation at Barachandroman. Tudor-arched windows with lattice glazing. The two-storey **manse**, also by Thomson, looks west down Loch Uisg.

### LOCHBUIE
An end-of-the-road estate on the wooded isthmus between Loch Uisg and Loch Buie. Some cottages, a mansion-house and a ruined castle.

173 **Lochbuie House**, 1793
A pedimented three-storey-and-attic house; classical orthodoxy stressed by flanking wings: a sound arrangement but *not very spacious or splendid*. Assimilated in the outbuildings is **Old Lochbuie House**, 1752. Not far away, a gabled **mausoleum**, 1777, bearing the arms of the MacLeans of Lochbuie, commemorates John, the 17th laird and builder of Old Lochbuie.

From top *Lochbuie House; Auchnacraig Bridge; Kinlochspelve Church; Armorial panel at Lochbuie House mausoleum.*

*Moy Castle.*

174 **Moy Castle**, early 15<sup>th</sup> century

Built by the MacLeans who had acquired the
Lochbuie estate from the Lords of the Isles in the
late 14<sup>th</sup> century. Constructed with beach
boulders and now much engulfed by vegetation,
this roofless tower-house seems to have grown
naturally out of the rock. The plan is square, the
section three storeys and a garret high. The
upper storeys, which are later, 16<sup>th</sup> or early 17<sup>th</sup>
century; rise to a parapet that finishes flush with
the walls below with no corbelling except under
windowed rounds at the north and east corners.
Vestiges of caphouses at the south and west
corners. The main hall, once roofed by timber
beams resting on corbelstones, is at second-floor
level. Below, chambers at ground- and first-floor
are barrel-vaulted in different directions. Over a
kilometre south-east is **St Kenneth Chapel**,
consecrated in 1500 but largely rebuilt as a
MacLean mausoleum in 1864 when the interior
was subdivided by a Gothic Revival screen.

From Strathcoil the Iona road runs on up the
valley of the River Lussa into Glen More.
Mountains press in. The landscape becomes
intimidating. It is as if the fearful sublimity of
nature casts a confessional claim on the traveller
before releasing him, chastened and shriven, onto
the shore of Loch Scridain and the last lap of the
pilgrimage down the long Ross of Mull

peninsula. Past the archetypal rural symmetry of **Rossal Farm**, early 19th century, the way becomes more open, winding west along the loch shore.

At Pennyghael there is a **cross**, dated 1582, which commemorates the Beaton family, famed locally as healers since medieval times when they served as physicians to the Lords of the Isles. **Pennyghael Lodge** dates from the 18th century but has been enlarged to dull pretension in the 1920s. No more remarkable is **Pennycross School**, 1872, an unexceptional work of an exceptional architect, Robert Rowand Anderson.

*Pennyghael Lodge.*

### CARSAIG

Reached by a narrow road climbing up from Pennyghael through Glen Leidle and down to the south coast. There are only a few estate houses in the wooded slopes above the bay. **Carsaig House**, built as Pennycross House, *c.*1800, follows the familiar three-bay gabled pattern enlarged by piended wings flanking a rear courtyard and linked to a crowstepped **Home Farm**. **Inniemore Lodge**, by David Thomson, 1877, is decidedly Victorian, gable-fronted with a battlemented tower. By the shore is a broad **pier** built by engineer Joseph Mitchell for the British Fisheries Commission in 1850, its splendid masonry subsiding into the sea. Nearby are two rubble **stores**, one gabled, one piended.

### BUNESSAN

Originally a fishing settlement planted by the 5th Duke of Argyll at the end of the 18th century, the village survives, tired and far from smart, a melancholy contrast to its picturesque setting on Loch na Lathaich. There is a **Parish Church**, 1804, no more than a buttressed hall; a **School**, 1869, and a **Baptist Church**, 1891, both in gabled Gothic; a ruined **mill**, early 19th century (?); and a

*Bunessan Parish Church.*

From top *Cottage in Salen; Craig Hotel; Salen Parish Church; Knock Bridge; Killiechronan House.*

number of rubble **cottages**, early 19th century, scattered along a side road at Ardtun. **Assapol House**, a kilometre south-east, is the former manse. About 3km. further on the same track are the 13th century walls of **Kilvickeon Old Parish Church**. But there is little else to delay the pilgrim *en route* to Iona.

Finally at Fionnphort the ferry is reached. It is a pleasant little place looking across the narrow Sound to Iona. A little apart, **The Columba Centre**, a turf-roofed interpretative centre with long white walls and a glazed café drum by John Renshaw, 1996-97, prepares the traveller for the sacred island (see below).

From Craignure the road north to Mull's only town, Tobermory, follows the shore. Close to Fishnish Point a ferry crosses the Sound to Lochaline in Morvern. Some 5km. further, shortly before the road crosses the River Forsa, is **Pennygown Chapel**, 13th century. Now no more than rubble walls with a few narrow, round-arched windows, it sits in a **burial ground** that contains some 17th and 18th century **slabs** and **table-tombs** and a MacLean memorial tablet, 1763, set in a finialled gable **monument**.

### SALEN
A village situated halfway from Craignure to Tobermory where a road branches west to Loch na Keal. There is a pleasant cluster of early 19th century cottages and, closer to the junction, the taller **Craig Hotel** and **The Coffee Pot**, both houses of the same period, the latter with a good corniced doorway. The former **Free Church**, 1883, by John C Hay, is sadly traduced by conversion. Still sadder, **Salen Pier**, 1904, consigned to dead-end dereliction *c*.500m. north of the crossroads.

**Salen Parish Church**, 1899, William Mackenzie Low nave, transepts and overlapping north porch in rough-faced granite with sandstone dressings. Plate tracery in the windows.

### GRULINE
Estate buildings about 5km. south-west of Salen in wooded grounds beside the winding course of the River Ba. Across the segmental arch of **Knock Bridge**, 18th century, close to the river's exit from Loch Ba, is **Knock House**, 18th century, a white piend-roofed mansion gently inflated by

Philip Graham

Left top *Knock House;*
Left bottom *Gruline House;* Below
*Macquarie Mausoleum.*

RCAHMS

RCAHMS

full-height semicircular bays on each side of a
piended porch. Just 2 km. north, where the river
begins its debouch into Loch na Keal, is
**Killiechronan House**, begun *c.*1840 but later
enlarged, bright and busy with bargeboarded
eaves dormers and canted bays.

176 **Gruline House**, 1861-65, Peddie & Kinnear
A Baronial mansion with a round angle tower,
built as Glenforsa House. A corridor connects
with **Old Gruline House**, erected in the late 18th
century and from 1804 the very plain three-bay
gabled home of Lachlan Macquarie, the so-called
Father of Australia. The **Macquarie
Mausoleum**, *c.*1825, sits in a rubble-walled
circular lawn in the estate, a rather dour tomb in
the form of a gabled Gothic block. Original
panelling from the house is now in the care of
Macquarie University, New South Wales.

**St Columba's Episcopal Church**, 1874, Alexander
Ross
Five-bay lancet Gothic with a gabled west porch.
The interior is of varnished pine with a tiled floor
to the raised sanctuary.

**AROS**
177 **Aros Castle**, 13th century
One of several fortresses built to command the

Mull did not escape **the religious conflicts of the 17th century**. In 1674 the Duke of Argyll invaded the island with a force of some 2,000 men. Intent on punishing the MacLeans of Duart for failing to support what he regarded as a common Protestant cause, Argyll occupied the MacLean castles of Aros and Duart. Campbell fury engulfed the island and many were killed and maimed in the confrontation of Protestant and Catholic clans. The Gaelic library held by the Beatons of Pennycross was destroyed. Thomas Kirke, an English traveller in Scotland in 1679, wrote with disgust of these terrible events.

*What strange butcheries have been committed in their feuds, some of which are in agitation at this day, viz., Argill with the Macclenes, and the Macdonnels about Mula Island, which has cost already much blood, and is likely will cost much more before it will be decided; their spirits are mean, that they rarely rob, but take away life first; lying in ambuscade, they send a brace of bullets on embassy through the travellers body; and to make sure work, they sheath their durks in his lifeless trunk, perhaps to take off their fine edges, as new knives are stuck in a bag pudding.*

Top *Aros Castle;* Below *Tobermory, Mull.*

passage through the Sound of Mull, Aros covered the central stretch of the channel in strategic partnership with Ardtornish Castle across the water in Morvern. Its location close to the Salen – Gruline isthmus gave it an additional significance in guarding the route west across Mull. The craggy promontory site, 15m. above the sea, is impressive but the few stands of thick rubble walling that survive give little clue to the castle's original appearance. There are some lintelled slit windows and a single pointed-arch opening with traces of Y-tracery. Built by the MacDougalls, it soon became a MacDonald stronghold and was later in MacLean and Campbell hands.

### TOBERMORY

A sheltered bay at the north end of the Sound of Mull, protected on the east by Calve Island and

Tobermory takes its name from the Gaelic *tobar-mhoire* meaning Mary's Well. It seems likely that the well was dedicated to the Virgin. In 1703, the traveller, Martin Martin, reported that the well had medicinal properties which probably encouraged pilgrims to visit it. Sir Walter Scott could only locate it somewhere in the middle of marshy ground and still today the site of the well cannot be accurately determined. Near the local cemetery a monument, erected in 1902 on the occasion of the coronation of Edward VII, records its existence but cannot be said to mark the precise spot. As for the ancient Chapel of St Mary, which even in the middle of the 16th century was described as a foundation of *long ago*, some scant footings near the cemetery gate may be the only surviving physical evidence.

*Left top Main Street, Tobermory; Left bottom Main Street including the Mishnish Hotel.*

lying in the lee of Mull itself, Tobermory was established as a fishing station in 1787. The shoreline was stabilised with a long **breastwork** of massive stone blocks, 1788-91, retaining reclaimed land to form Main Street. A 178 **Storehouse**, **Officers' Lodging** and **Custom House** were constructed in a U-plan facing the quay. The much abused piend-roofed building which today serves as the **Post Office** is unrecognizable as Robert Mylne's Custom House, 1789-90. Mylne's **New Inn**, built to the north-east of this central group, is invisible too (only a porthole window in the gable of the Co-op Building betrays its existence) but, running south-west towards Ledaig, a harbourside row of late 18th century, two-storey **houses**, all slated, survives. Above the scarp that ringed this coastal strip, an upper town developed on a simple grid-iron plan prepared by the British Fisheries Society agent, James Maxwell, in 1790.

The optimistic expectations of the Society failed to materialize but the kelp trade boomed and, with the opening of the Crinan Canal in 1801 and the Caledonian Canal in 1822, economic prospects were further improved. A new masonry jetty, **Fisherman's Pier**, *c.*90m. long, was constructed for the Commissioners for Highland Roads and Bridges under the direction of Thomas Telford in 1814, and a few years later **Ledaig Pier** was built privately to serve the Distillery, (see p.181) founded in 1822. Steamers arrived from

*Above from top Post Office; Nos. 24-26 Main Street.*

From top *Clydesdale Bank; Ferry Terminal Building; Former Free Church.*

Oban a few years later and soon the tourists, Mendelssohn and Queen Victoria among them, were adding to the town's prosperity. By *c.*1850, **Main Street** stretched round the northern edge of the bay in a series of gable-fronted, flatted houses - **Black's Land**, **Brown's Land**, **Portmore Buildings**, **Royal Buildings** and the **Mishnish Hotel** - varying in height between four and two storeys but more or less consistently peppered with eaves dormers. Even the **Clydesdale Bank**, by John C Hay, *c.*1880, which interrupts this parade, appropriately enough at a bend in the harbour front, does so intensifying eaves activity with an effusion of Baronial bartizans and dormers. Today many of these quayside properties are brightly painted with a calendar-conscious jauntiness that attracts the visitor and offends the purist. At the end of Main Street on the north side of the bay is the **Mishnish Pier**, 1864, and the former **Ferry Terminal Building** of 1936, flat-roofed with a concrete cantilevered balcony, unexpectedly *Moderne* and unequivocally white. At the opposite end of Main Street, is the former **Baptist Chapel**, 1862, a plain four-bay hall with some Gothic glazing bars in pointed-arch windows, now used as a Masonic Lodge. Beside Ledaig Pier are the buildings of the **Distillery**, 1822, reconstructed and extended, 1970-72, and a four-storey, rubble **warehouse**, late 18th century, converted to housing by Kinghorn Mee, 1992-93. (see p.181)

179 **Free Church**, 1877-78, John C Hay
Set back from the street front in the footprint of the Fisheries Society's Storehouse of 1790, Gothic gable, stair-turret and steeple face the harbour with lapsed conviction. Since 1964 the church has functioned as a craft shop. Next door, the former **United Free Church**, 1910, now serves the congregation.

**Town Clock**, 1905, Charles Whymper
A tapering granite tower at the pierhead. Under a pyramid cap is a leaded clock box with dials on four faces. Erected in memory of the traveller Isabella Bird, its design is not unlike the Village Shelter Whymper designed for Houghton in Huntingdon.

Steep braes wind uphill from Main Street. **Breadalbane Street**, the main avenue of the upper town's tiny grid-iron plan, is wide and tree-lined with tidy two-storey rows of gable-to-

gable houses down each side. At the north end is **Mansefield**, a former Telford manse of 1827-28 by William Thomson. The Parliamentary kirk, a standard two-door design, has gone, replaced by the **Parish Church** on Victoria Street, a five-bay Gothic nave with pinnacled tower by John Robertson, 1895-97. Gothic, too, the former **Tobermory Public School** on Argyll Terrace; tower, tall chimneys and classrooms with lancets and roundels, by Alexander Ross of Inverness, 1875-76, with additions by Alexander Shairp of Oban, c.1897. It is now an Arts Centre, its Victorian view of education superseded by the freer forms of a new **Tobermory High School** built in the 1980s by Strathclyde Regional Council.

180 **Western Isles Hotel**, 1882-83, John C Hay
A ponderous building constructed in whinstone rubble with red sandstone dressings, its intimidating bulk seems overburdened with bedrooms. Commissioned by the owner of Mishnish Estate, Frederick Caldwell, who had earlier built the town's third pier, it was erected at a time when it seemed that Victorian tourism might make Tobermory *one of the most fashionable watering places in the west*. High above the Mishnish Pier at the east end of Back Brae, its grim skyline dominates the bay.

181 **Court House**, 1861-62, Peddie & Kinnear
Brutal Baronial, no less implacable but less immediately visible than the Western Isles Hotel. A heavy symmetry, repeated on all four sides, dulls the edge of romantic allusion.

**St Mary's Chapel**
Barely discernible footings of a medieval chapel of uncertain date. Nearby, signposted by a granite cross, 1902, is the site of **St Mary's Well**, the Gaelic name for which, *Tobar Mhoire*, has given its name to the town.

Top left *Breadalbane Street*; From top *Parish Church; Tobermory High School; Court House.*

For four centuries the search for the treasure of **the Tobermory Galleon** has proved a consistent aspect of Mull's appeal. The ship which fled from the defeat of the Spanish Armada only to sink in Tobermory Bay in November 1588, whether by accident or sabotage, has, however, failed to release anything other than cannon, guns and a variety of other maritime appurtenances of no more than archaeological value. Research now maintains that contrary to tradition it is not the pay ship of the fleet but an armed merchantman out of Ragusa (now Dubrovnik), the *Santa Maria de Gracia y San Juan Bautista*. But when the Duke of Argyll claimed the rights to its salvage in 1608 the lure of gold was strong. Attempts to recover the *San Juan's* putative cargo followed and have continued ever since.

*Glengorm Castle.*

**Erray House**, late 18<sup>th</sup> century
A five-bay gabled house with small window openings at the end of a road 1km. north of town.

182 **Glengorm Castle**, 1858-60, Peddie & Kinnear
A lonely Baronial mansion sitting on grassy terraces high above the north coast. A tall square entrance tower with offset stair turret rises at the centre of the composition. There are the usual canted bays, bulging corner bows and crowstepped gables but the sea-front façade is surprisingly and disappointingly symmetrical. Closer to the shore, 1km. to the north-west above Sorn Point, are the ruinous vestiges of **Dun Ara Castle**, a stronghold of the MacKinnons in the 14<sup>th</sup> century. Masonry traces indicate an irregular curtain wall, an oblong hall structure and a number of smaller buildings which may have originated as a dependent **township**.

**DERVAIG**
A village established by Alexander MacLean of Coll in 1799 and laid out with low cottages lining each side of a single street. The street is a delight, architecturally ordered, with a two-storey house closing the axis, yet picturesque and charming in scale and detail.

Below from top *Dervaig, c.1940; Kilmore Parish Church.*

183 **Kilmore Parish Church**, 1904-05, Peter MacGregor Chalmers (?)
A small harled kirk beautifully placed on a rocky knoll just south of the village. Romanesque Revival distilled it seems to perfection, its formal simplicity – gabled nave, round apse and cone-capped tower – as potent spiritually as sculpturally.

## CALGARY

On the northern slopes of Calgary Bay are the ruinous walls of **Inivea township**, a community of some 20 dwellings with barns and stores. The settlement is shown on Pont's late 16th century map but the drystone walls still to be seen are likely to be those of the village cleared in the early 19th century. On the coast below is the small rubble **jetty** from which emigrant families set out for Canada where they would name another more prosperous Calgary. In an ancient **burial ground** at the head of the bay, dedicated to the Virgin Mary, two Early Christian **grave-markers** cut with Latin crosses, have been found.

The **deserted village** of Crackaig lies on the peninsula to the west of Calgary. Like many in the Highlands and Islands this township fell into ruins in the 19th century when rural populations were cleared from the land. Two hundred people were evicted, one villager hanging himself. Many found a new life across the Atlantic, an emigration in some way honoured when, in 1883, Colonel J E MacLeod of the Royal North-West Mounted Police, having spent an agreeable vacation at Calgary House, named the Canadian city eponymously.

Above *Inivea township;*
Left *RCAHMS plan of Inivea township.*

184 **Calgary House**, 1823, James Gillespie Graham (?)
Built by Captain Allan McAskill of Skye and known for more than a century as Calgary Castle. A symmetrical, two-storey-and-basement mansion constructed in basalt rubble with sandstone dressings. The style is battlemented Gothic, the classical tripartite composition stressed by bartizans lugged on a raised centre and octagonal turrets at the outer corners.

*Calgary House.*

From top *Torloisk House; Kilninian Parish Church; Ulva Parish Church; Inch Kenneth House.*

## KILNINIAN
**Torloisk House**, *c.*1760
A tall five-bay gabled mansion facing Loch Tuath, and the principal residence of the village. It was extended, 1811-12, and again in 1863-64 when Baronial bays and gables reworked its three-storey front.

185 **Kilninian Parish Church**, 1755
Simple harled kirk with three round-arched openings in the south wall, one the entrance. Birdcage bellcote. A forestair on the west gable rises to a gallery, early 19th century. Several **burial enclosures** step up the west boundary of the churchyard. Some carved **slabs**, Iona school, 14th-16th century, in the vestry.

## ULVA
The road continues along the north side of Loch Tuath until, past Laggan Bay, a track leads west to the Ulva ferry. Across the narrow Sound on the island is the **Ferry House**, a small early 19th century inn with three gabled dormers.

186 **Ulva Parish Church**, 1827-28, William Thomson
Standard T-plan Parliamentary kirk without galleries. Alterations to divide the interior into church and community hall, *c.*1950, added a boiler house between the principal windows and eliminated one of the two doorways. The Parliamentary **manse**, 1828, single-storeyed and piend-roofed is adjacent.

187 **Ulva House**, mid 1950s, Leslie Grahame MacDougall
Harled symmetrical T-plan mansion replacing an early 19th century house. Flat-roofed wings fill the re-entrants. Pediment-like, a gable rises at the centre of the south-west front carrying urns at apex and skews. (see p.181)

From the Ulva ferry the road follows the north shore of Loch na Keal to Gruline. There, a branch leads on to Salen on the east coast while the shore road returns west in the shadow of Ben More. It is a spectacular route, crimped between cliffs and sea.

## INCH KENNETH
A small island lying off Gribun at the mouth of Loch na Keal. Dr Johnson found it *verdant and grassy, and fit for both pasture and tillage.* By the time of his visit with Boswell in 1773, **Inch**

Kenneth Chapel, the Parish Church of the 13th century, was already a ruin; it still stands to eaves height, preserving a few lancets, aumbries and an altar base. Some **tapered slabs**, Iona school, 14th-16th century, a ring-headed **Cross**, early 16th century, and the **burial enclosure** of the MacLean family, hosts to Johnson and Boswell. **Inch Kenneth House**, c.1840, has altered its appearance several times. Burnt out in 1882, it was updated with a flat roof in the early 20th century only to be recast in dull battlemented mould, 1934-35.

188

## KILFINICHEN

Leaving the peninsula of Ardmeanach to the west, the road crosses south to Loch Scridain. A track leads to **Tiroran House**, late 19th century, and, still more isolated, **Tavool House**, a tacksman's dwelling typical for the late 1700s, enlarged during the 19th century and now a youth hostel. On the main road east is **Killiemore House**, again late 18th century, its five-bay breadth later extended to seven under a piended-roof.

189 **Kilfinichen Parish Church**, 1804, repaired 1828 Gabled simplicity with pointed-arch windows. Divested of dignity by the bargeboards and shutters of residential conversion. A short distance south-east is the Old Parish Church, a medieval **chapel** reduced to a few turf-covered courses. In the **burial ground**, the **MacLean Monument**, 18th century, an armorially enriched gable carrying ball finials.

At the head of Loch Scridain the road connects with the route coming through Glen More to Brolass and the Ross of Mull (see above).

## IONA

A place of pilgrimage, beautiful and sacral. The island lies off the south-west tip of Mull, a brief ferry crossing from Fionnphort. Set in a sometimes turquoise sea, its hilly terrain is fringed with white sands and a rocky coastline once quarried for white marble. A single settlement, little more than a one-sided village street established by Argyll Estates at the beginning of the 19th century, stretches north from the ferry jetty. Set apart is the Abbey. Begun by the Benedictines c.1200, it rose from the ruins of an earlier Celtic monastic foundation. Now

When Dr Johnson and Boswell visited the island of **Inchkenneth** in 1773 their host was Sir Allan MacLean. The laird's house seems to have been little more than a cottage yet the pleasure of their stay was memorable. Johnson wrote: *Romance does not often exhibit a scene that strikes the imagination more than this little desert in these depths of western obscurity, occupied not by a gross herdsman, or amphibious fisherman, but by a gentleman and two ladies, of high birth, polished manners, and elegant conversation, who, in a habitation raised not very far above the ground, but furnished with unexpected neatness and convenience, practised all the kindness of hospitality, and refinement of courtesy.* So enraptured was Dr Johnson that he composed 22 lines in Latin verse in honour of *The Island of St Kenneth.* These concluded *Quo vagor ulterius? quod ubique requiritur hic est; / Hic secura quies, hic et honestus amor* (Why go further? Here is secure quiet and honest love).

In 1810 Sir Walter Scott found the MacLean cottage in ruins. By 1840 a small mansion-house had been built. This, too, fell into neglect after a fire until, in the early 20th century, it was remodelled. Somewhat unusually, the house had a flat roof, provided to collect rainwater. In 1933, a new owner, Sir Harold Boulton, baronialized the property, adding an extra storey and new wing. Six years later Lord Redesdale purchased Inchkenneth and here Lady Redesdale lived with her ill-fated daughter Unity Mitford.

RCAHMS

*Kilfinichen Parish Church.*

restored, it remains sacred to the memory of St Columba whose missionary zeal brought Christianity from Ireland in the 6th century.

RCAHMS

*Iona Abbey.*

**190 Nunnery**, early 13th century

Conventional claustral layout with church to the north and chapter house to the east. The original cloister garth was, however, reconstructed and much enlarged in the late 15th century. A century later in the aftermath of the Reformation the buildings were abandoned and by the late 1700s were in ruin. By the 1830s the chancel vault had fallen leaving the church almost entirely roofless. Some repairs were carried out by Robert Rowand Anderson, 1874-75, and again by Peter MacGregor Chalmers in 1917, though the latter's proposals for a major restoration were never realised.

A three-bay arcade, blocked with early 16th century masonry, separates the nave of the **Church** from the aisle to the north. Both nave and aisle extend east into chancel and chapel, though only the small square chapel retains its quadripartite vault. Only the west gable and the north wall of the church survive more or less intact. Windows are round-arched, those above the moulded arches of the arcade aligned with

Left *Engraving of the Nunnery by R W Billings;* Below *Iona Nunnery.*

the piers below. Of the **East Range** only footings remain to indicate the three-room plan of a ground floor which would have supported the dormitory. The **Cloister** is all but invisible, though moulded fragments now held in the Nunnery and Abbey Museums suggest that the reconstruction of the late 15th century created an arcade of ogee arches on coupled colonettes.

**St Ronan's Church,** *c.*1200
The medieval parish church of Iona, oblong in plan, built over a still earlier place of worship and burial (possibly 8th century). Ruins stabilised and partially reconstructed by Robert Rowand Anderson, 1874-75, became the Nunnery Museum in 1922-23 with a glazed roof below the wallhead. A similar roof, now carried on delicate laminated timber beams and timber posts, introduced by John Renshaw in 1992-94. The collection of funerary monuments includes a **ringed cross** fragment, late 8th or 9th century, and several **tapered slabs**, 14th-16th century.

**Iona Parish Church,** 1828, William Thomson
Twin-doored gabled kirk built in pink Ross of Mull granite to Telford's standard Parliamentary

model. Bellcote on the south gable. In 1938-39, internal north vestibule and vestry were created, separated from the recast interior by a screen panelled with four-centred arches. Adjacent single-storey **manse** (now a Heritage Centre), 1828, given a central upper floor by Neil & Hurd, 1934. (see p.182)

*Bishop's House.*

**Bishop's House and St Columba's Chapel**, 1893-94, Alexander Ross
All but symmetrical village Gothic with attic dormers flanking central gables on the west and east fronts. West entrance, below a traceried window in the gable, leads through a cusp-arched screen to the Chapel. In the east gable, which projects slightly, a pointed-arch niche with a **statue** of the saint carved by Andrew Davidson, 1893.

**Reilig Odhrain**
An ancient graveyard, approximately square in plan (the enclosure dates from 1875), in use from Early Christian times until the present. 12th century burial place of the kings of Scotland, Ireland and Norway. In 1859 an attempt was made by the 8th Duke of Argyll to bring some order to the chaotic assemblage of grave markers. The more important stones were rearranged in railed enclosures in two parallel lines: the *ridge of the chiefs* and *ridge of the kings*. Many **tombstones**, several with carved effigies, are now in the Abbey Museum. But a number of weathered **tapered slabs**, 12th-16th century, can be seen as can the simple oval sandstone slab marking the grave of the 20th century politician John Smith.

191 **St Oran's Chapel**, 12th century
A severe skew-gabled oblong, its stark, implacably solid masonry seems calculated to shelter and preserve the flame of faith. Sited on the north edge of the Reilig Odhrain, it may have been founded as a mortuary chapel by Somerled, Lord of Argyll, or his son Reginald. Later it

*St Oran's Chapel.*

became the burial place of the Lords of the Isles. In decay but still in use, it was repaired 1855-56, again by the Office of Works, 1921-26, and finally fully restored by Ian G Lindsay in 1957. The austere rubble of the chapel's west gable is penetrated by a Romanesque doorway at once modest but architecturally powerful. Bold chevrons shadow the round-arched opening under a ring of chamfered voussoirs carved with animal and human heads. The interior is simple; sandstone paving, white plastered walls, two robust scissors-tie trusses, a stone block altar of 1957 set on a medieval base. In the south wall a splendid 15th century cusped arch **tomb-recess**, its ogee-arch hood moulding terminating at the apex in a carved figure of the crucified Christ.

192 **Iona Abbey**, from *c.*1200

Restored medieval church, cloister, domestic buildings, infirmary and Michael Chapel. The Benedictine buildings of the 13th century superseded an earlier Columban, or at any rate

*Iona Abbey.*

*Iona Abbey site plan surveyed by Alexander McGibbon in 1893.*

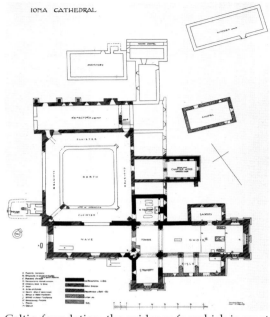

It is something of a glib simplification that **St Columba** brought Christianity to Scotland. An early Christian presence is, in fact, attested by 5th century architectural evidence at Whithorn in the south-west of the country and it is more than likely that Irish Christianity had penetrated Argyll by about 500AD, though Columba's landfall on Iona in 563 remains the familiarly significant date. He was born of noble blood in Donegal in 521 or 522. *Wishing to be a pilgrim for Christ*, he arrived in Argyll with 12 companions. A visit to the king of Dalriada secured royal patronage through which he may have been granted Iona – though a separate tradition suggests the island was a later gift from the Picts whom he had brought to Christ. In any event he founded a monastery there, the nature of which is dimly indicated in Adamnan's *Life of Columba, c.*690. Probably predominantly constructed of wood, wattle and thatch, the church, dormitory, workshops and other buildings stood within an earthwork enclosure or vallum, part of which still survives as the only visible vestige of this early settlement. Columba died in 597 and is said to be buried on the island, though his grave is unknown.

Celtic, foundation, the evidence for which is scant but compelling. Archaeological investigation in the 20th century revealed traces of the original monastery vallum to the north-west and west of the Abbey. The excavation of the remains of some early timber buildings, the survival of three High Crosses from the 8th century and the continued existence of an Early Christian oratory (now incorporated into the fabric of the restored Abbey) all provide further tantalising if problematical clues to the configuration of the pre-Benedictine settlement. The Abbey buildings incorporate successive intermittent phases of enlargement and alteration while restoration too has engrossed several campaigns of repair. Ruinous by the 18th century, the fabric was only saved from total degeneration in 1874-76 when Robert Rowand Anderson stabilised the structure. In 1902-04, the choir, crossing and transepts were rebuilt under the direction of Thomas Ross and John Honeyman. Peter MacGregor Chalmers then restored the nave, 1908-10. Reginald Fairlie produced further proposals for reconstruction in 1931 but it was not until 1938 that the Iona Community finally ensured the site's renewal as a place of worship while Ian G Lindsay began a programme of restoration of the monastic buildings which was not completed until the mid 1960s. (see p.182)

The plan of the aisleless **Nave** is essentially 13th century. The West Front incorporates a hooded pointed-arch doorway and the lower structure of a north-west tower, both 15th century. Abutting this tower masonry is the so-called '**St Columba's Shrine'**, a diminutive oratory cell from the 9th or 10th century, originally detached but assimilated to the Abbey fabric by Lindsay in 1962. The five-light, trefoil-headed window over the Abbey entrance door, the corbelled horizontal wallhead and the equilateral gable behind are by Chalmers. So, too, is most of the south wall, the hooded three-light traceried window similar to a 15th century window on the north side of the presbytery.

The gable, walls and corbelled parapets of the **South Transept** are all 15th century. Tracery in the hooded pointed-arch window in the gable dates from 1875 but is based on a 15th century window on the south side of the presbytery. The **North Transept** was rebuilt in 1904 but retains masonry from the early 13th century at the lower levels, notably around the round-arched windows in the east wall. Over the crossing is a square 15th century **Tower**. A bold string course wraps itself around all four sides above the roof ridges. On each face, lintelled belfry openings with elaborately carved tracery grids; above these, doocot openings under corbelled wallhead parapets laid in 1904. Caphouse completed by John Renshaw in 1996. Finial cross on the south gable by Graciela Ainsworth.

The **Choir**, rebuilt in the later 15th century, seems to reflect the nave in dimension and form. Corbelled parapets continue at the wallheads while the clearstorey windows are still small. To the north is the sacristy, in effect an adaptation of the original 13th century aisle. On the south, a

Left *Interior view of the Choir;* Below *Capital detail in the Choir.*

*Abbey interior.*

15th century aisle, largely restored in 1904. Both aisles stop short of the east gable which allows the presbytery to be lit by three tall pointed-arch windows, their tracery restored by Anderson, 1874-75.

**Interior**. Through the east door, a timber screen with Perpendicular tracery defines a small lobby, by Chalmers, 1910. Five steps down to 15th century flagstone paving in nave. Rubble walls with dressed stones to all openings. Boarded ceiling with 12 bays of curved struts on corbelstones. Pointed arches open to the crossing from nave, choir and transepts, that to the north surviving from the 13th century above the rebuilt 15th century opening. Fine plant, animal and figural carving on the pier capitals by 15th century master mason Donald O'Brolchan. Arcade of three round arches on the east wall of the north transept, *c.*1200. Over the choir, a roof of seven arch-braced trusses by Ross, 1902. The north wall (13th century to the clearstorey sills but 15th century above) is penetrated by a two-arch arcade stranded at an elevated level when the floor was lowered during 15th century changes which eliminated an earlier undercroft. The arcade, blocked when the sacristy was formed, was re-opened in 1904. Above, the original clearstorey windows line up with the piers of the arcade, as in the contemporary Nunnery. This relationship repeats on the south wall over a three-arch arcade, 15th century, with wonderfully carved capitals illustrating biblical themes.

Iona marble communion table, oak choir stalls and lectern by Chalmers, *c.*1910. The sandstone and marble font located at the west end is also by Chalmers. Stained glass in the north clearstorey by Douglas Strachan, 1939; SS Columba, Bride and Patrick. Two sandstone **effigies** of Iona abbots, 15th century, in the presbytery. Screened in the south transept, **effigies** the 8th Duke of Argyll and his third wife carved in white Carrara marble by Sir George Frampton, early 20th century.

The recreation of the abbey's **Monastic Buildings**, almost wholly the work of Ian G Lindsay, began in 1939 with the **East Range** where the 13th century west wall still stood. Extending north from the north transept gable of the church, the building houses the chapter house and adjoining rooms at ground floor and, above,

a library with a segmental ceiling, 1938-40, and dormitory, 1953-54. In the **North Range**, restored 1942-49, the undercroft, with 13th century walling north and south, serves as a shop. The refectory added above has a semicircular boarded ceiling with exposed roof ties. An entirely new **West Range**, completed in 1965, contains offices, kitchens and residential accommodation. The **Cloister** arcade of coupled octagonal shafts was reconstructed by Lindsay in 1959 drawing on earlier investigations and partial rebuilding by Anderson, 1875-76, Honeyman, 1904, and the Office of Works in 1921. The former **Reredorter** or privy to the north of the East Range has been converted to a house for the caretaker, 1950. The original 13th century drainage channel survives. Linked to it is the **Abbot's House**, recast as additional residential accommodation and laundry, 1956-57.

**Michael Chapel**, late 12th or early 13th century Skew-gabled rubble oblong lying east of the north end of the East Range. Lindsay's restoration, 1959-61, comprises a boarded ceiling of elliptical cross section, plastered walls with a boarded dado, and a stone-flagged floor. At the east end, a pointed-arch window with Y-tracery.

### Abbey 'Infirmary'

A long gable-ended building set parallel to the Michael Chapel immediately east of the Abbot's House. Its original form remains unclear for low walls were all that existed prior to Lindsay's 'restoration' of 1964. The building is now the Abbey Museum in which a rich collection of salvaged funerary stones, crosses and other architectural fragments is retained. Many **tapered slabs**, 14th-16th century, carved with plant

RCAHMS

From top *The Monastic Buildings before 1874; cloister with sculpture by Jacques Lipchitz.*

motifs, plaitwork, swords and galleys, some with inscriptions, can be seen. There are several high relief **effigies**, 14th-15th century, most of men in armour. Broken fragments of the **St John Cross**, 8th century, displayed as a re-assembled structure, 1990.

**High Crosses**

The fragmentary remains of several freestanding Early Christian crosses and cross bases can be seen in the Abbey Museum. These appear to be the work of Pictish stone carvers active on Iona between the 8th and 10th centuries. Three crosses, all dating from the second half of the 8th century and sharing common stylistic detail, survive in whole or in part. **St John's Cross** has been intelligently re-erected in the Museum, the early strengthening of its mortice-and-tenon construction by the introduction of a curved stone ring around its armpitted crossing clearly evident. A fine concrete replica stands some 12m. north-west of the Abbey's west door. **St Martin's Cross** remains in its position 21m. west of the south-west corner of the Abbey. It is ringed and armpitted and carved with bosses. Animal and figural motifs, some biblical, adorn both faces. Broken pieces of **St Oran's Cross** are in the Museum. It has a transom holed to receive the shaft and upper arm.

Also in the Museum, fragments of **St Matthew's Cross**, 9th or early 10th century. Though much weathered, its carved scenes are similar to those on the St Martin Cross.

*RCAHMS drawing of St John's Cross.*

**MacLean's Cross** is located 40m. south-south-east of Iona parish Church (see above). It is disc-headed, its carved ornament similar to that of the MacMillan Cross at Kilmory and thus probably dating from the 15th century.

**MacLeod Centre**, 1984-88, Feilden Clegg design Competition-winning, two-storey, gabled T-plan hostel, the south-west re-entrant forming an approach courtyard. Vernacular aspiration is evident but the north façade with its chevron roof line of eight bedroom dormers and studied repetitive disposition of fenestration, downpipes and render change is perhaps too self-consciously designed to convince.

**Dhu Heartach Lighthouse**, 1867-72, David and Thomas Stevenson

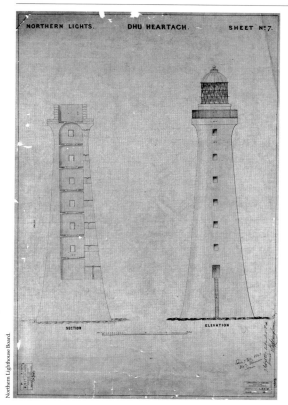

*Dhu Heartach Lighthouse drawn in 1867.*

**The building of the lighthouse on Dhu Heartach** (Dubh Artach) presented an immense challenge to the engineers David and Thomas Stevenson. Despite their considerable experience, which included the completion of Skerryvore Lighthouse beyond Tiree, it was a daunting task. For centuries, the Torran reef, a long archipelago of treacherous rocks lying close to the shipping lane to the west of Mull, had claimed many ships and lives. Between 1800 and 1854, 30 ships had been wrecked and more than 50 lives lost. It was here that David Balfour and Alan Breck came to grief in *Kidnapped*, the adventure novel written later by Robert Louis Stevenson, kinsman and apprentice to the engineers whose expertise would finally raise a warning light on this maritime danger. Describing his sight of this infamous hazard, Stevenson wrote *The full Atlantic swell beats upon it without hindrance, and the tides sweep round it like a mill-race. . .*

Work began in 1867. At a land base on Earraid, a small island connected to Mull at low water by a sand spit, a pier, sheds, cranes, working platform, bothies, cottages and an *iron house* for the resident engineer were set up. From here dovetailed granite blocks were ferried the 15 miles or so to the perilously smooth outcrop of black basalt chosen on the reef. A cylindrical iron barracks was established on the rock. Work could only be undertaken during the summer months and even then foul weather was frequent. Not until 1872 was the lantern finally fitted. A century later in 1971 the lighthouse ceased to be manned.

Granite tower rising 44m. out of the Atlantic 23.5km. south-west of Iona. Unmanned since 1971.

## TRESHNISH ISLES

A cluster of small islands strung across the sea west of Mull. None is now inhabited but the two islets at the north-east end of the chain retain 193 evidence of **fortification** consonant with their

*Plan of the Treshnish Isles drawn by Robert Johnson in 1741.*

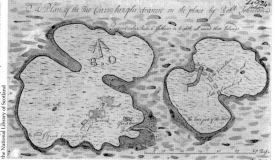

strategic position. Cairn na Burgh More is naturally protected by high cliffs but these have been made still more impregnable by a defensive curtain wall, 16th or 17th century, traces of which survive especially along the east side of the island. Evidence of a stone stairway and probable entrance gate can be detected. The walls and gables of a **chapel**, perhaps 15th century, survive. A second oblong building, longer and divided in plan by a rubble partition, served as a **barracks**, 16th or 17th century. On the neighbouring island of Cairn na Burgh Beg, which is smaller, but equally favoured by natural defences, there are more signs of rubble fortification and enclosures.

## ISLAY

### PORT ELLEN

One of several planned settlements established by the Campbell lairds of Islay, Port Ellen was founded in 1821 by Walter Frederick Campbell and named for his wife. Favoured by a fine natural harbour, it soon became the island's main port and today provides roll-on roll-off facilities for car ferry connections to the mainland at Kennacraig on West Loch Tarbert. From the pier, **Frederick Crescent** curves east around the bay in a ring of white harled 19th century houses, though not without aberration and intrusion. Most dwellings are of two-storeys with gabled eaves dormers recurring frequently. **No.79**, a former manse, 1847-48, has a good doorpiece

**Walter Frederick Campbell** (1798-1848) inherited estates in Islay in 1816 at the age of 18. Intent on radical improvements to the island economy, he reorganized land holdings, dispossessing many in the rural townships in order to reduce the number of people dependent on the land while at the same time introducing better methods of husbandry to improve agricultural production. His was not a heartless clearance for those displaced were re-housed and re-employed in new planned villages. It was a precedent set by Daniel Campbell the Younger, brother to Walter Frederick's grandfather, who, in the second half of the 18th century, had founded Bowmore to absorb the population of the old community of Kilarrow thrown off their land to enhance the setting of Islay House.

*Port Ellen Harbour.*

with fluted pilasters and a cornice on consoles. As the ring of building bends south and then south-west, the scale drops; **Fisher Row** is a short but crisp and simple series of early 19th century cottages. Two-storey, gable-to-gable houses, early 19th century, face each other across **Charlotte Street**, a severely urban path running north from the pier, grim and gruff but architecturally consistent. The street starts badly: at the pierhead, the rough rubble corner of the **Islay Hotel**, 1888, is drab and neglected. At the north end, the white-walled **White Hart Hotel**, mostly late 19th century, taller and more decoratively ambitious.

194 **St John's Parish Church**, 1897-98, Sydney Mitchell

Modelled on a church at Leulinghen-Bernes, near Boulogne, but none the better for this provenance. A strangely round-shouldered hipped belfry with a short slated spire sits over the gabled sanctuary. Behind this the nave roof falls to low eaves. Lean-to timber entrance porch on the rear gable.

195 **Ramsay Hall**, 1901-02, Sydney Mitchell & Wilson Arts and Crafts with free classical detailing. An asymmetrically set square tower with an undulating parapet gives the building its churchy feel. In this white-walled West Coast world, Dorset pea render hardly seems appropriate (though an edge-of-town site mitigates the misfortune). (see p.183)

**Port Ellen Distillery**, from 1825
Ten piend-roofed warehouses, erected between 1846 and 1907, and three pagoda-capped kilns. Malting plant buildings, 1973, rise 30m. in blue profiled metal sheeting, oblivious to context.

Four roads leave Port Ellen. Two run north in more or less parallel tracks across 12 bleak

The early 19<sup>th</sup> century improvements were carried out with the help of the surveyor William Gemmill who prepared maps of the reorganized holdings and of the new settlements. Port Ellen, named after Lady Eleanor Charteris, daughter of the 8<sup>th</sup> Earl of Wemyss, was founded in 1821 and a distillery established there in 1825. New cottages were built at Keills in 1826. Port Charlotte, intended like Port Ellen as a base for a fishing fleet and provided with a distillery also, was laid down in 1828. Port Wemyss appeared in 1833. Following the lead of his nephew, Campbell's uncle, Captain Walter Campbell, was also active in the renewal of Islay during the 1820s and 1830s. At Portnahaven he built rows of neat new houses on each side of a picturesque creek, replacing an untidy cluster of insanitary hovels. These unassuming but visually co-ordinated ventures in planning, carried out by the Campbell lairds over a period of some 50 years or so, have left Islay its legacy of white waterside villages wrought from a simple vernacular of harl and slate.

From top *St John's Parish Church;* *Ramsay Hall;* Left *Lagavulin Distillery.*

kilometres of peat moss to Bowmore and on to Bridgend. One follows the rocky coast east to Kildalton passing the distilleries at **Lagavulin** (founded 1816-17), **Laphroaig** (1820) and **Ardbeg** (1794), each with its own white cluster of warehouses, malt barns and peak-roofed kilns. A fourth goes west by Kilnaughton Bay to The Oa peninsula.

*Dunivaig Castle.*

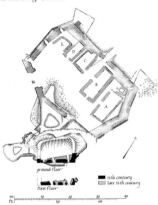

*RCAHMS ground floor plan of Dunivaig Castle.*

196 **Dunivaig Castle**, early 16th century
Traces of a polygonal curtain wall are scarcely distinguishable from the natural profile of a rocky knoll on the east side of Lagavulin Bay; sure, if eroded, evidence of the characteristic Gaidhealtachd stronghold. Still less visible is a series of small oblong buildings ranged along the inner face of the castle's north wall. The site was an important fortress of the MacDonald Lords of the Isles in the 14th century and may well have been fortified earlier, perhaps by the Norse. The castle passed into royal hands in the 16th century but continued unrest and successive sieges marked the ongoing struggles between Clan Donald and the crown. By the end of the 17th century Dunivaig was in ruins. Offshore, on Texa, the walls and gables of a small **chapel**, possibly 14th century, still stand.

### KILDALTON
An estate on the south-east edge of the island. The road from Port Ellen continues north, but only as far as Artalla.

**Kildalton Old Parish Church**, late 12th or early 13th century.
Though roofless, walls and gables still define a simple oblong plan which may have been divided into nave and sanctuary by a timber screen. The east end is lit by coupled round-arched windows in the north and south walls and two lancets in the gable. In the graveyard are many **tapered slabs**, 14th and 15th century, but

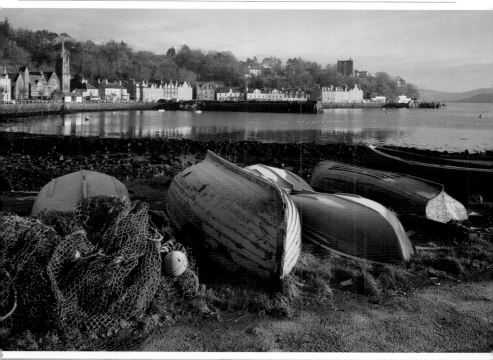

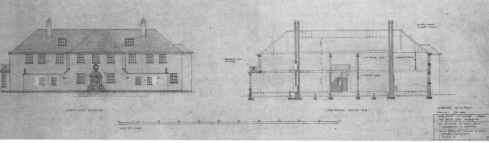

Top *Tobermory, Mull;*
Middle *Ulva House by Leslie Grahame MacDougall, 1955;*
Bottom *'Old Mull' whisky illustration showing Ledaig Distillery in Tobermory.*

The Celebrated "OLD MULL"

ESTD. 1823

Tobermory Distillery
Isle of Mull - SCOTLAND

SCOTCH WHISKY

JOHN HOPKINS & CO., LTD., Distillers.
GLASGOW, LONDON and ISLE OF MULL.

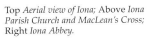

Top *Aerial view of Iona;* Above *Iona Parish Church and MacLean's Cross;* Right *Iona Abbey.*

Top left *Kildalton Cross, Islay;*
Middle *Painting of Port Ellen
Lighthouse, Islay, c.1850;*
Bottom *Ramsay Hall, Port Ellen, Islay;*
Top right *Bowmore Distillery, Islay;*
Below right *McArthur's Head
Lighthouse, Islay.*

183

RCAHMS

RCAHMS

RCAHMS

RCAHMS

Top *Lithograph of Craighouse, Jura by William Daniell, 1817*; Middle *Ruvaal Lighthouse, Islay*; Bottom *Hynish pier, Tiree*; Right *Sorisdale Cottages, Coll.*

*Kildalton Old Parish Church.*

the monument that makes the single-track
197 journey memorable is the **Kildalton Cross,** (see
p.183) dating from the second half of the 8th
century, the finest Early Christian high cross in
Scotland. Carved from one piece of epidiorite, it
stands 2.65m. high in a damaged socket-stone.
The ringed cross-head and shaft are alive with
delicately cut figural scenes of biblical events
wound up in a rich sculptural texture of bosses,
spirals and plaitwork. Outside the churchyard is
the **Kildalton Small Cross**, a disc-headed Iona
school cross, 14th or 15th century.

It is well worth making the trip along
the single-track road north-east from
Port Ellen to discover the **Kildalton
Cross**. This, the outstanding example
of a free-standing cross in Scotland, is
a Christian monument of memorable
beauty. Carved from a single piece of
grey-green stone sometime in the
second half of the 8th century, its only
rivals are the high crosses of Iona – St
Oran, St John and St Martin. On one
face the shaft is carved with roundels
and spirals over which are the Christ
Child and the Virgin seated between
angels. On the cross head is a central
boss of coiled snakes and lizards
inside a cable-moulded ring and in
the arms biblical scenes. On the other
side are more coiled serpents, lions,
plaitwork and knobbly bosses. At
2.65m. high, it compels reverence.

*Kildalton Castle, c.1900.*

198 **Kildalton Castle**, 1867-70, John Burnet
A Baronial mansion reduced to dereliction.
Gables and crowsteps mass around the
customary turreted tower though the roofs are
neither so steep nor the upward surge of the
composition so exaggerated as was envisaged in
a proposal prepared by James Ingram in 1863.

**McArthur's Head Lighthouse**, 1861, David and
Thomas Stevenson
A short white cylinder perched on the flank of
Beinn na Caillich at the entrance to the Sound of
Islay. Equally white against the green slopes,
low walls snake around an inner precinct in
dipping curves. (see p.183)

**THE OA**
A hilly, off-the-beaten-track, peninsula west of
Port Ellen. At Lurabus and Tockmal, deserted
early 19th century **townships** retain evidence of
rig cultivation and cruck-roofed dwellings.
There are a few farms but The Oa is a wild and
lonely corner of Islay.

**Kilnaughton Chapel** and **Burial Ground**,
late medieval
A simple oblong cell with much of its rubble
walling swallowed up in soil and sand on the
western shore of Kilnaughton Bay opposite Port
Ellen. There are a few **tapered slabs,** Iona
school, 14th –16th century, one carved with the
effigy of a mailed warrior.

**The Oa Parish Church**, 1828-29, William
Thomson
One of 32 churches built in the Highlands at
Parliamentary behest. The programme was co-
ordinated by Thomas Telford but the churches
and manses effectively designed to standard
models by his surveyor subordinates. There are
two in Islay, both T-plan with Tudor arched doors
and windows. At Portnahaven (q.v.) the kirk still
serves the community but here, at Risabus, there
are no worshippers, the church a sad empty shell
since 1930.

**Port Ellen Lighthouse**, 1832
A memorial to Lady Ellinor Campbell, first wife
of Walter Frederick Campbell. A white square
tower forming a stepped L-plan relationship with
a lower stair tower. Both are flat-roofed with a
block cornice and parapet. Set above a hooded
Gothic doorway is an oblong tablet bearing an
inscription in verse. (see p.183)

The Museum of Islay Life

*Drawing of American War Memorial.*

199 **American War Memorial**, 1918, Robert Walker
Raised in what seems pilgrimage isolation, a high
cylindrical cairn of polychromatic rubble
dramatically sited above the Mull of Oa cliffs.
The monument commemorates those American
sailors and soldiers lost in the wreck of the
transport ships *Tuscania* and *Otranto* off Islay.

**BOWMORE**
A planned settlement, laid out in 1768 after the
laird, Daniel Campbell II of Shawfield and Islay,
had razed the old village of Kilarrow as part of
the improvements made around Islay House. A
decade later a distillery was established. The
new town (scarcely a village) grew, housing
estate workers, fishermen and a few weavers,
and by the middle of the 19th century the
population had reached *c*.1,200. Since then there
has been a decline but Bowmore remains the
focus of the island's administrive and commercial
activities.

**200 Kilarrow Parish Church**, 1767

Islay's best known building – and justifiably so, for the white geometrical sophistication of its architecture is wholly unexpected in such a provincial setting. A harled drum roofed with a slated cone and fronted by a dumpy ashlar tower, more tolbooth steeple than church spire, it sits at the top of the town looking down Main Street to Loch Indaal. The axial tower has an octagonal belfry capped by a stone cupola and carried on a square base which is pedimented at the eaves height of the church behind. A Latin inscription in the tympanum acknowledges the patronage of the laird. The designer is not recorded; tradition asserts the possibility of a French architect, perhaps encountered by Campbell on the Grand Tour, but the conscription of a proposal for a round church at Inveraray, prepared by John Adam in 1758 but never used, is much more likely. At the centre of the church interior, the builder, Thomas Spalding, has placed a stout timber pillar to support the complex radial roof structure hidden above a flat plastered ceiling. Whatever its maritime allusions, this mast-like column is architecturally disconcerting. In 1828 a U-plan gallery was added and 50 years later the interior seating recast.

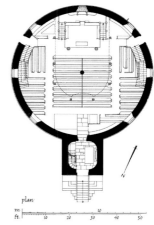

plan

From top *Kilarrow Parish Church;*
*RCAHMS plan of Kilarrow Parish*
*Church;* Below *Bowmore Main Street.*

**Main Street** is the backbone of the new town plan, linking church and pier. The **Old Town Hall**, late 18th century, is little more than a house with taller than usual windows at first floor and a roughly pilastered doorway. Once used as the sheriff court, it is now a Masonic Lodge. **Ileach**, one of several early to late 19th century dwellings on the north side of the street, is distinguished by buckle-ended strapwork hood mouldings. Nearer the pier is **The Harbour Inn**, mid 19th

*Shore Street, Bowmore.*

century, three storeys high with bipartite windows to the street. Finally, a few late 18th century **stores** with forestairs giving access to dwellings above. A few streets cross the Main Street axis at right angles to create a simple grid-iron plan. The scale of building is generally two-storey but architectural consistency is lacking. Groome, writing in 1882, noted the town's *regular plan* but regretted *the medley character of its private houses*. Over a century later his observations are still pertinent. **Shore Street**, which bends subtly with the Loch Indaal coastline, is best, houses packed gable-to-gable along each side under a common eaves height.

**Whisky** is perhaps Islay's main claim to fame. Two centuries or so ago illicit production was legalised but no duty charged. Drunkenness was rife and a major concern to the local clergy. Today there are eight distilleries on the island – Ardbeg, Lagavulin, Laphroaig, Port Ellen, Bowmore, Caol Ila, Bunnahabhainn, Bruichladdich – each producing its own distinctive malt. Flavours vary but, born of the peats and waters of the island, a certain smokiness characterises the flavour of most Islay whiskies, from the soft rounded hints of Bowmore to the robust tanginess of Laphroaig.

**Islay High School**, 1876, William Railton
An unremarkable Victorian school, enlarged by Argyll County Council in 1964 and greatly enlivened by additions made by Strathclyde Regional Council, 1985-86. Behind a smart glazed link is a pyramid roof with a pagoda-topped belfry ventilator, evidently an echo of nearby distillery forms.

**Bowmore Distillery**, founded 1779
Warehouses, maltings and kilns grouped in a courtyard plan between School Street and Loch Indaal. **Reception Centre**, 1974, by McKay & Forrester. (see p.183)

*Bowmore Distillery.*

*Bridgend.*

**BRIDGEND**
The green heart of the island. A Victorian inn with timbered eaves and gables, **Bridgend Hotel**, *c.*1850, some early 19th century dwellings, barn and former stables picturesquely parallel on the banks of the River Sorn, and a bowling green under the trees. Across the two segmental rubble arches of **Sorn Bridge**, 1860, the road from Bowmore divides; west to the Rinns and north-east to Port Askaig. At Redhouses a water-driven **woollen mill**, 1883, retains much of its original machinery and is still in production. The iron wheel, installed in 1928, replaced a wooden undershot wheel.

*Islay House.*

## 201 Islay House, begun 1677

Hidden in wooded grounds is the island's principal country house. Begun as Kilarrow House, an L-plan mansion built for Sir Hugh Campbell of Cawdor, it was transformed by Daniel Campbell of Shawfield and Islay into a U-plan arrangement, with a three-bay, three-storey centre sandwiched by broad crowstep-gabled wings, *c*.1731. Later in the century, *c*.1760, half-octagon stair towers were added on each flank. William Playfair built a Baronial service wing to the east in 1841-45 but this was subsequently remodelled by Detmar Blow, 1909-11, who recast its south-west front in sympathy with earlier work. Though there is some deference to classical manners in all of this (elongated windows at the centre of the main south-west façade, Venetian windows lighting the stair towers, and an elegant Edinburgh New Town doorpiece added *c*.1825) the vernacular simplicity of harled walls and steep slated roofs succeeds in unifying repeated aggrandizement. Estate buildings include a **Home Farm** range, late 18th century; an octagonal **East Tower**, *c*.1775; a Gothic **West Tower**, late 18th century, crenellated on a square plan; and the **Forester's House** (or Bluehouse), a small three-bay dwelling with lower flanking wings, three porches, and a roadside wall carrying urns.

## 202 Eallabus House, late 18th century

A plain but impressive double-gabled house,

**Daniel Campbell** (*c*.1670-1753), known as 'Great Daniel' to distinguish him from his grandson, Daniel Campbell the Younger (1737-77), who inherited the Islay Estates from him, was the founder of modern Islay. A shipowner and trader with the New England states before he was 30, he became an early and important member of the *Tobacco Lord* oligarchy who ruled Glasgow in the 18th century. He acted as Collector of Customs at Port Glasgow and was a Member of Parliament in the Scots Parliament and, after 1707, in the Union Parliament. In 1711 he commissioned the building of a large town house in the city's Trongate, the Shawfield Mansion, which set a pattern for a new, classical style of residence. His support for the introduction of a Malt Tax led, however, to the sacking of this house by the mob in 1725. He claimed compensation, won his case, and with the money gained purchased the Islay and Jura Estates. From 1726, spending the summers on the island at Islay House, he was Laird of Islay until his death.

*Islay House West Tower.*

*Eallabus House.*

*Kilmeny Parish Church.*

*Hall-House, Finlaggan.*

The idea of the Argyll and the Hebrides being a separate domain from that of mainland Scotland has a long history. The Dark Ages kingdom of Dalriada stretched across the Irish Sea. The Norsemen also established their rule from the Isle of Man north to the Western Isles. In the 12th century Viking suzerainty was superseded by that of Somerled, progenitor of the Clan Donald. It was Somerled's son, Reginald of Islay, who adopted the title *Rex Insularum, Dominus de Argil*. In the 14th century his successor, *Good John of Islay*, signed himself **Dominus Insularum – Lord of the Isles**. The MacDonald Lords had their seat of government at Loch Finlaggan on Islay where, on two small islands, the council of state met and the Lords were installed in power. Islay became the most important of the Hebridean islands and a centre of Gaelic culture. Not until the end of the 15th century, when James IV finally extended the rule of the Scottish monarchy over the western seaboard, was the Lordship abolished and Finlaggan abandoned.

harled with sandstone dressings. There is a very squat pilastered porch at the centre but above that, emphasising the *piano nobile*, a fine tripartite window with moulded architraves and cornice. Two-storey canted bays left and right are probably 19th century additions but the coupled lights to the second floor are original.

## BALLYGRANT
A cluster of houses on the road between Bridgend and Port Askaig

### 203 Kilmeny Parish Church, 1828-29
A remodelled late 18th century (?) kirk. The date of this rebuilding, commissioned by Walter Frederick Campbell, points to a possible link with the building of Telford's Parliamentary Churches, two of which were erected at the time on Islay (see Portnahaven and The Oa). The skew-gabled, T-plan arrangement is also suggestive. On the other hand, two tall Venetian windows indicate other influences. The central gabled porch was added in the second half of the 19th century. Adjacent is the **manse**, 1828, which is certainly to the standard Parliamentary model produced by Telford and his surveyor assistant Joseph Mitchell.

### 204 FINLAGGAN
Known to be the power-base from which the MacDonalds exercised their dominion over much of the western seaboard until the forfeiture of the Lordship of the Isles at the end of the 15th century, Finlaggan is of great archaeological importance. Its architectural impact is, however, disappointing. The settlement developed on two small islands at the north end of Loch Finlaggan. On Eilean Mor, originally ringed by a wooden palisade from which a series of towers projected, there is evidence of rig cultivation and the remains (little more than grass covered footings) of some 20 small buildings. The ruined walls of **Kilfinlaggan Chapel**, an oblong cell of 14th century date, are readily seen. Less evident is a slightly larger building, probably a **hall-house** of similar date, though modified in the 15th century. It is difficult to relate these remnants to a hindsight view of 1549 that this was a place *well biggit in palace-wark*. A second isle, Eilean na Comhairle, which seems to have been reached by a stone causeway, is even less revealing – at least, above ground. Excavation does, however, suggest a sequence of dun or broch, a small stone

castle, and latterly three buildings which may include the Council Chamber implied by the island's Gaelic name.

## PORT ASKAIG

A tiny harbour on the Sound of Islay with car ferry connection to Jura, Colonsay and Kennacraig on the mainland. The intermittent bustle on the pierside apron is surrounded by a green cyclorama of wooded cliffs at the base of which is a ring of white early 19th century buildings – post-office, piermaster's office and piend-roofed stores. **Port Askaig Hotel**, an agitated cluster of 19th century gables, has a drovers' inn core said to date from the 16th century.

*Dunlossit House in 1906.*

**205 Dunlossit House**, 1865; rebuilt by John Burnet & Son, 1909-11
Robust Baronial rising from falling lawns in a polychromatic sandstone surge of bartizans and crowstepped peaks.

North of Port Askaig on the Sound of Islay shore are two distillery settlements. At **Caol Ila**, founded 1846, there is 20-bay long warehouse, a late 19th century wall of pilastered brick stretched along the quay. Beside it, a **Still House** by G L Darge, 1972-74, fully glazed to the sea. Behind the distillery, some neat rows of terraced housing landscaped on the grassy slopes. At **Bunnahabhainn**, further north, the distillery buildings, 1880-83, stretch along the shore, robust and uncompromising like the gateway to some Victorian industrial suburb.

**Ruvaal Lighthouse**, 1857-59, David and Thomas Stevenson (see p.184)
White marker at the northern entrance to the Sound of Islay. 36m. high round tower set in a rectangular precinct bounded by low rubble walls. Gabled **Stores** and **Keepers' Houses**.

*From top* Kilnave Chapel; Ardnave
*House;* Foreland House; *Right*
*Bruichladdich Distillery.*

## ARDNAVE

A tapering peninsula at the north-west tip of
Islay. On the west shore of Loch Gruinart is
**Kilnave Chapel**, *c.*1400, a small gabled oblong,
roofless but intact to the wallhead. Standing
almost 3m. high in the **burial ground** is the
**Kilnave Cross**, the east face much weathered but
carved with roundels and spirals similar to those
on the grander and better known Kildalton Cross
(q.v.). On Nave Island is another ruined **chapel**
with a two-light round-arched window and
shelved aumbry; probably early 13th century,
though the oval-shaped **burial ground** may be
earlier.

206 **Ardnave House**, late 18th century
Tacksman's house of two harled storeys with a
full-height bow-fronted projection flanked by
chimneys at the centre of the south front. The
contemporary **steading** has a crenellated screen
with three blind Gothic arches.

## BRUICHLADDICH

A shoreline hamlet which developed in the late
19th century after the building of the distillery.
The **Distillery** itself, built in concrete in 1881, has
a courtyard plan with a vented pyramid roof over
the kiln and a 12-bay malt-barn range laid along
the coast road.

207 **Foreland House**, *c.*1820
Harled three-bay dwelling with pretension to
grander things. The north façade is broad but
low, the first floor windows pressed down by the
eaves course. A columned doorpiece carrying

*Foreland Tileworks.*

entablature and pediment seems strangely pinched in width. Various additions and remodellings. To the north-east are the rubble remains of an early 19th century **tileworks**.

*Aerial view of Kilchoman Old Parish Church and Burial Ground.*

## KILCHOMAN

208 **Old Parish Church** and **burial ground**, 1825-27
Remote and isolated above Machir Bay, the site has ancient religious associations and settlement may date from Early Christian times. There are records of a medieval church in the 14th century. The present church, closed 150 years after it was built, is a derelict gabled box with simple Gothic windows and a buttressed and battlemented north tower. Panelled U-plan gallery supported on timber columns. The **burial ground** is busy with medieval and post-Reformation **slabs** and **headstones**. Not far from the church's south gable is the disc-headed **Kilchoman Cross**, 14th - 15th century, Iona school, carved with a Crucifixion scene, several figures, plant whorls and interlacing.

**Kilchoman House**, 1825-26
The former manse. A plain piend-roofed house, the central entrance bay pedimented under an apex chimney.

*Kilchoman House.*

**Loch Gorm Castle**, late 16th and early 17th century
An island stronghold already much reduced by the 17th century, barely enough survives to discern its toy fort plan; a quadrangular curtain with four circular bastions at the corners. The remains of some smaller later structures built within the walls show evidence of cruck roofing.

## PORT CHARLOTTE
Established as an agricultural and distilling settlement in 1828 by Walter Frederick Campbell.

*Shore Street, Port Charlotte.*

Whisky production ceased a 100 years later but the village remains popular with holiday makers. The plan is subtle and contingent rather than geometrical, bending with the shoreline on the west coast of Loch Indaal. Three-bay, two-storey houses, built *on the scale of the manses of the clergy*, pack picturesquely in short gable-to-gable ranges along **Main Street**, **Saddler's Brae**, **Shore Street** and **School Street**, making this the most charming and least altered of Islay's white-walled villages. Beside a small bay, **Port Charlotte Hotel** stands to three storeys.

*St Kiaran's Church.*

209 **St Kiaran's Church**, 1897, Peter MacGregor Chalmers
Rubble Romanesque dressed with red sandstone. The conically roofed apse is attractive but the gabled transept and porch seem to compromise rural simplicity.

**Kilchoman Free Church**, 1843
Harled gabled box speedily built with Disruption fervour. Birdcage bellcote on the south-east gable similar to one on Kilmeny Parish Church (q.v.). In 1977, 50 years after worship had ceased, the church was converted to the Museum of Islay Life. A small library and splendid collection of local artefacts provide a fascinating picture of the island's past.

**Loch Indaal Lighthouse**, 1869, David and Thomas Stevenson
A low round tower on the Loch Indaal shore at Ruadh'an Duin. Two-storey, T-plan **Keepers' Houses** are, surprisingly, built in facing brick.

*Loch Indaal Lighthouse and Keepers' House.*

**Port Charlotte School**, 1830
Pedimented gable with an apex bellcote and porch, placed at the head of School Street. Extended and altered, it now serves as the Village Hall.

Close to the shore, at **Nereabolls**, some 5km. south-west of Port Charlotte on the road to Portnahaven, is a ruined **chapel** and **burial ground**, probably 15th century. The rubble remains of the small cell are scant but suggest a raised floor at the east end.

**KILCHIARAN**
A remarkable farm, ruined chapel and the detritus of 19th century slate workings.

**Kilchiaran Chapel** and **Burial Ground**, late medieval

The east gable with its three aumbries is substantially original; the north, south and west walls were, however, partially reconstructed and stabilised in restoration work carried out 1972-73. A medieval **font** survives, its ribbed stone basin supported on a modern base. Several carved **tapered slabs**, 14th-16th century.

*Kilchiaran Farm.*

210 **Kilchiaran Farm**, *c*.1826

The two-storey piended farmhouse is unexceptional; simple symmetry with a corniced doorpiece. The **steading**, however, makes an unexpected architectural impact. Two parallel east-west ranges of byres and stables enclose an oblong courtyard. Projecting from the centre of the north range is a threshing mill powered by a breastshot iron water-wheel. Attached to the south range is a semicircular cattle court divided by two radial walls and edged by a band of pitched-roof stores. Despite the insensitivity of later alterations and additions, the geometry is still strong, a clear reminder of the rational thinking that lay behind the agricultural improvements of the Campbell lairds.

## PORTNAHAVEN

Originally founded as a fishing settlement in 1788, the village was further developed by Walter Frederick Campbell in the 1820s. Gable-to-gable harled cottages line each side of a narrow rock-flanked inlet protected from the treacherous Rinns of Islay currents. Most are now holiday homes.

211 **Portnahaven Parish Church**, 1828, William Thomson

Sited monitorially at the head of the village. Characteristic Telford Parliamentary kirk; T-plan with north, west and east galleries. The

*Portnahaven Parish Church.*

symmetrical south front has two, tall, four-centred arched windows and two doorways reputedly used with proprietorial exclusivity by the villagers of Portnahaven and nearby Port Wemyss, respectively and respectfully. A short distance east is the former Parliamentary manse, 1828, now known as **Brookfield** and much altered.

### Portnahaven Free Church, 1849

Built to a gabled T-plan as the Free Church School, it became a church in 1875. Arched belfry on the main gable. The adjoining **manse**, which is taller, was added in 1892.

### Portnahaven Primary School, 1878, William Railton

Another T-plan, with convex entrance porches – one for boys, one for girls – tucked into the re-entrants. Three-bay **Schoolhouse** also by Railton.

*Aerial view of Port Wemyss.*

## PORT WEMYSS

Planned village, founded in puzzling proximity less than a stroll from Portnahaven, by Walter Frederick Campbell in 1833. There is no church, no school and no shop, only houses, still predominantly single-storey, the whole laid out on a D-plan with the stem of the D ranged along the rocky coast opposite Orsay.

*Orsay Chapel.*

## ORSAY

A small island separated from Portnahaven and Port Wemyss by a narrow channel at the southern tip of the Rinns of Islay. To the north of the island is a ruined **chapel**, possibly 14th century, with two small lancets in the lateral walls. A tiny medieval **mortuary chapel** survives.

212 **Rinns of Islay Lighthouse**, 1824, Robert Stevenson.

Five-stage cylindrical tower surmounted by a corniced balcony and lantern. It stands 45m. above high water level. The lens mechanism of 1896 was modernised in 1978. At the base of the tower are the **Keepers' Houses** and **Stores** arranged symmetrically. These are flat-roofed with pedimented parapets and octagonal chimney stacks.

*Rinns of Islay Lighthouse.*

## JURA

An island low in population but high in elevation; the scree-crusted Paps of Jura rise in spectacular silhouette to just under 800m. A single road, constructed by the Commissioners for Highland Roads and Bridges, 1805-12, follows the shore for almost the entire length of the eastern coastline, much as it did in cattle-droving days. It begins at Feolin where the rubble block **jetty** and **slipways** of 1809-10, designed by David Wilson of Lochgilphead, have been superseded by the modern car ferry link across the Sound of Islay to Port Askaig.

**Claig Castle**, 15th century (?)
Ruined tower-house of the MacDonald Lords of the Isles. Built on the rocky summit of a small

RCAHMS

island off the south coast, it commanded the southern entrance to the Sound of Islay. Only the ground floor walls survive.

**Jura House**, 1878-83, Alexander Ross
A very vertical house with piended gables, bay windows, and a balustraded tower; seat of the Campbells of Jura.

### CRAIGHOUSE
The island's only village. The curving rubble **pier**, 1812-14, by surveyor John Sinclair for Thomas Telford and the Commissioners for Highland Roads and Bridges, survives at Small Isles Harbour. A few dwellings are strung along the coast. **Caigenhouse**, or Mariners' Row, makes a gentle bend of gable-to-gable cottages. **Frisco** and **Lac-na-Bruich** date from the 1870s; **Lorne Cottage** and **Mulindry** were built as weavers' cottages, c.1840. The **Distillery** dominates the scene. Founded in 1810, it was rebuilt in 1884, extended by W Delme-Evans, 1961-63, and further enlarged in the 1970s when warehousing was added and the number of stills increased from two to four. (see p.184)

The Museum of Islay Life

RCAHMS

*Top right Jura House; Above Jura Parish Church; Right Craighouse, c.1900.*

**Jura Parish Church**, 1777
Small gabled kirk with round-arched windows. Altered to a T-plan in 1842 when galleries with forestair access were added. The gabled belfry may also be part of these changes. In 1922 the north gallery and stair were removed, the seating recast and a porch built.

Left from top *Keils township;*
*Corran River Bridge; Lagg pier.*

The road continues passing **Keils township**, a cluster of dwellings, byres and stores, some with cruck–trussed roofs and thatching. In **Killearndale Burial Ground** there are several **tapered slabs**, 14th-15th century, and the **Campbell Mausoleum**, a buttressed and vaulted Gothic Revival cell by William Burn, 1838. Past the abandoned Gothick of **Jura Free Church**, 1866, the road crosses the **Corran River Bridge**, an impressive rubble-built structure of three segmental arches, erected 1809-10 to a design by David Wilson of Lochgilphead.

## LAGG

Here the droving road ended and cattle crossed to Knapdale on the mainland. The rubble **slipway** and **pier**, built 1809-10 to the design of David Wilson, remain. Both curve slowly in plan; the way to the slip channelled between parapet walls in a 60m. long approach, the 35m. pier battered on the convex seaward side. The **drovers' inn**, now a farm, sits solidly at the head of the bay, a plain two-storey, three-bay, early 19th century house.

For many years the ferry at Lagg carried the drovers and their beasts from Jura to the mainland. Joseph Mitchell's *Reminiscences of my Life in the Highlands*, published in 1883, recounts one such crossing.
*On arriving at the ferry we found every corner of the inn crowded with drovers who had been detained by the weather for several days, and were passing their time as was their wont, in riotous and continuous drinking. We felt it no agreeable sojourn to stay at the inn with these noisy and half-intoxicated men, for the very air was impregnated with an odour of whisky. We appealed to the ferrymen to take us across. At first they positively refused on account of the storm, but with some persuasion and a handsome present, their scruples were overcome . . . [the drovers] got excessively angry, talked in Gaelic long and loud and insisted that we should take at the same time a cargo of their cattle. This the boatman could not refuse, and eighteen cattle were put on board. . . . The wind was quite in our favour, but it blew furiously and the sea was high . . . The men tried to lower the sail, which they could not effect, and all looked helpless. On this, the drover seized the helm, and with sharp and decisive words he took command of the boat . . . and in no time he landed us in the shelter within the little bay. The time we took to make the crossing – nine miles – was little more than half an hour.*

*Lagg slipway.*

*Ardlussa House.*

Immediately beyond the northern tip of Jura is the notorious **whirlpool of Corryvreckan** (*coire bhreacain* – the speckled cauldron) where many vessels have come to grief. The sinister threat to sailing craft is at its worst when a spring tide is running (at a speed of as much as 10 knots) against the west wind, a surging conflict best safely observed from the land on Scarba island to the north or from above the rocks of Carraig Mhor on Jura. George Orwell (1903-50), who wrote his novel *1984* at nearby Barnhill, has recorded how he came close to losing his life here in 1949 when attempting to sail round Jura.

In 1814 the road was continued to Tarbert, where the island narrowed to permit a link to the crossing then made down Loch Tarbert to Colonsay. Today the road goes on to Ardlussa estate. **Crossman Bridge**, a naively battlemented rubble construction of 1912, spans the Lussa River *en route* to **Ardlussa House**, *c.*1843, a pleasant, gabled and bayed agglomeration wrapped around an earlier U-plan dwelling. 10km. further north a rough track arrives at Barnhill, the remote dwelling where George Orwell wrote his novel *1984*. Beyond, off the northern tip of Jura, is the whirlpool Gulf of Corryvreckan.

### GARVELLACH ISLES

An archipelago of small islands north-west of Scarba and Lunga. Now rather remote and deserted, three of the four main islands preserve traces of earlier settlement. On Dun Chonaill, which lies at the north-east of the chain, there are the footings of the rubble curtain wall that surrounded the **castle** crowning the cliff-edged summit. Described as the *great castle of Dunquhonle* by John of Fordun in the 14th century, the fortress was probably constructed a 100 years earlier. Several gateways defended the ascent from a boat-landing and there are the remains of a number of smaller structures both within the curtain and at the north-east end of the island. On Garbh Eileach, the walls of a roofless **dwelling** and byre or barn, late 18th or early 19th century, are recessed for a cruck-couple roof. But it is the Early Christian monastic settlement on Eileach an Naoimh which has left the most

*Eileach An Naoimh, double beehive cell.*

interesting evidence of a pre-Norse community. The oldest structures are a double **beehive cell**, one chamber roofless, the other with half of its corbelled rubble dome in place, and the so-called **Eithne's Grave**, now no more than a ring of stones but said to be the burial place of St Columba's mother. There are several ruinous oblong cells: one, roofless, is believed to have been a **chapel**, 11th or 12th century; another, built in flagstone masonry like the first, is designated **monastery** but may be no more than a 17th or 18th century farm; a third is thought to be all that remains of a medieval **church**.

## COLONSAY

A small hilly island lying west of Jura. At low tide it is linked across The Strand to the neighbouring island of Oronsay. Car ferry connection with Oban and, in the summer, with Kennacraig on West Loch Tarbert and Port Askaig on Islay.

## SCALASAIG

The village focus of island life gathered around pier, hotel and church. A long concrete pier of steel and concrete, 1988, provides roll-on roll-off facilities. Beside it is the harbour of *c*.1850 with its L-plan **pier** of exquisitely jointed masonry, skilfully curved in the re-entrant. **Colonsay Hotel** is a white harled inn begun *c*.1750, probably by Michael Carmichael, and since extended and altered several times. The A-frame **chalet block** behind, which is timber-boarded on the gables and terraced to the west between cross walls, is by John Fox. Crowning the hill south of the village is the **Lord Colonsay Monument**,1879, a tall obelisk of pink Mull granite commemorating Duncan McNeill, 6th laird of the island.

*Colonsay Hotel.*

*Colonsay Parish Church.*

From the 15$^{th}$ century, if not before, Macphees or MacDuffies were **Lairds of Colonsay**. Some time soon after 1615 they were ousted by MacDonalds who in turn were supplanted by their enemies the Campbells. In 1700 Malcolm MacNeil of Knapdale acquired Colonsay and Oronsay. Legend has it that the MacNeils came to the islands in an open boat along with their cattle. They proved liberal landowners and Colonsay did not suffer from the same clearances that affected many other estates in the Highlands and Islands. Nevertheless, over the second half of the 19$^{th}$ century the population dropped from almost 1,000 to around 350. Debts forced the MacNeils to sell the islands and in 1905 Lord Strathcona became the new owner. His planting in the sheltered Kiloran valley extended the work begun by his predecessors; many species of trees were cultivated, rhododendrons, azaleas and magnolias blossomed, even figs and peaches have ripened. Meanwhile, though landscape and climate draw faithful holiday-makers, the population continues to fall. By the early 1990s, there were only 100 or so permanent residents.

Middle *Colonsay House;*
Bottom *Kiloran Mill wheel.*

213**Colonsay Parish Church**, 1801-04, Michael Carmichael

A composition of simple solid geometries given added dignity by its elevation on a grassy rise. The oblong church is piend-roofed and fronted on the east by a narrow pedimented centrepiece carrying an elongated birdcage belfry. Below the pediment is a blind oculus and below that a round-ended vestry projects under a conical slated roof. Flanking this sculptural assembly are two tall round-arched windows which are repeated on the west front. Forestairs to galleries on the north and south were provided but that to the south was removed in 1922 (a similar fate befell Jura Parish Church in the same year). Light and timber panelled within.

214**Colonsay House**, from 1722

Originally known as Kiloran House, the compact three-bay core, seen best at the centre of the north front, can lay claim to be the earliest classical mansion in Argyll. During the first half of the 19$^{th}$ century, the house was enlarged to Palladian status with quadrant links to piended pavilion wings and a central north porch gabled over a Venetian window. This feature was repeated in grander style to the south lighting bow-fronted rooms added on each gable of the original house. Service buildings spreading east were raised to two storeys, *c.*1910. Fine lawns and **gardens**. **Home Farm**, 18$^{th}$ century (?).

Scattered around the island are the ruinous vestiges of several medieval **chapels** and **burial grounds**: those near Balnahard in the north and Garvard in the south may be 13$^{th}$ or 14$^{th}$ century in origin. West of Scalasaig is **Machrins Farm**, a gabled T-plan dwelling, part 18$^{th}$ century (?), with an octagonal horse-gang and U-plan steading; perhaps originally a tacksman's house. The **Mill** at Kiloran has been reconstructed as a dwelling but retains its iron wheel on the gable.

215**Oronsay Priory**, 14$^{th}$ century

A religious community may have been established by St Columba or St Oran as early as the 6$^{th}$ century but the roofless ruins which

RCAHMS

Top *Oronsay Priory;* Left *Oronsay Priory by T Pennant, 1772.*

survive in remarkably substantial condition are those of the Augustinian house founded by John I, Lord of the Isles, in the second decade of the 14th century. The Priory was ruinous by the 1730s and it was only in the 1880s that restoration was begun by William Galloway. Further consolidation and repairs were carried out by the Office of Works in 1927.

The plan is claustral. Of the **Cloister** itself, only the round-headed south arcade is original, though all four corner piers remain. The west arcade of triangular arches is a second reconstruction, 1883, which incorporates two carved piers from the early 16th century. The **East Range**, standing to the wallhead, is 14th century. In the late 18th century, however, the Chapter House was divided to create the **McNeil Burial Aisle**, extended east in an oblong gabled cell with a pointed arch doorway, mid 19th century. The west and east walls of the **North Range** are two storeys high and it may be that here were located the kitchens with the refectory above and perhaps a chapel linked to the East Range. The so-called '**Prior's House**' at the north-east corner of the plan was repaired in 1927 to house a rich collection of funerary monuments. Built at an angle off the east gable of the North Range are the stabilised walls and gable of the '**Prior's Chapel**', its sanctuary extended in the early 16th century.

RCAHMS

*Oronsay Cross.*

In his **Journey to the Western Islands of Scotland**, Dr Johnson devotes a long description to his visit to the small island of Coll in autumn 1773. Forced by poor weather to remain on the island, he and Boswell found their hosts hospitable. At Grissipol, where Johnson *saw more of the ancient life of a highlander, than I had yet found*, they were entertained by Mrs Macsweyn who spoke no English but spread a liberal table. Thereafter, as guests of the local laird, MacLean of Coll, they put up *very commodiously* at New Breacachadh Castle, *a neat new house, erected near the old castle* then *still very strong, and having not been long uninhabited, . . . yet in repair.* But it was the landscape rather than the few buildings on the island which impressed the travellers most. *Col is not properly rocky; it is rather one continued rock, of a surface much diversified with protuberances, and covered with a thin layer of earth, which is often broken, and discovers the stone. Such a soil is not for plants that strike deep roots; and perhaps in the whole island nothing has ever yet grown to the height of a table. The uncultivated parts are clothed with heath, among which industry has interspersed spots of grass and corn; but no attempt has yet been made to raise a tree.*

*Right Arinagour cottages.*

On the south side of the Cloister is the Priory **Church**, an aisleless nave of 14th or early 15th century date. Walls are largely intact, though much restored; in the east gable, a three-light window with plain Y-tracery. The **MacDuffie Aisle**, late 15th century, abuts the south wall. The thick-walled chamber added against the west gable in the late 15th century seems to be the base for an intended tower. A number of arched and lintelled openings along the south wall of the nave remain difficult to interpret; their differing levels suggest the possibility of a gallery. At the east end, a re-assembled sandstone altar, late 15th century (?).

The **burial ground** contains many grave-markers. In the 'Prior's House' there are numerous **tapered slabs**, 14th-16th century, most carved with animals, plants or swords but several bearing effigies of religious and military figures. The **Oronsay Cross**, Iona school, late 15th century, stands close to the west wall of the Church. Carved in the disc-head on a background of interlacing is a crucified Christ; floral roundels and plaiting fill the shaft.

## COLL

A small outlying Argyll island to the north-west of Mull. The low landscape is broken with a rash of rocky outcrops in the north-east but more is fertile in the south-west with machair, dunes and wide strands of sandy shore. Car ferry connection with Oban and nearby Tiree.

216 **ARINAGOUR**

Village founded by Alexander MacLean of Coll in the first years of the 19th century. Two short rows of gable-to-gable **cottages**, *c.*1814, overlook the **Old Pier**, early 19th century, on the upper reaches

RCAHMS

of Loch Eatharna. A second, rubble and concrete, **Mid Pier** was built, *c.*1968, a little to the south; but the present roll-on roll-off facilities are at the **New Pier**, 1987-92, almost a kilometre south in deeper water. Invitingly white, the **Isle of Coll Hotel,** a double-gabled, 19th century house, extended 1968, looks south down the loch to the sea.

**Coll Parish Church**, 1907
Simple Gothic with pointed-arch windows and a
finialled tower. Its humble architecture
fortuitously dignified by an elevated location but
genuinely enhanced by a splendid boarded
ceiling of unexpectedly complex joinery.

At **Acha** there is a 19th century **mill**, now
converted to residential use. **Acha House**, also
19th century, is thoroughly Scottish, harled and
gable-ended. Reached across 2km. of dune-
backed shore at the south end of the island,
**Crossapol House**, late 18th century, is beautifully
situated above a deserted graveyard tumbling to
the rocks and sand below. In the west,

Left *Grishipoll House;* Above *Thatched
cottage in Sorisdale.*

217 **Grishipoll House**, mid 18th century, is a ruin,
though the robust rubble walls are still intact
enough and the site green enough to evoke
thoughts of that *house and farm* where Dr Johnson
*saw more of the ancient life of the highlander, than I
had yet found.* Evidence of a harder Highland life
survives, though barely, at Sorisdale; an
abandoned **township** (see p.184) with a few
rubble cottages derelict but still thatched. Proof
that the tradition of limewashed simplicity lives
on is to be found at Ballyhaugh where Richard
Avery's **Hebridean Centre**, 1992, has a measured
farmyard modesty.

218 **Breacachadh Castle**, 15th century
Tower-house stronghold of the MacLeans of
Coll. A curtain wall bulging to the south-east
enfolds an inner yard on the southern side of
which a single-storey hall was constructed. At
the end of the 16th century the level of the yard
was raised and the wall heightened with
machicolation over the entrances on the east and
south-west. An artillery battery was begun in
the early 17th century on the landward side of the

*Aerial view of Breacachadh Castle and New Breacachadh Castle.*

tower but was never completed. Late in the same century the single-storey hall was raised to three storeys as a dwelling; its crowstepped gables still appear above the curtain parapet. Finally, in 1750 the castle was abandoned and New Breacachadh built. Intermittent repairs failed to arrest decay and it was not until 1961 that Ian G Lindsay began a programme of restoration. This was completed by Richard Avery in 1993 and the castle is again a residence.

### 219 New Breacachadh Castle, 1750
Built by Hector Maclean of Coll in a simple if unsophisticated classical manner, the house failed to impress Dr Johnson in 1773. It had, he averred, *nothing becoming a chief about it*. More than a little unfair for a hip-roofed mansion of three storeys with quadrant wings and Venetian windows. More justified censure might fall on

later impairment, *c.*1860, which included the addition of a fourth storey, a crenellated parapet and corner bartizans. By the middle of the 20th century the building was empty and in decay. The crenellated **steading**, late 18th or early 19th century, is now in occupation. About a kilometre to the south is the **MacLean Burial Ground**, *c.*1835, an empty Gothic enclosure, lonely and neglected above Crossapol Bay.

### TIREE
The most westerly of the Argyll islands, edged by long arcs of sandy coastline held between rocky fringes. The land is flat and swept by wild Atlantic winds, but fertile enough for good farming. There is an air link with Glasgow and car ferry connection with Coll and Oban.

### SCARINISH
What appears to be an ill-conceived scatter of dwellings is the island's principal settlement, founded to promote the fishing industry in the mid 18th century. Though the Duke of Argyll provided the island's first harbour, there seems to have been no plan for the village. Houses appear at random as varied in materials and form

*From top New Breacachadh Castle; MacLean Burial Ground.*

**Archaeological remains** are plentiful on Tiree. There are standing stones, stone circles, souterrains, cists, crannogs. The broch at Dun Mor Vaul, constructed *c.*100AD and excavated in the early 1960s, has a diameter of *c.*11m., the low wall structure showing cells, galleries and stairs in its 4m. thickness. A wattle and daub hut, perhaps erected in the late 5th or early 6th century BC, probably preceded the broch on the site. The ruinous vestiges of many dun forts can be found around the island's shores. On the north coast between Vaul Bay and Balephetrish Bay is the so-called *Ringing Stone*, a large erratic boulder thought to have come from Rhum during the Ice Age. It is ovaloid in shape, has many cup markings and, if struck with a small stone, emits a strangely metallic ringing sound. Were it to be shattered, tradition warns that Tiree will sink into the sea.

*Scarinish harbour, c.1900.*

The **vernacular housing of Tiree** is characterised by several different types: thatched rubble cottages, whitewashed dwellings with black-tarred roofs, corrugated iron houses, partly whitewashed *spotted* masonry buildings, adapted Nissen huts, modern bungalows and kit houses, etc. Of these the most fascinating are those thatched cottages, byres and barns which still survive, as, for example, at Sandaig Museum. The plan of the dwelling is long and narrow with rounded ends but no raised gables. Two parallel dry-stone rubble walls constitute the outer walls, the gap between being filled with packed sand. The height of the stonework is approximately six feet, the overall width roughly the same. Windows are inevitably small and deeply set. Rough roof timbers rest on the inner wall and are fitted together at the ridge with wooden pins. A slightly steeper pitch is contrived on the rear or windward side of the house. Cross timbers and branching form a base for turfs laid overlapping from wallhead to ridge. Thatch is similarly laid and the finished roof secured against the high winds with weighted cross-ropes.

as in siting: limewashed or heavily mortared walls; thatched, slated or corrugated iron roofs; upper storeys with eaves dormers or black tarred attics. The **pier** is an L-plan of rubble, *c*.1835, but the harbour used only by small craft. The recent roll-on roll-off **pier** is a kilometre north, a long finger pushing out into the deep water of Gott Bay.

## KIRKAPOL

A hotel and a cluster of churches at the middle of Gott Bay. Two churches are ruinous, both 220 probably late 14th century. The larger is the **Old Parish Church**, a gabled rubble shell rectangular in plan. The other is a smaller **chapel**, also oblong and no less degraded. Adjacent is the medieval **burial ground** with a few **tapered slabs**, 14th-16th century, and many grave-markers eroded to stone stubs. The former **Free Church**, 1880, now a guest house, is betrayed by lancet windows.

**Kirkapol Church**, 1843-44, Peter McNab
A piend-roofed kirk with a pedimented south-east projection carrying an obelisk-topped belfry. Four-centred arched windows. Inside, a curved gallery carried on cast-iron columns.

The east end of the island has few habitations. Some traditional rubble dwellings barely survive at **Ruaig**. At **Milton** and **Vaul**, there are **brochs**, the latter relatively well preserved for a few courses above ground level. Crofting settlement is more extensive in the fertile west. A little 221 beyond the untidy hamlet of **Crossapol**, **Island House**, built for the Duke of Argyll's factor in 1746-48, is still approached down a man-made causeway in Lochan Eilein, though its unpretentious 18th century character has been elaborated by gabled additions in the 19th century. Near **Cornaigmore** the **mill**, mid 19th century, is

From top *Kirkapol Old Parish Church*; *Kirkapol Church*; Right *Island House*.

in ruins but retains its iron wheel and a few paddle blades on the north gable. Worship here centres on **Heylipol Church**, 1901-12, by William Mackenzie, a cruciform Gothic kirk built in rough granite with a parapetted tower and some plate tracery. At **Sandaig** on the west coast, The Hebridean Trust have preserved some of Tiree's unique vernacular buildings in the form of a **Folk Museum**: double-skin drystone walling and turf-covered roofs restored by John Wilson Associates, 1989-93. Another of the island's vernacular styles – white-walled cottages with black-felted, timber-framed upper storeys – gives a stark beauty to the trim hamlets of **Balemartine** and **Mannel**. In the **burial ground** at Soroboy there are several **tapered slabs**, Iona school, 14th-16th century, and a host of later **headstones** including four for the families of the men who worked on Skerryvore Lighthouse (q.v.).

## HYNISH

A group of granite buildings with an unexpectedly strong architectural presence. Constructed 1837-43 by engineer Alan Stevenson to support the lighthouse at Skerryvore. A **pier** (see p.184) and **tidal dock**, both stepped and battered in section, are built of massive stone blocks quarried in the Ross of Mull. A range of former stores, now known as **Taigh Alan Stevenson**, has been converted to residential use by John Wilson Associates, 1988-89. Above the harbour, **workers' houses** in the Lower Square and a range of **Keepers' Houses** have been restored by A R P Lorimer and Associates, 1995-99, for The Hebridean Trust. The same architects have converted the cylindrical **Signal Tower** to a museum.

Tiree was famously caught up in demands for **Land Reform** in the 1880s. In 1886 the Land League called on the Duke of Argyll to parcel out a vacant farm to as many tenants as possible. When, however, the secretary of the League bought the whole farm for himself, 75 islanders staked their claim by putting animals on the land. Interdicts were issued but enforcement proved a problem. The Duke enlisted a force of police and others but they were obliged to return to the mainland without success. A scurrilous press report that the islanders had attacked the Duke's messengers at arms led to over-reaction by the government. Two naval ships, the *Assistance* and the *Ajax*, and a third chartered vessel, the *Nigel*, sailed to Tiree and an armed force was landed. The situation became confused but, instead of conflict, marines and islanders seem to have established some kind of *rapport*. Soldiers helped with the harvest, a golf course was laid out, while the marine band proved popular. Only a handful of men were arrested but, although given short prison sentences, the fame of the island's fight for land was now so widespread that they were soon released to return as heroes.

Above *Hynish Signal Tower before conversion*; Left *Conversion drawings of the Old Barracks in Hynish.*

**Skerryvore Lighthouse**, 1838-44, Alan Stevenson
Remote on a reef 20km. west-south-west of Tiree.
The tower is 42m. high, nine storeys tapering in a
slow curve to a cavetto cornice under the balcony.
Appropriately enough, the cast-iron walkway
around the lantern is ornamented with dolphin-
shaped hand-grips.

From top *Aerial view of Skerryvore
Lighthouse; Drawing of Skerryvore
Lighthouse.*

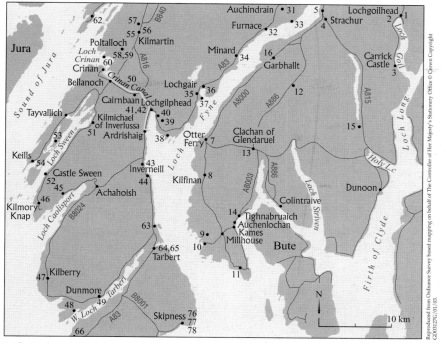

## 1. Cowal and Mid Argyll

ACKNOWLEDGEMENTS

Many people have helped in the compilation of this book. Charles McKean and David Walker have both read the text and as always I am especially grateful for their criticisms and suggestions and for the ready way they have shared their encyclopaedic knowledge. Much of the information gleaned could not have been uncovered were it not for the efforts of Murdo Macdonald, archivist at Lochgilphead, and Michael C Davis, librarian and local historian formerly at Sandbank and now at Helensburgh. Having written the *Argyll and Bute* volume in The Buildings of Scotland series published by Penguin Books (and now by Yale University Press), my task for this book was made easier, thanks largely to the research work carried out for that series by John Gifford and his team. To my former students, whose work constitutes the curate's egg of AHAUS, the Archive of Historical Architecture at the University of Strathclyde, my thanks are due. I am also grateful to Simon Green, Diane Watters and the staff of the library at the National Monuments Record of Scotland and Simon Montgomery and Debbie Mays at Historic Scotland. Needless to say many fellow architects have assisted me with information; among them are David Anderson, Shauna Cameron, Philip Flockart, Stephen Hunter, Brian Leech, Diana Maclaurin, Bill Murdoch, David Page, Brian Park, John Renshaw, Fiona Sinclair, Donald Wilson, and John Wilson. Others who have helped, often with generous hospitality, include Douglas and Allison Fairbairn, Peter and Moira MacGillivray, Gordon and Efric McNeil, Allan Millar, Bill and Caroline Murdoch. I am indebted, too, of course, to those many owners of property, ministers, priests and local residents who opened doors, literal and metaphorical, for me. I must hope that those whom I have forgotten to mention here will forgive me.

Long in its gestation, this book would not have taken final shape were it not for the indulgent support afforded me first by Helen Leng and Susan Skinner at The Rutland Press and later, in the design and production period, by Rebecca Bailey and Philip Graham at the Royal Commission on the Ancient and Historical Monuments of Scotland. Special thanks are also due to John Stevenson and Georgina Brown of RCAHMS for the layout and maps respectively.

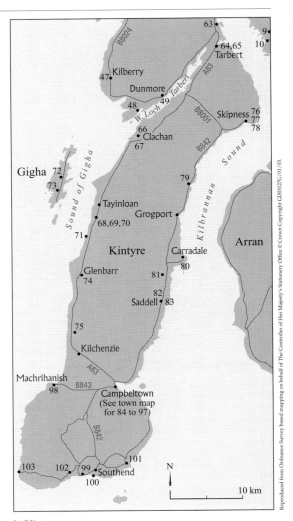

2. Kintyre

SOURCES

The seven volumes of the Inventories on *Argyll* published by the RCAHMS (1971-92) have been of fundamental value. Scarcely less vital, the *Lists of Buildings of Special Architectural or Historic Interest* prepared by Historic Scotland, particularly those more recently revised and more informatively descriptive. *The Statistical Accounts of Scotland* published in the 1790s and 1830s-1840s have also been helpful. Besides these the following sources have been regularly consulted. Colvin, H, *A Biographical Dictionary of British Architects, 1600-1840* (1978); Cruden, S, *The Scottish Castle* (1960); Dunbar, J, *The Historic Architecture of Scotland* (1966); Glendinning, M, MacInnes, R, and MacKechnie, A, *A History of Scottish Architecture* (1996); Groome, F H, *Ordnance Gazetteer of Scotland*, 6 vols. (1882-85); Hume, J R, *The Industrial Archaeology of Scotland*, 2 vols. (1976-77); Lindsay, I G and Cosh, M, *Inveraray and the Dukes of Argyll* (1973); MacGibbon D and Ross, T, *The Castellated and Domestic Architecture of Scotland*, 5 vols. (1887-92) and *The Ecclesiastical Architecture of Scotland*, 3 vols. (1896-97); Maclean, A, *Telford's Highland Churches* (1989); Ritchie, G, *The Archaeology of Argyll* (1988); and Walker, F A, *Argyll and Bute* (2000).

Many local histories, guides and fragmentary references relating to regions, towns, villages, buildings or individuals have been read; to name them all here would be impossible. But in this respect I must again particularly acknowledge the generous help of Murdo Macdonald at Lochgilphead and Michael C Davis formerly at Sandbank. The pages of the *Oban Times* frequently proved informative as did those of *The Kist*, the magazine of the Natural History and Archaeological Society of Mid-Argyll. For many years this latter publication was edited by the late Marion Campbell of Kilberry whose knowledge and love of Argyll is now legendary. I regret never having met her but hope that this little book would have met with her approval.

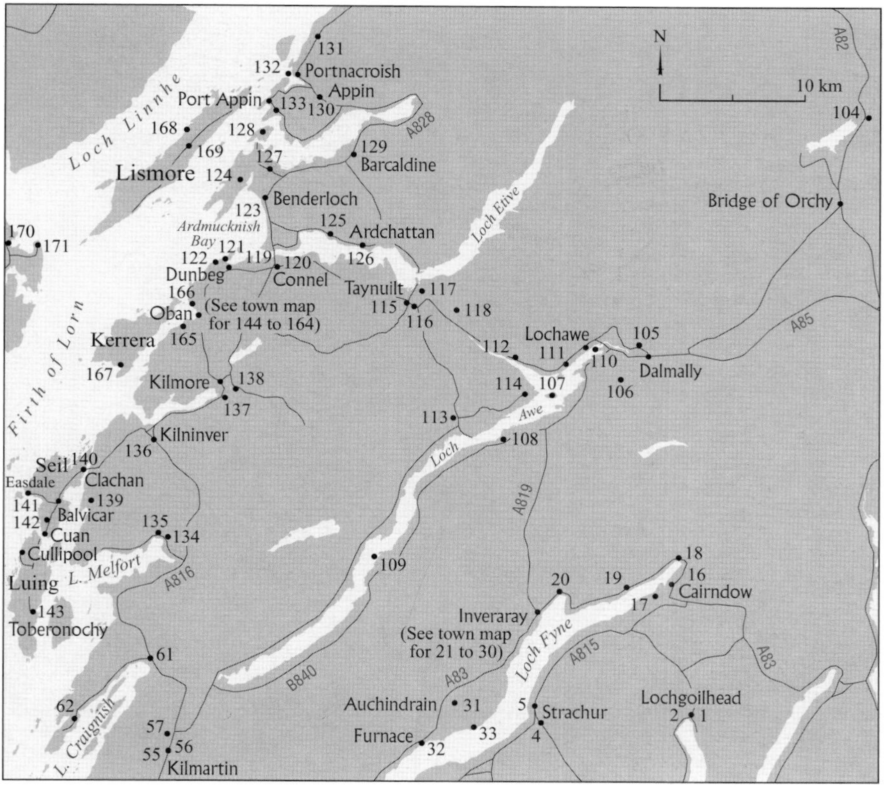

N

10 km

A82

104

131
132 • Portnacroish
Port Appin 133 130 307 Appin
168 • 128 •
169 •
127
Loch Linnhe
129
Lismore 124 • Barcaldine

123
Benderloch
Ardmucknish 125 Ardchattan
Bay 121 126
170 122 119 120
• 171 Dunbeg 166 Connel Taynuilt • 117
Oban (See town map 115 118
for 144 to 164) 116
Kerrera 165 112 Lochawe 105
167 111 110
Kilmore • 138 114 107 106 Dalmally
137 113 •
Kilninver • 108
Seil 140 136
Easdale Clachan Loch Awe
141 • 139
142 Balvicar
• Cuan 135
Cullipool • 134
Luing L. Melfort 109
• 143 20 18
Toberonochy 19 16
17 Cairndow
61 Inveraray
(See town map
62 for 21 to 30)
L. Craignish Auchindrain • 31 5 Strachur Lochgoilhead
57 Furnace 33 2 • 1
55 • 56 32 4
Kilmartin

Firth of Lorn

Loch Etive

Bridge of Orchy

A828

A85

A819

A816

B840

A83

A815

A83

Loch Fyne

3. Lorn and Mid Argyll

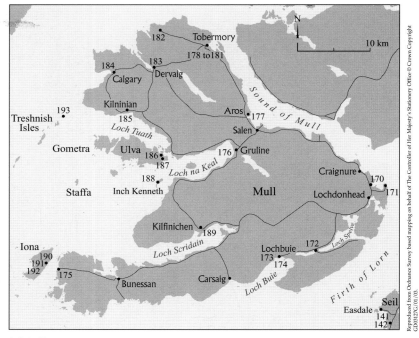

4. Mull

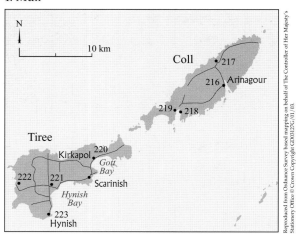

5. Coll and Tiree

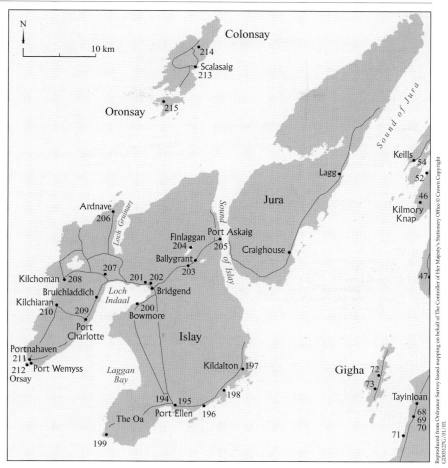

6. Islay, Jura and Colonsay

# GLOSSARY

1. Architrave (projecting ornamental frame)
2. Astragal (glazing bar)
3. Barge (gable board)
4. Basement, raised
5. Bullseye, keyblocked (circular window with projecting blocks punctuating frame)
6. Buttress (supporting projection)
7. Caphouse (top chamber)
8. Cartouche (decorative tablet)
9. Cherrycocking (masonry joints filled with small stones)
10. Channelled ashlar (recessed horizontal joints in smooth masonry)
11. Chimneycope, corniced
12. Chimneycope, moulded
13. Close (alley)
14. Cobbles
15. Console (scroll bracket)
16. Corbel (projection support)
17. Crowsteps
18. Cutwater (wedge-shaped end of bridge pier)
19. Doocot, lectern
20. Dormer, canted & piended
21. Dormer, pedimented (qv) wallhead
22. Dormer, piended (see under 'roof')
23. Dormer, swept wallhead
24. Fanlight (glazed panel above door)
25. Finial (crowning ornament)
26. Fly-over stair
27. Forestair, pillared
28. Gable, wallhead
29. Gable, wallhead chimney
30. Gable, Dutch (curved)
31. Gibbs doorway (framed with projecting stonework)
32. Harling
33. Hoist, fishing net
34. Hoodmoulding (projection over opening to divert rainwater)
35. Jettied (overhanging)
36. Lucarne (small dormer on spire)
37. Margin, stone
38. Mercat Cross
39. Marriage Lintel
40. Mullion (vertical division of window)
41. Nave (main body of church)
42. Pavilion (building attached by wing to main building)
43. Pediment (triangular ornamental feature above windows etc)
44. Portico
45. Quoins, rusticated (corner stones with recessed joints)
46. Refuge (recess in bridge parapet)
47. Ridge, crested
48. Roof, flared pyramidal
49. Roof, leanto
50. Roof, ogival (with S-curve pitch generally rising from square plan and meeting at point)
51. Roof, pantiled
52. Roof, piended (formed by intersecting roof slopes)
53. Roof, slated
54. Skew (gable coping)
55. Skewputt, moulded (lowest stone of skew, qv)
56. Skewputt, scroll
57. Stair jamb (projection containing stairway)
58. Stringcourse (horizontal projecting wall moulding)
59. Transept (transverse wing of cruciform church)
60. Transom (horizontal division of window)
61. Voussoir (wedge-shaped stone forming archway)
62. Tympanum (area within pediment qv)
63. Window, bay (projecting full-height from ground level)
64. Window, oriel (corbelled bay qv)
65. Window, sash & case (sliding sashes within case)

For further terms see *Dictionary of Scottish Building*, Glen Pride, The Rutland Press, 1996.

# INDEX

Royal
Commission on the
Ancient and
Historical
Monuments of
Scotland

# RECORDING AND PROMOTING SCOTLAND'S BUILT HERITAGE

A good proportion of the images used in this guide have come from the collections of the Royal Commission on the Ancient and Historical Monuments of Scotland. RCAHMS records and interprets the archaeological sites, monuments and buildings of Scotland's past and promotes a greater appreciation of their value through the National Monuments Record of Scotland (NMRS).

RCAHMS carried out an extensive survey of the county of Argyll from 1960 onwards, publishing the seventh and final *Inventory of Monuments* in 1992. In addition to these seven volumes, the NMRS holds a wide range of material relating to Argyll including a selection of RCAHMS publications: *Kilmartin - Prehistoric and Early Historic Monuments* (1999), *Argyll Castles in the care of Historic Scotland* (1997), and *Early Medieval Sculpture in the West Highlands and Islands* (2001).

In 1999 RCAHMS began the Scottish Architects' Papers Preservation Project, an extensive programme of cataloguing and conservation supported by the Heritage Lottery Fund and the Royal Incorporation of Architects in Scotland. Several collections in the project feature surveys and designs for buildings in Argyll, particularly the *Ian G Lindsay, Lorimer and Matthew, Leslie Grahame Thomson MacDougall, Shearer and Annand, Monro and Partners, J and J A Carrick,* and *Dick Peddie and McKay* Collections.

The NMRS library is open to the public from Monday to Friday 9:30am – 4:30pm.

Researchers can consult a range of archive material including historic, survey and aerial photographs, architects' drawings, reference books, manuscripts and maps. Copies of many of the items can be supplied in a variety of formats.

## SEARCH THE WEBSITE

The RCAHMS website (www.rcahms.gov.uk) gives access to CANMORE, the NMRS database, which contains details of the collections held in the NMRS, along with information on Scotland's architectural, archaeological and maritime sites.

The recent addition of CANMAP enables a geographical search to be made of the NMRS database with the results displayed on a map.

## CONTACT
RCAHMS
John Sinclair House
16 Bernard Terrace
Edinburgh EH8 9NX
**Tel: +44 (0)131 662 1456**
**Fax: +44 (0)131 662 1499**
**Email: nmrs@rcahms.gov.uk**
**Website: www.rcahms.gov.uk**

# PROMOTING ARCHITECTURE IN SCOTLAND

The Rutland Press is dedicated to producing books which stimulate awareness of Scotland's built environment in an entertaining and informative way. The publishing division of the Royal Incorporation of Architects in Scotland (RIAS), it is Scotland's leading architectural publisher with three-quarters of the Illustrated Architectural Guides to Scotland series now published in a venture unmatched elsewhere in the world.

PUBLISHED TITLES: 1. Edinburgh, 2. Dundee, 3. Stirling and The Trossachs, 4. Aberdeen, 5. The South Clyde Estuary, 6. Clackmannan and the Ochils, 7. The District of Moray, 8. Central Glasgow, 9. Banff & Buchan, 10. Shetland, 11. The Kingdom of Fife, 12. Orkney, 13. Ross & Cromarty, 14. The Monklands, 14. North Clyde Estuary, 16. Ayrshire & Arran, 17. West Lothian, 18. Borders and Berwick, 19. Gordon, 20. Sutherland, 21. Midlothian, 22. Caithness, 23. Dumfries and Galloway, 24. Perth & Kinross, 25. Deeside and The Mearns, 26. Falkirk and District, 27. Argyll and the Islands.

FORTHCOMING TITLES: 28. Western Seaboard, 29. Angus, 30. Inverness, Nairn, Badenoch & Strathspey, 31. Greater Glasgow, 32. Lanarkshire, 33. Cumbernauld, Kilsyth & the Campsies, 34. East Lothian.

THE RUTLAND PRESS

"Good armchair reading with their exotic mixture of fact and personal comment"
**Colin McWilliam, *The Scotsman***

These and other RIAS titles and books on world architecture are all available from: RIAS Bookshop, 15 Rutland Square, Edinburgh, EH1 2BE. Tel 0131 229 7545  Fax 0131 228 2188
email: rutland@rias.org.uk  website: www.rias.org.uk
The Rutland Press is part of RIAS Services Limited